WITHDRAWN

HARVARD LIBRARY

WITHDRAWN

From Birth to Old Age

The Human Life Cycle in Medieval Thought, 1250–1350

Michael E. Goodich
University of Haifa

UNIVERSITY
PRESS OF
AMERICA

Lanham • New York • London

Copyright © 1989 by

University Press of America,® Inc.

4720 Boston Way
Lanham, MD 20706

3 Henrietta Street
London WC2E 8LU England

All rights reserved

Printed in the United States of America

British Cataloging in Publication Information Available

Library of Congress Cataloging-in-Publication Data

Goodich, Michael, 1944–   .
From birth to old age : the human life cycle in medieval thought, 1250–1350 /
Michael Goodich.
   p.   cm.
Bibliography: p.
Includes index.
1. Social history—Medieval, 500–1500.   2.   Life cycle, Human—Social aspects—
   History.   3. Developmental psychology—History.   I. Title.
HN11.G66   1989   305.2'09'02—dc20   89-34169 CIP

ISBN 0-8191-7486-6 (alk. paper)

HN
11
.G66
1989

All University Press of America books are produced on acid-free paper.
The paper used in this publication meets the minimum requirements of American
National Standard for Information Sciences—Permanence of Paper for Printed Library
Materials, ANSI Z39.48–1984.   ∞

ACKNOWLEDGEMENTS

This work is a natural outgrowth of my interest in medieval hagiography. In the course of reading innumerable pious biographies, I have been impressed by the stereotypical structure found in the saints' lives, and by the nearly universal agreement concerning the virtues and vices, and the critical junctures of the human life cycle from birth to death. My aim has been to determine to what extent the truisms voiced by the hagiographer were echoed in contemporary medical, theological and pedagogical sources. Concentrating on a period of great economic and social advance just prior to the crises of the fourteenth century, I have sought to discover whether the theoretical musings of the medieval 'developmental psychologists' were the product of changing material and demographic circumstances.

This study has forced me to conclude that an appreciation of the physiological, psychological and spiritual characteristics of each stage of life found in the late thirteenth and early fourteenth centuries, although based on theological assumptions, bore a remarkable resemblance to more contemporary theories of developmental psychology. Relying on such traditional notions as the four humors, the parallel between the earthly and heavenly worlds, the microcosmic nature of man, and the stereotypical characteristics of each stage of life, a fully formed theory of human psychology was created which took into account such contemporary factors as the sacramental character of marriage, greater longevity, and the rise of the individual.

While I naturally accept full responsibility for the book's contents, I have invariably benefited from the observations of friends and colleagues, whose suggestions and comments have helpfully guided my work. Among those whose assistance has encouraged me to rethink and refine my work, I wish to thank Robert Brentano, the late John D'Amico, Ann Edelman, John Mundy, Aryeh Grabois, Benjamin Z. Kedar, Zvi Razi, Paul Rose and Myriam Yardeni, along with many other unnamed persons whose fruitful remarks have assisted me in reformulating my thinking. I wish to acknowledge the kind and gracious service extended by numerous librarians at the University of Haifa, Columbia University, the University of California at Berkeley, the University of California at Los Angeles, the Graduate Theological Union, Oxford University, the New York Academy of Medicine, the Wellcome Institute, the Bibliothèque Nationale, and the British Library. A special thanks is due to Heather Kernoff for typing the many drafts of the manuscript with patience and fortitude; to the staff of the University Press of America for its help; and to the University of Haifa for its kind and generous assistance.

Finally, my wife Marian has provided the editorial and moral assistance which has invariably seen me through many a crisis; my daughter Claudia has supplied the living example of successful passage from one stage of life to another; and my parents, Sylvia and William, often unwittingly, have taught me to appreciate the necessary balance between the theoretical and practical, the earthly and spiritual, which eases the transition from one age to another.

Haifa
1989

TABLE OF CONTENTS

FROM BIRTH TO OLD AGE:

THE HUMAN LIFE CYCLE IN MEDIEVAL THOUGHT, 1250-1350

I. **Introduction: Study of life cycle in the late middle ages** 1

    A. Earlier studies
        1. Enlightenment and 19th century
        2. 20th century
    B. Medievalists on life cycle
        1. Recent research
        2. Classical sources
    C. Special character of 13th and 14th centuries
        1. Demographic Change
            a. Population rise
            b. Life expectancy
        2. Philosophical Optimism
            a. Rise of philosophy
            b. Idea of progress
        3. Syncretism
            a. Translation of Arabic sources
            b. Mutual influences
        4. Rise of the individual
            a. Breakup of family
            b. Penance and confession

II. **Prolegomena to the Sources** 27

    A. Hagiography
        1. Stereotypes and classical precedents
        2. Exemplary function
    B. Autobiography
        1. Earlier precedents
        2. 13th century proliferation
    C. Hortatary Material
        1. Aristotelianism
        2. Mirrors for princes
        3. Pseudo-Aristotle
        4. *Oecumenicus*
    D. Encyclopedism
        1. Classification
        2. Sources and methods
    E. Popularization of learned theory

III. Common Themes of Life Cycle Theory 59

    A. Age-oriented terminology
        1. Classical sources
        2. Lexicography
        3. Jewish precedents
    B. Natural history
    C. Dignity of man
    D. Analogical thinking
        1. Biblical commentary and sermon
        2. Ages of man and history

IV. Infancy and Childhood 83

    A. Prenatal images
        1. Prophecy and dream
        2. Symbolism of prenatal biology
    B. Childhood vices and virtues
    C. Child education
        1. Monastic precedents
        2. Secularization of education

V. Adolescence 105

    A. Virtues and vices of youth
    B. Images of youth
        1. *Assimilatio*
        2. Natural history
    C. Monastic education
        1. Gregorian precedents
        2. Hagiographical examples
    D. Lay education
        1. Parental love
        2. Tutors and students

VI. The Sexual Strains of Late Adolescence and Early Adulthood 121

    A. Control of male and female passion
        1. Male sexuality
        2. Women's vices and virtues
        3. Late medieval sexual ethics
    B. Resolution of male sexuality
        1. Gregorian precedents
        2. Male chastity
    C. Female chastity
        1. Desireability of marriage
        2. Holy marriage
    D. Jewish late adolescence

VII. Adulthood and Old Age 143

    A. Middle Age
        1. Man's virtues
        2. Regimens for health
    B. Weakness and strength of old age
        1. Fear of death
        2. Confession
    C. Extension of life
        1. Aristotelian corpus
        2. 13th century commentaries

VIII. Conclusion 159

Bibliography 163

Index 207

ABBREVIATIONS

AB	= *Analecta Bollandiana.*
ADH	= *Annales d'histoire démographique.*
AF	= *Analecta franciscana.*
AHDLMA	= *Archives d'histoire doctrinale et littéraire du moyen âge.*
ASS	= *Acta sanctorum quotquot tote orbe colluntur*, ed. Socii Bollandiani, new ed., 66 vols. to date (Paris, 1863-1940).
Beiträge	= *Beiträge zur Geschichte der Philosophie des Mittelalters.*
B.M.	= *British Museum*
B.N.	= *Bibliothèque Nationale*
BS	= *Bibliotheca sanctorum*, ed. Filippo Caraffa et al., 12 vols. (Rome, 1962-1970).
CCL	= *Corpus christianorum latinorum.*
CSEL	= *Corpus scriptorum ecclesiasticorum latinorum.*
DDC	= *Dictionnaire de droit canonique*, ed. Raoul Naz et al., 7 vols. (Paris, 1924-1965).
DHGE	= *Dictionnaire d'histoire et de géographie ecclésiastique*, ed. Alfred Baudrillart, 20 vols. to date (Paris, 1912-1985).
DSB	= *Dictionary of Scientific Biography*, ed. Charles C. Gillespie, 16 vols. (New York, 1970-1980).
DTC	= *Dictionnaire de théologie catholique*, ed. A. Vacant et al., 15 vols. (Paris, 1908-1950).
EETS	= *Early English Texts Society.*
MGH	= *Monumenta germaniae historica.*
MPG	= J.P. Migne, ed., *Patrologiae cursus completus. Series graeca*, 161 vols. (Paris, 1857-1905).
MPH	= Polska Akademia, *Monumenta poloniae historica*, 6 vols. (Cracow, 1864-1894).

MPL	= J.P. Migne, ed., *Patrologiae cursus completus . Series latina*, 221 vols. + 4 Suppl. (Paris, 1844-1905).
Sarton	= George Sarton, *Introduction to the History of Science* 3 vols. (Baltimore, 1953).

I. Introduction: Study of Life Cycle in the Late Middle Ages

One of the most persistent notions underlying the study of human life cycle is the classical theory of the ages of man, which has remained the framework of developmental psychology since ancient times. The great Enlightenment physician Cabanis (1757-1808) in a series of lectures delivered at the National Institute in 1796/7 dealing with the relations between the moral and physical condition of man, divided the proverbial seventy years of life into stages during which one or another organ dominates. The controlling emotions and sensibilities are a result of the vital humors coursing through the body and their concentration in one region or another.[1] The nervous system, he argued, gradually impregnates various parts of the body, transforming one's character. Cabanis noted that the ancients likewise linked the moral and the physical development of man, and identified the age of reason as seven. Infancy is followed by a phase which ends sometime between fourteen and twenty-one, when one's judgement is refined and the moral relations between the child and the outside world are fixed. If in childhood the humors are concentrated in the head, approaching adolescence they gravitate toward the chest, and finally rest in the genitals, whose appetites become a decisive influence on one's life, until displaced in middle age by the stomach. After twenty-one the mind is subject to the greatest number of impressions emanating from the outside world, and the imagination takes flight. The high point of maturity is reached between twenty-eight and thirty-five; as the movement of fluids in the body is gradually reduced, one feels the need to marshal one's resources and economize for the future. This mature period comes to an end between forty-nine and fifty-six, when a certain melancholia and hypochondria may be apparent, and the mind becomes timid and hesitant; in some this may give way to a "second childhood" before death.

Cabanis had thus summarized the traditional view of the human life cycle which, with small modifications, had survived since classical times. After Cabanis, in the nineteenth century, anthropologists observed the hierarchy of age (sometimes as an analog to the class system) and recognized the different capabilities of each period of life as a central feature of tribal societies.[2] While the number of discretely separated ages may differ, and while certain individuals may develop more quickly and prematurely achieve a higher status, the irreversible, chronological division of life into ages appeared to be universally recognized in all cultures. Cohorts segregated by age often play a significant role in the religious, military, economic and political organization of society. As anthropologists have observed, the process of maturation may be punctuated by collective ceremonial rites, whereby tribal members pass from one stage to another. Each chronological stage initiates the members of an age-defined group into both a new level of the maturation process, and into greater social and political responsibility. Such groups may cut across family or kinship structures, but are characterized by feelings of corporate solidarity which are a product of shared common experiences. Each age may possess its own rules and obligations, conferring a new status, exacting a different conformity to certain long-established norms.

The phases of life may be delimited by a series of sign-posts which conclude one age and usher in another; in fact, each individual will develop independently, and one phase may overlap another, containing the seeds of its successor. In the middle ages, the Christian sacraments may be regarded as such rites of passage, initiating the believer into another stage and reaffirming his allegiance to family, community and Faith. In medieval and Renaissance literature, this life cycle found its spiritual reflection in the metaphorical journey of the pilgrim from birth to old age and death.[3]

In recent years, the study of the life cycle in history has gained momentum, as evidenced by the creation of the new Interdisciplinary Center for Historical Research on the Human Life Span at the University of Louvain, devoted to encouraging the study of such subjects as the family, youth, aging, childhood, women, death, etc.[4] Scholars from a variety of disciplines have already reacted favorably and have submitted reports of current research. The continuing interest in the theme of seven ages -- which in recent years has tended to supersede all other schemes -- is indicated by a symposium held under the auspices of the British journal *New Society*, during which groups of scholars were invited to present the biological and psychological changes undergone during the seven decades of life. Many of their observations echo the remarks found in classical and medieval sources.[5]

Medievalists on Life Cycle

The publication by Philippe Ariès of his by now classic *Centuries of Childhood* has been especially instrumental in encouraging consideration of the perception of the life cycle in the past.[6] Medievalists have been attempting to correct the misconception voiced by Ariès that the middle ages possessed no clear notion of childhood as a separate developmental phase.[7] As a result, over the past several years an increasing number of studies have appeared in which such subjects as wet-nursing, infant care, oblation and infant mortality have been studied in greater depth. Such works have proven that infancy and childhood were clearly recognized as identifiable phases of the life cycle: obstetrical care and childhood diseases and diet were standard themes of medical inquiry; rules governing oblation occupied considerable space in monastic statutes; and secular law protected and recognized the rights of minors.[8] Hagiography and its companion, *exempla* literature, have proven to be particularly valuable sources for evidence of attitudes toward childhood, the family and education. Although adhering to traditional precedents, saints' lives often contain details which possess a ring of authenticity; and such an *exempla* collection as Johannes Gobi's *Scala coeli*, for example, contains a chapter devoted to the virtues of children, with didactic examples.[9] Less thoroughly studied have been the miracle collections, in which the symptoms of childhood disease and the grief caused by a stricken or dying child were described in great detail.[10]

Adolescence has likewise been the object of some interest, as the period when the social, political and familial responsibilities of adulthood were first experienced, and when the religious coming to consciousness was at its height. The works of such social historians as Duby and Boutruche have led the way in showing how the population rise of the eleventh century and the attendant changes in the laws of inheritance, created a class of dissatisfied youth whose energies did much to generate the new forces of Crusade, settlement, religious reform and intellectual ferment which characterized the central middle ages.[11] Another stage in the life cycle which has recently received increasing attention is death, whose image dominated the fourteenth century, as the catastrophic specters of famine, pestilence, depopulation and war haunted Europe.[12] The statistical evidence of demographic decline in the late fourteenth century has been confirmed in the *Ricordi*, which document the relatively sharp drop in life span, by perhaps as much as ten years, following a continuous rise in life expectancy during the previous several hundred years.[13]

Thus far several studies have appeared which examine the ancient and medieval foundations of the concept of the 'ages of man', namely Böll (1913) on classical antiquity, Wackernagel on the medieval German tradition (1862) and Löw (1875) on the Jewish sources. These works traced various schemes based on three, four, five, six and seven ages of life, along with their cosmic parallels in the stages of history and the heavenly constellations.[14] The persistence of the notion of the ages of man as a framework for speculation on the life cycle in the medieval period has been admirably addressed by Hofmeister (1926) and de Ghellinck (1948), who brought together most of the classical and medieval monastic and patristic literary sources.[15] But despite the mass of available material, both admit the imprecision with which such terms as *iuvenis* and *senex* were employed, and the rather unsystematic approach of most thinkers.

More recently, a masterly account by Elizabeth Sears surveys a large range of hitherto unexamined sources, many in manuscript, including sermons, Biblical exegesis and computistic works on time reckoning, as the bases for artistic illustrations of the ages of man.[16] The virtue of Sears' work lies in its integration of both visual and literary sources, indicating the degree to which the concept of life cycle had been communicated to a very wide audience. A thirteenth century architrave at San Marco in Venice, for example, could initiate a wide public into the images of developmental change associated with the ages; as Chew notes, it illustrates "carefree childhood, the sports of youth, the perils of manhood, the authority acquired by experience, and the wisdom of old age and its consolations found in family affection." The paralleling of the seven ages and periods of history was to be found in the thirteenth century west portal of the baptistry at Parma, illustrating the exegetical interpretation of the laborers in the vineyard of the Lord (*Matthew* 20). While the image of the wheel of fortune, in which youth rested on the upward slope of the wheel, and old age on the downward, graphically brought home the vagaries of the human condition. In Michael Scot's astrological *Liber introductorius* (1236?) figures of the planets were pictured as various ages.

J.A. Burrow's recent work, which surveys many of the relevant medieval and classical sources concerned with the ages of man, is particularly valuable as a guide to the vernacular material, especially in the fourteenth and fifteenth centuries, when the speculations of the natural philosopher and theologian reached a wide, non-learned audience.[17] His placement of man's behavior and physical constitution in the broader context of the natural order lays the foundation for a clearer comprehension of the ages of man as an organic, all-embracing scheme of human psychology and physiology which underlay much medieval thought and writing. Burrow presents a vast panorama of sources drawn from literature, natural philosophy and the plastic arts in which different frameworks for the ages of man appeared, and he notes the growing domination of a seven-age scheme in the later middle ages.

All of these works have indicated the vast body of classical speculation concerning the ages of man and the life cycle on which the medieval tradition rested. The church fathers, occasionally without acknowledging their sources, passed this material on to their medieval successors. One group of transmitted sources dealt with the ages as a literary *topos*, like the remarks of Lactantius; another concentrated on the characteristics of a particular age, e.g. Cicero on old age, or Virgil on the youth of Aeneas. This material often reached the middle ages through the agency of *florilegia* or Latin dictionaries containing selected citations from the classics arranged by topic, although this filter might be rather eclectic. A collection of *Sententiae morales* associated with Engelbert of Admont (ca. 1250-1331), for example, contained quotations dealing with such rubrics as the ages (*de etatibus*), adolescence and youth (*de adolescentia et iuvenibus*) and childhood (*de puericia et puerilitate*); here Seneca and Cicero were the most often cited.[18] Engelbert was himself the author of two works, the *De regimine principum* and the *Liber de causis longaevitatis hominum ante diluvium*, which bear directly on the medieval theory of the life cycle, and which may well have made use of the pithy sayings he had collected. Several of the more comprehensive ancient sources dealing with the cycle of life, on the other hand, such as Varro, Censorinus or Philo, rarely showed up in medieval discussions. The astrological tradition represented by Martianus Capella, although revived by the twelfth century cosmographers, particularly in the *Liber Hermetis Mercurii triplicis VI rerum principiis* (1135/4), found little echo until the early fourteenth century.

The present volume, unlike its predecessors, is confined to the late thirteenth and early fourteenth centuries (ca. 1250-1350 A.D.).[19] This period was characterized by a number of conditions which heightened interest in the life cycle, its overall structure, the critical passages from one age to another, and the possibility of improving and prolonging the span of human life. Four factors appear to have played a decisive role in focusing attention on the life cycle: 1) a vast demographic rise which reached a peak during this period, and its attendant effect on the quality of life; 2) an optimistic assessment of humanity and the possibilities for its progressive advancement; 3) the unprecedented absorption of non-Christian philosophical and medical speculation in the schools, which transformed the terms of reference and greatly enriched the sources from which the theologian and natural philosopher could draw; and, 4) a heightened sense of the individual's responsibility for his own spiritual destiny.

Demographic Change

As John Noonan has noted, much fruitful research may be undertaken concerning the impact of moral theology on issues of population. In the middle ages, theological views concerning abortion, equality of the sexes, contraception and matrimony could directly encourage demographic rise by providing the intellectual underpinnings to a Christian strategy of marriage, fertility and child-rearing.[20] On the other hand, contrariwise, one could argue that it is rather the material conditions which led to a rise in population, encouraging theologians and philosophers to provide suitable solutions to the kinds of problems which demographic change engendered. The demographic conditions prevalent in the late thirteenth and early fourteenth centuries naturally fostered concern for such subjects as the care and rearing of children and adolescents, the maintenance of good health, and the extension of life.

Recent observers are unanimous in identifying a continuous rise of population from the eleventh to the late thirteenth centuries which, although unevenly distributed and not always adequately documented, goes far to explain the great political and economic energy displayed by Europe during this period.[21] Among its ramifications were: a geographic and demographic revolution in the older cities, along with the creation of new towns; the *Reconquista* in Spain and the colonization of central and eastern Europe, which brought merchants, artisans, peasants and noblemen to formerly sparsely populated regions, sometimes at the expense of the former inhabitants; the creation of new settlements in former wastelands and inaccessible areas; the unprecedented construction of bridges, roads, canals, ports and other facilities; and the vastly increased treasuries of Church and State. By about 1300 Catholic Christianity was to reach the acme of its geographical expansion in Europe. At the same time hopes of converting the Mongols to the Faith had not yet been dashed and embassies were sent to the Far East in order to forge economic and political ties, and perhaps to convert the non-believers.

While precise figures may never be available because the middle ages lacked the lists of taxpayers, parish registers and large scale censuses which are the stock-in-trade of the historical demographer, some tentative conclusions concerning the population of Europe as a whole in the late thirteenth century have been reached through measuring urban dimensions, analyzing grave sites, and studying manor rolls, heriot lists and inquisitions post mortem. As Leopold Génicot has noted, "taken by itself, each piece of evidence is debatable... It is the consistency of the evidence that brings conviction."[22] Somewhat more accurate figures reflect the mortality of the wealthier and more privileged classes, such as the nobility and beneficed clergy. J.C. Russell, for example, has provided some rough estimates illustrating the growth of population between 1000 and 1340 A.D.[23] In Italy the population rose by about 100%; in Iberia, by about 30%; by 215% in France and the Low Countries; by 150% in the British Isles; and by 187% in Germany and Scandinavia. Such increases were experienced in both rural and urban areas, although some towns increased more than 300% in size.[24] For Europe as a whole the annual rate of increase has been estimated at 0.2 percent per annum. The most dramatic rise seems to have occurred between 1150/1200 and 1300 A.D., with the first signs of a slowdown appearing in the late thirteenth century. In addition to an increased fertility rate, it has been speculated that this population rise could have been caused by such factors as the absence of any major plague until the fourteenth century, a rising standard of living which enhanced life expectancy, and early marriage.

The slowdown which preceded the catastrophic conditions of the mid-fourteenth century may have been caused by late marriage, a reduced standard of living and economic productivity, and a lower fertility rate, which had already appeared in some areas by the late thirteenth century. The famine of 1315/7 was one of the first of a series of natural catastrophes which were to result in a sharp drop in Europe's population, so that the late medieval peak was not reached again in many regions until the late seventeenth century. While precise dating may not be possible, it has been argued that by about 1300 much of Europe had begun to exhibit the first signs of a Malthusian crisis of overpopulation, for the low level of technology could no longer support a growing population.[25] Europe's agricultural resources were inefficiently exploited, leading to: 1) a sudden reduction in the standard of living after a long period of rising expectations; 2) increasing prices for basic commodities; and, 3) food shortages, which helped to prepare a physically weakened population for the onslaughts of the plague. With the onset of the "Little Ice Age" and its attendant poor harvests in the early fourteenth century, Europe's ability to support its population reached a critical stage. Thus the relative political and social stability which had prevailed during the late twelfth and early thirteenth centuries was shattered, and Europe was confronted with increasing personal, class and national conflict over its dwindling resources.

The demographic rise which was to reach its peak sometime between 1280 and 1300 brought in its train several consequences which bear directly on the perception of the life cycle. Firstly, the admittedly sparse evidence points to a continuing increase in the number of children and adolescents up to this period.[26] One may assume an infant mortality of about 15-20% during the first year of life, with a continuing high death rate till twenty. The considerable concern in the medical and encyclopedic literature with the care of the neonate may represent an attempt to reduce the high incidence of death among infants. But despite high infant mortality rates, a rapid demographic rise had insured the survival of large numbers of children. In some areas, the number of persons under twenty-one had reached half the total population, and those under fourteen about a third. Figures provided by Higounet-Nadal for Périgeux indicate the high rate of 4.3 children per family between 1280 and 1300, dropping thereafter. In Taunton, Somerset, for example, there were 612 inhabitants over twelve in 1248, and 1,448 in 1311, despite the fact that the arable land had been only marginally increased by 10%.

The selective replacement rate (i.e. the number of children, usually male, who survive the death of one or another parent, generally male) cited by Russell and Hollingsworth, based on inquisitions post mortem, indicates a rate of 1.64 until 1265, with a drop in the late thirteenth century (1266-1290 A.D.) to 1.26 and the early fourteenth century (1291-1315) to 1.28; this was followed by a slight rise to 1.40 between 1316 and 1340.

Afterwards, the replacement rates remained negative until the late fifteenth century, which reflects the precipitous population drop.[27] If these rates were applied to England as a whole, it would mean that the number of children demanding parental and clerical attention reached a high point around 1260, which is precisely the time when a vast proliferation of educational manuals and handbooks of advice occurred. Indirect evidence for the larger number of youths is the increasing number of colleges and the promulgation of new educational statutes.[28] This was followed in the 1290s by the publication of handbooks of health directed at adults, which would confirm the demographic patterns of the late thirteenth century, when the "baby-boomers" of mid-century had reached maturity.[29] This golden age of youth was, however, not to last long since there is evidence that the death rates for children, adolescents and young adults were higher during the fatal plagues of the late middle ages than they were for adults.[30]

Another consequence of the demographic rise was a concurrent increase in life expectancy, no doubt aided by the economic prosperity which characterized the thirteenth century. Although precise figures are elusive, Russell has suggested that a high life expectancy of about 35.3 years at birth was achieved by about 1276.[31] For those who reached age ten, life expectancy was about 36.3. The life expectancy for adults lay roughly somewhere between forty and sixty years of age. One may assume a shorter life span among women under the age of forty due to the perils of childbirth. After 1276, these figures began to drop and it was not until the late nineteenth century that such a long life expectancy was reached again. Evidence drawn from the privileged classes indicates large numbers of persons surviving into their sixties and seventies. There therefore appears to be some tangible evidence for the contention voiced by Roger Bacon and Engelbert of Admont that, despite the shortened life span which mankind inherits because of the expulsion from Eden, life expectancy may nevertheless be extended through a proper regimen of health and the application of artificial means.

The paucity of fully reliable figures in the short run does not allow us to determine with any certainty whether the publication of large numbers of manuals for health was caused by the suddenly worsening state of health and mortality which began to afflict some parts of Europe by the turn of the century. Nevertheless, as often happens, society may have responded belatedly to changing material conditions, and the meliorism displayed in intellectual circles may merely be a delayed reaction to the optimal conditions which had obtained several years earlier. By 1300 signs of social, political and economic dislocation had appeared: the loss of the Holy Land in 1291; the failure of the Mongols to accept Christianity; the devaluation of the currency; the critical conflict between Boniface VIII and Philip the Fair; industrial strikes and civil disorder. The many *regimina* for the maintenance of good health which appeared may be read in conjunction with contemporary schemes for political and religious reform, suggested by Alexander of Roes, Pierre Dubois, Dante, Raymund Lull and others.

Philosophical Optimism

The palpable economic and demographic expansion which dominated much of the late thirteenth and early fourteenth centuries found expression in the rational exploitation of philosophy as a means of improving the human condition. Roger Bacon (1214-1292) described the goal of temporal welfare as providing "what individuals and people required to insure their health, to prolong their life, to acquire the goods of fortune, virtue, judgement, peace, justice, and to triumph magnificently over all that was an obstacle to this..."[32] The chief means of achieving these ends was to be the study of philosophy, which applies reason to the understanding of nature, and which teaches us to know the Creator through a knowledge of what He has created. The saints and wise men of antiquity, he argued, in their exposition of Scripture, had collected together literal meanings (as Isidore of Seville had done) from the nature of things and their properties, from which one could elicit the spiritual sense of those words by applying the appropriate adaptations and similarities.[33] As Augustine had declared in his *De doctrina christiana*, citing Jesus' call to learn prudence from the serpents and simplicity from the doves, one may derive an infinite number of Christian moral principles from an observation of nature.

To Bacon, the wisdom acquired through philosophy, which encompassed all the natural sciences and was based largely on the Aristotelian corpus, could assist in the conversion of the non- believers and combat the machinations of the Antichrist. Philosophy teaches us how to lead an honest life and organize the community through the practical application of those principles which the Christian perceives through his Faith, but which require confirmation through reason.[34] Bacon adduced the example of the saints, who diligently made use of the doctrines of the philosophers in their arsenal of polemical tools. He praised Seneca's treatises on anger and on the shortness of life, in particular, as pagan sources which confirm the moral teachings of Christianity. This same suggestion that the rational arguments found in philosophy could boost the claims of Christianity was found in Aquinas; for both Jerome and Augustine had argued that one must know one's enemy in order to destroy him.[35] At the same time, since natural reason, which is divinely imparted to us, cannot contradict faith, so philosophy cannot contradict revelation. Based on reason, it serves three functions: 1) to demonstrate the axioms of the Faith; 2) to teach the Faith with the aid of analogies drawn from nature; and 3) to disprove what is contrary to the Faith.

This tendency to apply reason and the wisdom of the non-believer to an understanding of human development was strengthened by a progressive view of human history which pervaded thirteenth century thought. The optimistic estimation of human destiny, which contrasts with the Augustinian stress on sin and its baleful results, perhaps had its genesis in the Western need to fend off the attacks of Byzantine Christianity, Judaism and heresy in the twelfth century, which accused the Church of introducing unwarranted novelties. In the twelfth century, Anselm of Havelberg, Hugh of St. Victor, Gerhoh of Reichersberg, and Honorius of Autun had all argued that, despite the fatal consequences of the Fall from Eden, man progressively receives new divine revelations which expand his knowledge of God and perfect the work of the Holy Spirit.[36] Anselm of Havelberg had argued in his *Dialogi* (ca. 1135) that God teaches us by degrees, progressively (*paulatim, quasi furtim*) adapting His pedagogy to man's capacity to learn. Just as the physician applies a different medicine to each complaint, so God provides different revelations in each period in accordance with man's power to comprehend. Hugh of St. Victor in his *De sacramentis* (ca. 1140), for example, had demonstrated the organic development of the Christian sacraments from pagan and Jewish ritual. This theory of progressive revelation often sought the basic governing principle characteristic of each age. Gerhoh of Reichersberg (ca. 1160), for example, expounding on the four vigils of the night in *Mark* 6.46, argued that each vigil represents a period of history, and each period is characterized by its own virtue -- prudence, fortitude, justice and temperance -- and is symbolized by a particular creature.[37] In Thomas Aquinas' (1226-1274) commentary on *Hebrews*, history was divided into three periods paralleling the ages of man, namely childhood, adolescence and old age.[38] The final historical age had begun some time ago and, although its duration was uncertain, the consummation was approaching. In the same way, old age commenced at sixty, but is of indeterminate length, unlike the other ages, in some persons ending at one hundred and twenty.

The most widespread such scheme of history in the late thirteenth century, when many Biblical prophecies appeared on the verge of fulfillment, was the trinitarian plan suggested by Joachim of Flora and his disciples, which divided history into three ages -- the Age of the Father, the Age of the Son, and the Age of the Holy Ghost -- in accordance with the Christian Trinity which suffuses history, since the world was created in God's image.[39] Joachim optimistically characterized the Old Testament period as one when the maturity of age (like the Jewish patriarchs) taught men to distinguish the eternal from the transitory; during the age of the New Testament, man was taught by the patience of the young; in the evangelical third age, initiated in the thirteenth century, the innocent sincerity of the child would be humanity's teacher.[40]

The radical Joachitic claim that the young would convert the world to the Faith found its most extreme expression among the Apostolic Brethren, who allowed children to preach.[41] The Joachitic vision foresaw a spiritual renewal which would commence in the late thirteenth century and would bring about a radical reorganization of society, wherein Church and State would operate in tandem. This "fluid upward motion in man's affairs"[42] would be guided, according to different interpreters of the Calabrian prophet's words, by an angelic pope, a secular ruler, a new sect of *viri spirituales*, or the Franciscan order. Ubertino da Casale in his *Arbor vitae crucifixae* (1305) stated that the present, decisive, sixth period of history, was a "new age in which a new church would be created". This would entail "the renovation of the evangelical life and the destruction of the cult of the Antichrist through the agency of those who undertook voluntary poverty in this life." The last, seventh age would be a time of "rest and miraculous participation in future glory, during which the Heavenly Jerusalem would come down to earth."[43] Such Utopian optimism bred a host of reform schemes aimed at hastening the salvation of humanity: Alexander of Roes' dream of a revived Empire; Dante's plan for a universal monarchy; Bacon's program for the reorganization of learning; Lull's suggestions for the conversion of the Infidel; and Pierre Dubois' design for the reconquest of the Holy Land.

Perception of the life cycle was likewise affected by faith in man's possibilities. The Augustinian stress on the sinfulness of man was now complemented by an understanding of the dynamic development of the whole human being from birth to death, in which the foibles and weaknesses of each stage of life are balanced by virtues and opportunities for improvement which allow for spiritual, physiological and emotional growth. Suggestions for the improvement of man's political and social life were complemented by programs for the amelioration of his spiritual and physical condition which abound in the hortatory and medical traditions.

Syncretism

Apparently associated with the Franciscan Spirituals and the Joachitic apocalypticists, Bacon's proposed reform of learning, which emphasized the observation of the natural world, was directed at neutralizing the Antichrist by arming Christians with the same mathematical and scientific knowledge possessed by the Antichrist. He even argued that the Church should study the proscribed prophecies of the Sybil, Merlin, Aquila and Joachim, along with other books of history, philosophy and astronomy, in order to determine exactly when the Antichrist would arrive.[44]

Such an attitude fostered the intellectual syncretism which permeated this period. Many of the figures whose voices will be heard speculating on the life cycle or contemplating their own spiritual development straddled several complementary, but competing cultures. Among those who wrote autobiography, Raymund Lull, Pope Celestine V, Angelo of Clareno, Abraham Abulafia and his disciple displayed an openness to oriental influence, partly as a consequence of their Mediterranean orientation, and partly due to their missionary and apocalyptical instincts, which demanded confrontation with and knowledge of the foe. The cosmopolitan environment of Catalonia and Southern Italy, for example, afforded opportunities for fertile intellectual and spiritual contact between Islam, Judaism and Christianity, along with their sectarian and heretical permutations.[45] Angelo of Clareno, for example, spent several years in Greece as an exile, and translated Johannes Climacus' *Scala paradisi* into Latin; Celestine V's form of Benedictine monasticism owes much to Greek precedents. Abulafia travelled widely in Italy and Spain in search of pupils, reaching the papal court in 1285; while his anonymous student admitted the influence of Sufism and of Avicenna on his spiritual transformation. Raymund Lull was well-acquainted with the Sufi al-Farabi, engaging in polemical battles with his Moslem opponents and suggesting the creation of schools of oriental languages to convert the non-believer; while Arnold of Villanova, Maimondes, ibn Falaquera and Bernard Gordon differ little in their prescriptions for health, for all shared the same tradition of Arabic medicine mixed with empirical observation.

One cannot ignore the reintroduction of Greek learning and the translation of Arabic sources on all speculation in natural philosophy, which had begun to be felt after about 1120; around that time Adelard of Bath began to elucidate the "causes of things" from Arabic sources; while Hermann of Carinthia had spoken of "the deep treasuries of the Arabs" as a great fountain of wisdom.[46] Within a span of about fifty years those sources which were to have a major impact on speculation concerning the ages were to be translated into Latin: the *Liber de medicina ad Almansorem* by al-Razi (865-932), translated by Gerard of Cremona; the *Liber regalis* of Haly Abbas (d. 995) translated by Stephen of Antioch; and Avicenna's (931?-1037) *Liber canonis*, translated by Gerard. Also published were Nemesius of Emesa's *De natura hominis* (390/400) in a translation by Alfano of Montecassino, and Hippocrates' *Aphorisms* with Galenic commentary. Such long-neglected occult sciences as astrology and onerology experienced a revival. The *Liber Hermetis...* (1135/47), for example, noted how the influence of the dominant planet during the months of conception and birth could affect one's destiny.[47] Daniel of Morley believed that because of the interrelatedness of the heavens and the earth, astrology could be employed by physicians.[48] The man who lives under Jupiter's benign rule, for example, will achieve immortality. A work such as the *Liber thesauri occulti* (1165) by Paschalis Romanus classified dreams and noted the messages hidden within them, depending on the age and condition of the subject.[49]

Beginning in 1210, the *libri naturales* of Aristotle, along with the commentaries of Averroes, were repeatedly condemned as a means of stemming a perceived threat to Christian dogma. But even the 1277 condemnation by Bishop Stephen Tempier of Paris of several Aristotelian and Averroistic propositions did little to stem the infiltration of Arabic and pagan learning in the schools.[50] The search for non-Christian sources to buttress the tenets of the Faith often led theologians/philosophers in the discussion of such themes as the ages of man and their ramifications, to rely on Avicenna, Averroes and Aristotle as a means of illustrating the physiological parallels of the moral traits of each age found in Isidore, Augustine or other Christian moralists.

This religious syncretism may be illustrated by two contemporary examples of Jewish autobiography, one by the great Kabbalist Abraham Abulafia (1240-1292?) and another by an anonymous follower, perhaps of Palestinian origin, which have much in common with their Christian counterparts. This includes: dependence on direct revelation; wandering and spiritual quest as a preparation for initiation into the secrets of mysticism; and an ecumenical openness bordering on religious syncretism. These works indicate a familiarity with the autobiographies by the philosopher and physician Avicenna and the Sufi mystic al-Ghazzali, which play the same kind of paradigmatic role often played by Augustine's *Confessions* as the stereotypical Christian autobiography.

Abraham Abulafia's autobiographical remarks were composed in 1285, five years after his abortive attempt to confer with Pope Nicholas III, when he was imprisoned for a month by the Franciscans.[51] Abulafia had been born in 1240, which in Kabbalistic thought, characterized as it is by messianic expectations and numerological speculations, corresponds to the year 5000 since the Creation, and the commencement of the last Millennium. This fact presumably added to Abulafia's prophetic pretensions. The same kind of messianic Apocalypticism, often based on the theology of Joachim of Flora, animated much of the evangelical fervor found in contemporary Christianity.[52] At twenty, after his father's death, Abulafia apparently had his first spiritual experience which moved him to cross the sea to Palestine in search of the legendary river Sambation, site of the Lost Ten Tribes. Like all other contemporary autobiographers, Abulafia was very vague about dates; he catalogues some of the places he taught, including Capua, Rome, Barcelona, Burgos and Messina, along with the names of some of his outstanding students and expressions of disappointment with those who were apparently forced unwillingly to study, and who may have converted to an alien faith. At the age of forty-one (1281) at Barcelona Abulafia began to record his revelations and prophetic visions. Like Raymund Lull,[53] Abulafia reported that he sometimes had Satanic, imaginary visions, and experienced some difficulty distinguishing truth from falsehood. In 1285 at Messina in Sicily, all his uncertainties were finally resolved and he reached the pinnacle of mystical understanding.

Abulafia's autobiographical remarks represent a kind of cathartic recapitulation of the stages through which he passed until reaching what he regarded as spiritual wisdom. His personal revelations, a rare phenomenon in medieval Judaism, were in fact attacked by his rival Solomon ben Adret, who accused him of declaring himself a Messiah and attributing his literary labors to the inspiration of a higher force. Modesty was certainly not one of Abulafia's virtues, and his character shares much in common with his fellow countryman Raymund Lull. The same flirtation with heresy is found among such Christian autobiographers as Lull, Angela of Foligno and Angelo of Clareno.

The second Jewish autobiographical text was composed by a disciple of Abulafia's in about 1295, and tells the same story of wandering, even abandonment of parents and native land, in search of wisdom - a theme which also appeared in Christian hagiography.[54] Like Abulafia himself, the study of Maimonides' *Guide to the Perplexed* represented an important stage in the author's intellectual growth, strengthening the desire to study logic and natural science. Another stage in his development entailed an encounter with Sufism. But only when he met a Kabbalist adept, became acquainted with the *Sefer Yetsirah* (also noted by Abulafia), having passed through a graded initiation, did he achieve a spiritual revelation whose character is described in great detail. The author indicates more than a mere nodding acquaintance with Avicenna's (980-1037) *Autobiography*; for he notes how when the great philosopher encountered difficulty solving a problem, he customarily took a drink of strong wine, fell asleep, and thereby aroused himself to even deeper thought, and the solution to his problem. This episode is taken directly from Avicenna's work. Abulafia's follower also seems to have been acquainted with the *Confessions* of the Sufi al-Ghazzali (1058-1111), who had likewise presented a catalogue of the schools of thought which he encountered before becoming a spiritual adept, explaining his grounds for rejecting each one.[55]

The Rise of the Individual

The demographic, economic and intellectual trends of the late thirteenth and early fourteenth centuries likewise had an impact on the perception of the individual and his place in both the family and the wider cosmos. Some have termed this development "the discovery of the individual", a phenomenon which had of course been apparent since the early twelfth century in clerical and noble circles. By the thirteenth century it had spread to other classes. As a result, the individual was liberated from the bonds of clan and village, free to seek his own fortune and salvation.[56] Its multiple causes have been long discussed: the breakup of the family; the loss of local communal or group identity; the social and geographical mobility of the central middle ages, as new social classes, regions of development, religious orders, came to the fore; the increased stress laid by the Church on individual responsibility, perhaps in response to heretical demands for personal accountability; and the appearance of minority and marginal groups which appeared to threaten Christian unity.

Many of the traditional constraints of clan solidarity, patriarchal authority and religious sanction had begun to break down by the late thirteenth century, not yet replaced by patriotic fervor and the nation-state. The social and geographic mobility which had paralleled the demographic revolution had separated many from their families and created the kind of independent personality whose goals are determined less by group pressure than by the need for personal economic, intellectual or spiritual fulfillment.[57] As Georges Duby has pointed out, younger sons were increasingly deprived of their inheritance with the introduction of the law of primogeniture, which was designed to conserve the resources of the family and prevent clan warfare in a time of population growth and land shortage. Among the phenomena linked to this increasing fragmentation of the family, brought on partly by economic necessity, were the Norman conquests, the Crusades, the proliferation of monasteries, the *Reconquista* and the eastern settlement. The literary symbol of this familial and social dislocation was the young knight who undergoes a series of tests to win his lady love, preferably an heiress.[58] The spirit of adventure evident in these enterprises had its religious parallel in the life of the saint who passes through a series of heroic spiritual trials in search of sacred truth. The break with one's family, followed by a period of wandering and pilgrimage, became a regular feature of contemporary biography. The adventure-packed autobiography of the former novelist Raymund Lull is perhaps the best example of the genre, filled with tales of violence, exile, captivity and shipwreck.[59]

A religious haven for those who had rejected family, friends and homeland in favor of spiritual fulfillment and penance, was to be provided by the Franciscan order, which was the moving force behind much of the life-cycle literature of the period. The heroic imitation of Christ espoused by Francis of Assisi (d. 1226) was posited on a forceful break with the past, which often paralleled the sexual crisis of late adolescence, which was to become standard fare in life-cycle theory.[60] The new mendicant order rejected the traditional partiarchal structure of monasticism, and transformed religious penance from a series of simple formulary acts into a continuing process of self-examination. This demanded "the conscious awareness of the singularity of each individual life,"[61] which is the cornerstone of the Christian doctrine of penance as it evolved in the thirteenth century. The kind of simple confession of faith one finds in Rather of Verona's (d.974) *Confessio*[62] was now to be replaced by a continuous introspective narrative which may be surprising in its frankness.

The confessional thus became the means whereby every Christian could periodically undergo the kind of re-evaluation which brought the stages of his own development into perspective. After 1215, the Church sought to exercise its control over wayward believers by imposing the sacrament of penance on all its communicants.[63] Such confessions became the raw material out of which much contemporary biography and autobiography were fashioned. We may thus compare the perceptions of the life cycle expressed by theologians, philosophers and physicians with individual attempts to place one's own life in some schematic perspective. The stress was naturally on emotional rather than physiological development, and on the crises of the spirit which accompany the passage from one to another stage of life. The autobiographical self-examination engendered by religious confession encouraged the believer to provide a rational structure to his life, imposing some periodization upon the organic passage from childhood to adolescence and adulthood.

The institution of regular confession was part of a longer process of penance requiring contrition, oral confession and satisfaction via a suitable penitential act.[64] The curative role of such penance was widely recognized, and the act of confession was akin to vomiting out a deadly poison in order to affect a cure of the soul.[65] Confession and penance are posited on the notions of correction and rehabilitation, somewhat akin to the meliorative, progressive theories of history current at the time. The Christian notion of confession and penance and the philosophical belief in progress share a common optimistic faith in man's potential for improvement.

While the confession was to be undertaken before one's local priest, the newly founded mendicant orders, especially the Dominicans and Franciscans, were accorded the papal privilege of hearing confessions, which enabled a larger number of believers to fall under the Church's scrutiny. Such figures as Humbert of Romans (1193/4-1277) undertook to counsel preachers concerning the means of composing a convincing sermon directed at a particular audience.[66] All theoreticians stressed the centrality of shame in confession -- an emotion voiced in turn by authors of autobiography. The many confessional manuals further contained much relating to such issues as childhood, baptism, oblation, child-marriage, sexual non-conformity, consanguinity, pedagogy and infanticide.

The institution of confession and its restorative character became more widespread through the new penitential or tertiary orders which attempted to regularize acts of penance among those pious faithful who could not entirely abandon the world for a monastery.[67] These groups invariably demanded more than the yearly confession required by the Fourth Lateran Council -- three or four times a year. Their greatest devotees allegedly confessed daily. The Dominican minister-general Humbert of Romans, founder of many confraternities intended for pious laymen, sought to achieve three stated aims: 1) the encouragement of the cult of the Virgin Mary; 2) the repression of heresy; and, 3) the improvement of morals. The second two goals, at least, could be achieved through the greater exposure of the believer to the clerical observation accorded by the practice of confession. Although the first such confraternities date from the time of Francis himself and received special impetus during the revivalist Alleluia campaign of 1233 under the leadership of Peter of Verona, among others, most of the extant regulations date from the 1260s, and all require the frequent confession of sin.[68]

Although the history of these movements has not yet been entirely mapped out, the impetus they gave toward critical self - examination is undeniable. Many of those who published autobiographies or were the subjects of contemporary hagiography, were associated with them. The earliest Franciscans, including the founder, were themselves penitents, who were eventually regularized and clericalized. In 1221, Pope Honorius III had indeed created an order of penitence (although the term 'order' clearly does not wholly apply to all the penitents) which required confession and communion at least three times a year (at Christmas, Easter and Pentecost), and obliged its members to refrain from resort to arms, dishonest acts and swearing, and to restore all ill-gotten goods. Those who could not join the order, particularly married couples, might carry out penitential exercises, although they were apparently at first not subject to a specific rule. By the late thirteenth century, such informal adherence was institutionalized with the creation of "sisters and brothers of penitence" -- the so-called tertiary orders -- constitutionally linked to the Franciscans and Dominicans. In addition, several religious orders were formed which began as penitential confraternities, such as the Servites, the Brethren of the Sack (later incorporated into the Augustinian order), and the Flagellants. Another group of penitents were the many *mulieres religiosae*, often called beguines, some of whom were cloistered, who had been observed by James of Vitry in the Low Countries and the Rhine basin in the early thirteenth century, and were responsible for much of the mystical, visionary literature now produced.[69]

Thus, the imposition of confession and penance upon the believers, along with the formal organization of confraternities of penitent laity, encouraged interest in the life cycle in the following ways: 1) much of the literature dealing with the stages of life was produced by the mendicant orders; 2) attention was directed toward the progressive development of the individual's physical, emotional and spiritual life, which was viewed as a microcosmic reflection of the dynamic progress of God's creation; and, 3) comprehension of the stages of life as understood in learned circles, and the transitional phases from period to period, reached a wider audience through the agency of the mendicants and the institution of penance.

Many of the conditions needed to reinforce interest in the stages of life and their spiritual, physiological and emotional ramifications were thus present in the late thirteenth century. The proliferation of classical and Arabic sources, which inundated the universities after 1240 and whose exploitation was justified as a tool in the rational support of Christianity, provided the raw material for the creation of a theory of developmental psychology. While still founded on the Christian notion of sin and its consequences, such a theory was informed by an optimistic appraisal of man's potential for development, and a recognition of the dynamic balance of biological and spiritual forces with which the individual must struggle. The demographic and economic improvement which had characterized the previous centuries had reached its highest point, and the material achievements of European civilization fostered a more comprehensive appreciation of man's potential. At the same time, the greater emphasis placed on penance created the institutional framework for a retrospective examination of each individual's personal development.

I. *Notes*

1. Pierre-Jean George Cabanis, *Rapports du physique et du moral de l'homme. Quatrième mémoire. De l'influence des âges sur les idées et sur les affections morales*, in *Oeuvres complètes*, 5 vols. (Paris, 1843), III, 158-191. This was first published in 1802. See Martin S. Staum, *Cabanis. Enlightenment and Medical Philosophy in the French Revolution* (Princeton, 1980), 211-217.

2. Michael Philibert, *L'échelle des âges* (Paris, 1968) 24 ff. contains a good summary of anthropological studies of life cycle; Leopold Rosenmäyr, "Die menschlichen Lebensalter: in Deutungsversuchen der europäischen Kulturgeschichte," in L. Rosenmäyr, ed., *Die menschlichen Lebensalter: Kontinuität und Krisen* (Munich, 1978), 23-79 for a survey of Western sources; see also Henry Fosbrooke, "Die Altersgliederung als gesellschaftliches Grundprinzip - Ein Untersuchung am Beispiel des Hirtenvolkes der Maasai in Ostafrika," in *ibid.*, 80-104; S.N. Eisenstadt, "African Age Groups. A Comparative Study", *Africa*, 24 (1954), 100-113; P.H. Gulliver, *Social Control in an African Society. A Study of the Arusha: Agricultural Masai of Northern Tanganyika* (London, 1963), 28 ff.; A.H.J. Prins, *East African Class Systems: An Inquiry into the Social Order of Galla, Kipsigis and Kikuyu* (Groningen, 1953).

3. Samuel Chew, *The Pilgrimage of Life* (Port Washington, N.Y., 1973), 144 ff.

4. "The Human Life Span in History", *Interdisciplinair centrum voor historisch onderzoek naar de menselijk levensloop Bulletin*, 1 (1984), 17.

5. Robert Sears and S. Shirley Fellman, eds., *The Seven Ages of Man* (Los Altos, Ca., 1973); for criticism of the alleged rigidity of the Western tradition, see Ashley Montague, *Growing Young* (New York, 1981), 123; cf. Colin Turnbull, *The Human Cycle* (New York, 1983); Daniel J. Levinson, *The Seasons of a Man's Life* (New York, 1978).

6. Philippe Ariès, *Centuries of Childhood*, trans. R. Baldick (New York, 1965) for shortened English translation.

7. Jerome Kroll, "The Concept of Childhood in the Middle Ages," *Journal of the History of the Behavioral Sciences*, 13 (1977), 384-393; Adrian Wilson, "The Infancy of the History of Childhood: An Appraisal of Philippe Ariès," *History and Theory*, 19 (1980), 132-153; L. Milis, "Het kind in de Middeleeuwen. Beschouwingen over methode en onderzoek," *Tijdschrift voor geschiednis*, 94 (1981), 377-90.

8. See especially the articles collected in *ADH*, 8 (1973).

9. Johannes Gobi, *Scala coeli* (Lübeck, 1476), cccxxvii. *puer*. For an example of loving parents, cf. Gervase of Tillbury, *Otia imperialia*, ed. F. Liebermann and R. Pauli, *MGH*. *Scriptores* (Hannover, 1885), 27:390; an excellent collection of sources is Klaus Arnold, *Kind und Gesellschaft im Mittelalter und Renaissance* (Paderborn, 1980).

10. An example of curial discussion concerning drowning children saved through the good offices of Thomas of Cantilupo (1318/20), representative of hundreds of such cases which arose, is found in André Vauchez, *La sainteté en occident aux derniers siècles du moyen âge d'après les procès de canonisation et les documents hagiographiques* (Rome, 1981), 633-647.

11. Georges Duby, "Structure de parenté et noblesse dans la France du Nord aux XIe et XIIe siècles," in *Hommes et structures du moyen âge* (Paris, 1973), 267-85; idem, *Rural Economy and Country Life in the Medieval West*, trans. C. Postan (London, 1968), *passim*; idem, *The Early Growth of the European Economy*, trans. H.B. Clark (London, 1973), 171-85; Robert Boutruche, *Seigneurie et feodalité*, 2 vols. (Paris, 1970), II, 224-34.

12. Philippe Ariès, *Images de l'homme devant la mort* (Paris, 1983) for a survey with much illustrative material; Jacques Chiffoleau, *La comptabilité de l'au dela les hommes, la mort et la religion dans la region d' Avignon à la fin du moyen âge (vers 1320-vers 1489)* (Paris, 1980) discusses the great upheavals of the period and their ramifications in the attitude to death; see also Jean Delumeau, *La peur en Occident (xive-xviiie siècles). Une cité assiegée* (Paris, 1978).

13. David Herlihy and Christiane Klapisch-Zuber, *Les toscanes et leur familles* (Paris, 1978), 200 ff.

14. Franz Böll, "Die Lebensalter, Ein Beitrag zur Ethologie und zur Geschichte der Zahlen," *Neue Altertumsgeschichte und deutsche Literatur*, 16 (1913), 89-145; Leopold Löw, *Die Lebensalter in der jüdische Literatur* (Szegedin, 1875); W. Wackernagel, *Die Lebensalter, Ein Betrag zur vergleichenden Sitten-und Rechtsgeschichte* (Basel, 1862); see also A.F. von Pauly and G. Wissowa, eds., *Realenzyklopädie*, 48 vols. (Stuttgart, 1958-1974), I, 691 ff. on the *aetates* in the ancient world.

15. Adolf Hofmeister, "Puer, Iuvenis, Senex. Zum Verständnis der mittelalterlichen Altersbezeichnungen," in *Papsttum und Kaisertum. Forschungen zur politischen Geschichte und Geisteskultur des Mittelalters. Paul Kehr zum 65. Geburtstag dargestellt*, ed. Albert Brackmann (Munich, 1926), 287-316; Joseph de Ghellinck, "Iuventus, gravitas, senectus," in *Studia mediaevalia in honorem admodum reverendi patris Raymundi Josephi Martin* (Bruges, 1948), 39-59; David Herlihy, "Veillir à Florence au Quattrocento," *Annales (Économies, Sociétés, Civilisations)*, 24 (1969), 1338-1352 contains citation of a large number of formerly unmentioned sources.

16. Elizabeth Langford Sears, *The Ages of Man. Medieval Interpretations of the Life Cycle* (Princeton, 1986); cf. Ukrike Bauer, *Der Liber Introductorius des Michael Scotus in der Abschrift Clm. 10268 der bürgerlichen Staatsbibliothek München* (Munich, 1983), 81-90, fig. 70. See also Fritz Saxl, "Beiträge zu einer Geschichte der Planetendarstellungen in Orient und Okzident," *Der Islam*, 3 (1912), 175; cf. Chew, *op. cit.*, 162 for quote.

17. J.A. Burrow, *The Ages of Man: A Study in Medieval Writing and Thought* (Oxford, 1986).

18. G.B. Fowler, "Manuscript Admont 608 and Engelbert of Admont (c. 1250-1331). Part II. Appendices 6-13", *AHDLMA*, 45 (1978), 250-306. The *Manipulus florum* attributed to Thomas of Ireland, *B.M. Royal* 7, C.III. on *iuventus* (fol. 100v), cites Ambrose, Bernard, Cyprian, Cassian and Seneca. *Senectus* (fol. 170r-v) cites Ambrose, Jerome, Augustine, Cyprian, Hugh of St. Victor, Seneca, John Chrysostom and Cassian.

19. For a general survey of the period see J.H. Mundy, *Europe in the High Middle Ages, 1150-1309* (London, 1973); H. Jedin, ed., *Handbuch der Kirchengeschichte*, III, pt. 2 (Freiburg, 1966-1968); Leopold Génicot, *Le XIIIe siècle européen* (Paris, 1968). For a survey of the economy til 1340, see Robert Henri Bautier, *The Economic Development of Medieval Europe*, trans. Heather Karolyi (London, 1971), 110-169. Michael Postan, et al., *Cambridge Economic History of Europe*, 7 vols. to date (Cambridge, 1941-1978), III, 155-191, 289-337, 372-398; Gerald A.J. Hodgett, *A Social and Economic History of Medieval Europe* (London, 1972), 88-105. On the growing acceptance of wealth, *Cambridge Economic History*, III, 558-70. Some of the following material is dealt with in Georges Minois, *Histoire de la viellesse* (Paris, 1987), 221-285, although different conclusions are often drawn.

20. John T. Noonan, "Intellectual and Demographic History," in V. Glass and R. Revelle, eds., *Population and Social Change* (London, 1972) 115-135.

21. A good summary is J.C. Russell, *Population in Europe 500-1500* (London, 1969), which summarizes his *Late Ancient and Medieval Population* (Philadelphia, 1958), along with modifications based on more recent findings. John Hatcher, *Plague, Population and the Economy 1348-1530* (London, 1977) summarizes the economic evidence; specific data on trends in urban population appear in Roger Mols, *Introduction à la démographie historique des villes d'Europe du XIVe au XVIIIe siècle*, 3 vols, (Louvain, 1954- 1956); for some of the problems in medieval demography, see R. Fossier, "La Démographie médiévale: problèmes de méthode (Xe - XIIIe siècles)," in *ADH*, 10 (1975), 143-165; E. Baratier, "Démographie médiévale dans le midi méditerranéen. Sources et méthodes," in E. Perroy, ed., *La démographie médiévale. Sources et méthodes* (Nice, 1970), 9-16. A

major survey of methods and results in historial demography is T.H. Hollingsworth, *Historical Demography* (London, 1969).

22. Leopold Génicot, "On the Evidence of Growth of Population in the West," in Sylvia Thrupp, ed., *Change in Medieval Society* (New York, 1964), 21. The Jewish family experienced a somewhat lower demographic rise. See Kenneth R. Stow, "The Jewish Family in the Rhineland in the High Middle Ages: Form and Function," *American Historical Review*, 92 (1987), 1085-1110.

23. Russell, *Population*, 19; cf. also M.K. Bennett, *The World's Food* (New York, 1954), 9, 10, 14.

24. Pierre Guillaume and Jean-Pierre Pousson, *Démographie historique* (Paris, 1970), 48; on the rural rise, based on a study of one hundred and seventy-seven villages, see J. Dupaquier and E. LeRoy Ladurie, "Quatre-Vingts villages (XIIIe - XX siècles)", *Annales (Économies, Sociétés, Civilisations)*, 24 (1969), 423-434.

25. On the loss of equilibrium around 1300 see George Bertrand et al., eds., *Histoire de la France rurale. La formation des campagnes françaises des origines au XIVe siècle* (Paris, 1975), 553 ff.; Barbara Harvey, "The Population Trend in England between 1300 and 1348," *Transactions of the Royal Historical Society*, 16 (1965), 23 ff.; Georges Duby, *Rural Society and Country Life in the Medieval West*, trans. Cynthia Postan (London, 1968), 118; Ian Kershaw, "The Great Famine and Agrarian Crisis in England 1315-1355," in R.H. Hilton, ed., *Peasants, Knights and Heretics: Studies in Medieval English Social History* (Cambridge, 1976), 85-132; *Cambridge Economic History*, III, 191-256, 338-354, 389-413, 456-8.

26. Russell, *Population*, 25 ff.; Fols, *op. cit.* II, 208, J.C. Chambers, *Population, Economy and Society in Pre-Industrial England*, ed. W.A. Armstrong (Oxford, 1972), 20; A. Higounet-Nadal, "Les facteurs de croissance de la ville Périgueux," in *ADH*, 17 (1982), 11-20; E. Miller, "The English Economy in the XIIIth Century. Implications of Recent Research," *Past and Present*, 28 (1964), 21-40; J.Z. Titow, "Some Evidence of the Thirteenth Century Population Increase," *Economic History Review*, 14 (1961/2), 217-223.

27. Hatcher, *op. cit.*, 26-9; Hollingsworth, *op. cit.*, 375-388.

28. Nicholas Orme, *English Schools in the Middle Ages* (London, 1973), 294 lists the number of English localities between 1066 and 1530 in which one or more schools are noted. Before 1500, the highest increase occurred first between 1250 and 1299 (an increase of 16, from 32 to 48), followed by 1300-1349 (an increase of 14, from 48 to 62); cf. A.F. Leach, *The Schools of Medieval England* (New York, 1915), 174: "At some time unknown before 1306 a new departure was taken in organizing the grammar schools of Oxford, which appears to point to a considerable increase in their number."

29. Wilhelm Berges, *Die Fürstenspiegel des hohen und späten Mittelalters* (Stuttgart, 1938), lists forty-six "mirrors for princes" which appeared between 1159 and 1387. The peak period for the appearance of such manuals of advice occurred in the second half of the thirteenth century. A similar convergence is found in Diane Bornstein, *The Lady in the Tower. Medieval Courtesy Literature for Women* (Hamden, Ct., 1983), which covers manuals of advice to young girls, many of which appeared ca. 1260-1320. Manuals of health, directed largely at adults, some of which are translations of Avenzoar, Maimonides or Pseudo-Galen, were concentrated in the period ca. 1290-1340. See Sarton, II.2, 832, 890, 894, 1087; III.1, 245, 285, 835.

30. G. Ohlin, "No Safety in Numbers: Some Pitfalls in Historical Statistics," in H. Rosovsky, ed., *Industrialization in Two Systems: Essays in Honor of Alexander Gerschenkorn* (New York, 1966) 68-70.

31. Russell, *Population*, 30-32.

32. Roger Bacon, *Compendium studii philosophiae*, ed. J.S. Brewer (London, 1959), 393.

33. Roger Bacon, *Opus majus*, ed. J.H. Bridges, 3 vols. (Oxford, 1897-1900) III, 51: "Item omnes sancti et sapientes antiqui in suis expositionibus sensum literalem colligunt ex naturis rerum et proprietatibus earum, ut per convenientes adaptationes et similtudines eliciant sensus spirituales". Cf. also *ibid.*, I, 301.

34. Roger Bacon, *Moralis philosophia*, III Dist. 5, ed. Eugenio Massa (Turici, n.d.), 142.

35. Thomas Aquinas, *Expositio super librum Boethii de trinitate*, ed. Bruno Decker (Leiden, 1959), 90-97; cf. Augustine, *De trinitate*, IX-XII, XIV, XV, in *MPL*, 42: 859ff., 1035ff.

36. Wilhelm Kamlah, "Apokalypse und Geschichtstheologie," in *Historische Studien*, 285 (Berlin, 1935), 57ff.; Alois Dempf, *Sacrum imperium* (Darmstadt, 1954), 229ff.; Michael Goodich, "Un dialogue entre occident et orient: Anselme de Havelberg et l'idée de progrès," *Actes du premier colloque franco-polonais d'histoire* (Nice, 1983), 173-181.

37. Peter Classen, *Gerhoch von Reichersberg* (Wiesbaden, 1960), 296.

38. Thomas Aquinas, *Super Epistolam S. Pauli Apostoli ad Hebraeos Commentaria*, IX, Lect 5, 2 vols. (Turin, 1929), 390.

39. Delno C. West and Sandra Zimdars Swartz, *Joachim of Fiore, A Study in Spiritual Perceptions and History* (Bloomington, Ind., 1983), 99-112; Bernard McGinn, *The Calabrian Abbot. Joachim of Fiore in the History of Western Thought* (New York, 1985); Marjorie E. Reeves, *Joachim of Fiore and the Prophetic Future* (London, 1976), 74ff.; idem, *The Influence of Prophecy in the Middle Ages* (Oxford,

1969) are some of the more recent works. Angelo of Clareno's *Historia septem tribulationum fratrum minorum* contains the Spiritual Franciscan version of history. See Ignaz von Döllinger, ed., *Beiträge zur Sektengeschichte des Mittelalters*, 2 vols. (Munich, 1890), II, 417-528; on the Spirituals see Decima L. Douie, *The Nature and Effect of the Heresy of the Fraticelli* (Manchester, 1932); Gordon Leff, *Heresy in the Later Middle Ages*, 2 vols. (Manchester, 1967), I.

40. Joachim of Fiore, *Tractatus super quattuor Evangelia*, ed. E. Buonaiuti (Rome, 1930), 92.

41. Eugenio Anagnine, *Dolcino e il movimento ereticale del trecento* (Florence, 1964) on Gerard Segarelli and his movement.

42. West and Zimdars, *op. cit.*, 112.

43. Ubertino da Casale, *Arbor vitae crucifixae* (Venice, 1485), f. 203 r, f. 200 r, cited in Reeves, *Joachim*, 44: "est renovationis evangelicae vitae et expugnationis sectae antichristianae sub pauperibus voluntariis nihil possidentibus in hoc vita," and "quedam quieta et mir participatio futurae gloriae ac si celestis Jerusalem videatur quoddam novum seculum seu nova ecclesia tunc formari." Cf. also Henri de Lubac, *La posterité de Joachim de Flore. I. De Joachim à Schelling* (Paris, 1978), 104-107.

44. Roger Bacon, *Opus maius*, I, 269.

45. Yitzhak Baer, "Ha-megama ha-datit chevratit shel 'Sefer ha-Hassidim'," *Zion*, 3 (1937/8), 50-51 notes the parallel between Franciscanism and early Hassidism; Shulamith Shahar, "Le catharisme et le début de la cabale," *Annales (Économies, Sociétés, Civilisations)*, 29.pt.2 (1974), 1185-1210 attempts to demonstrate the similarities between Catharism and early Kabbalistic tracts such as the *Sefer ha-Bahir*. For evidence of Jewish influence on Raymund Lull, particularly Judah Halevi and Kabbalism, see J. Ma Millas i Vallicrosa, "The Doctrine of the 'Lullian Dignities' and the Sefiroth," *Yitshak Baer Jubilee Volume*, ed. S. Ettinger, et al. (Jerusalem, 1960), 186-90 [Hebrew]; Eusebio Colomer, "Die Beziehung des Ramon Llull zum Judentum und Rahmen des spanischen Mittelalter," in Paul Wilpert, ed., *Miscellanea Mediaevalia. Jüdentum in Mittelalter* (Berlin, 1966), 183-227 notes Lull's relations with the Jews of Majorca and his polemical tracts against Judaism.

46. Adelard of Bath, *Questiones naturales*, ed. Martin Müller, in *Beiträge*, 31. 2 (Munich, 1934), i; Hermann of Carinthia, *De essentiis*, ed. Charles Burnet (Leiden, 1982), 70.

47. Theodore Silverstein, ed., "Liber Hermetis Mercurii triplicis de vii rerum principiis," *AHDLMA*, 23 (1955), 266.

48. Cited in Tullio Gregory, "La nouvelle idée de nature et de savoir scientifique au xiie siècle," in John Emery Murdoch and Edith Dudley

Sylla, ed., *The Cultural Context of Medieval Learning*, in *Boston Studies in the Philosophy of Science*, 26 (Boston, 1975), 202.

49. Simon Collin-Rosset, ed., "Le *Liber Thesauri occulti* de Pascalis Romanus (Un traité d'interprétation des songes du xiie siècle)," *AHDLMA*, 30 (1963), 111-198; Gerhart Hoffmeister, "Rasis' Traumlehre. Traumbücher des Spätmittelalters," *Archiv für Kulturgeschichte*, 51 (1969), 137-159 notes the influence of the four humors, qualities and elements on dream analysis. R.A. Pack, ed. "De prognosticatione sompniorum Libellus Guillelmus de Aragonia adscriptus," *AHDLMA*, 33 (1966), 237-93 contains a discussion of the sources for dream-analysis.

50. Aime Forest, et al., *Le mouvement doctrinal du XIe au XVe siècle* (Paris, 1956), 205-208, 321.

51. On Abulafia see Gershom Scholem, *Major Trends in Jewish Mysticism* (New York, 1964), 118-55; Abraham Berger, "The Messianic Self-Consciousness of Abraham Abulafia," in *Essays in Jewish Life and Thought presented to Salo W. Baron*, ed. J. Blau, et al. (New York, 1959), 55-62. For a reprint of the autobiographical sections of Abulafia's (1285) *Otsar Adon Genooz*, see G. Scholem, *Hakabbalah shel Sefer ha-Tmunah shel Avraham Abulafia*, ed. I. Ben Shlomo (Jerusalem, 1968).

52. See A. Tuaf, "Remazim le-Tnuah Meshichit be-Roma be-Shnat 1260," *Bar-Ilan. Sefer ha-Shana shel Universitat Bar-Ilan*, 14/15 (1976), 114-121; Aharon Ze'ev Eskoli, *Ha-Tnuot ha-Meshichiot be-Yisrael* (Jerusalem, 1956), 186-90 on Jewish messianism in the thirteenth century, which closely parallels Christian movements.

53. B. de Gaiffier, ed. "Vita beati Raimundi Lulli," *AB*, 48 (1930), 130-178 (cc. 24-5).

54. Scholem, *Major Trends*, 17-55 for translation; for original see *idem*, "'Shaarei Tsedek', Maamar be-Kabbalah mei-Ascolat R. Abraham Abulafia meyoohas le-R. Shem-Tov," *Kiryat Sefer*, 1 (1924), 127-139.

55. William Gohlmann, ed. and trans., *The Life of Ibn Sina* (Albany, 1974); Claud Field, ed. and trans., *The Confessions of Al-Ghazzali* (Lahore, n.d.).

56. See e.g., Adolf Rein, "Über die Entwicklung der Selbstbiographie im ausgehenden deutschen Mittelalter," *Archiv für Kulturgeschichte*, 14 (1919), 193-213; T.C. Price Zimmermann, "Confession and Autobiography in the Early Renaissance," *Renaissance Studies in Honor of Hans Baron*, ed. A. Molho and J.A. Tedeschi (Florence, 1971), 119-140; Marziano Guglielmiti, "L'Autobiographie en Italie, xve-xviie siècles," in James Olney, ed., *Autobiography: Essays Theoretical and Critical* (Princeton, 1980), 101-104.

57. Karl Joachim Weintraub, "Autobiography and Historical Consciousness," *Critical Inquiry*, 1 (1975), 821-848. See his survey in *The Value of the Individual. Self and Circumstance in Autobiography* (Chicago, 1978). A problem which has recently exercised historians has been the degree to which "individualism" may have existed as a praiseworthy characteristic in the middle ages. Some recent discussions are John F. Benton, "Individualism and Conformity in Medieval Western Europe," in *Individualism and Conformity in Classical Islam*, ed. A. Banani and S. Vyronis, Jr. (Wiesbaden, 1977), 145-158; Colin Morris, "Individuality in Twelfth Century Religion," *Journal of Ecclesiastical History*, 31 (1980), 195-206.

58. Robert Hanning, *The Individual in Twelfth-Century Romance* (New Haven, 1977), 3-50 on the appearance of the solitary hero in literature.

59. de Gaiffier, 130-78.

60. Michael Goodich, *Vita perfecta: the Ideal of Sainthood in the Thirteenth Century*, in *Monographien zur Geschichte des Mittelalters*, 25 (Stuttgart, 1982), *passim*. While there may be some conventional hagiography in the theme of familial opposition to one's break with the past, at around the same time two other well-documented cases of conflict over the turn to religion occurred, those of Thomas Aquinas and Salimbene de Adam. In both instances, quite legitimate family interests came into conflict with the desires of youth. Thomas' family preferred the influential Benedictines of Montecassino to the newly founded Dominicans. Salimbene's choice of the Franciscans left his family without a legitimate male heir. See *ibid.*, 106-109.

61. Georges Gusdorf, "Conditions and Limits of Autobiography" in Olney, *op. cit.*, 48.

62. Rather of Verona, *Confessio eiusdem*, in *MPL*, 136:393-444.

63. Nicole Beriou, "Autour de Latran IV (1215): la naissance de la confession moderne et sa diffusion," in Groupe de la Bussière, *Pratiques de la confession* (Paris, 1983), 73-93; Hervé Martin, "Confession et contrôle sociale à la fin du moyen âge," in *ibid.*, 117-134.

64. For some of the early confessionals see P. Michaud-Quantin, "A propos des premiers 'Summae confessorum'," *Recherches de théologie ancienne et médiévale*, 26 (1959), 264-309; idem, *Sommes de casuistique et manuels de confessions au moyen âge (xii-xvi siècles)* (Louvain, 1962) for a useful list of the major manuals; Thomas Tentler, "The Summa for Confessors as an Instrument of Social Control," in *The Pursuit of Holiness in Late Medieval and Renaissance Religion*, ed., C. Trinkaus and H. Oberman (Leiden, 1974), 123-5 on the confessional method; idem, *Sin and Confession on the Eve of the Reformation* (Princeton, 1977); Cyrille Vogel, ed., *Le pêcheur et la pénitence au moyen âge* (Paris, 1969) for a collection of relevant sources. Edmund of Abingdon (d. 1242) provided a standard

definition of penitence: "Penitencia enim cum cordis contricione, oris confessione, et operis penitentis, et destruit mortale peccatum, et retraxit hominem ad suum creatorem, et ducit animam ad magnam gaudium et claritatem." (*Speculum ecclesie*, ed. Helen P. Forshaw [London, 1973], 67.)

65. As Pope Celestine V (d. 1294) wrote in one of his *Opuscula, De Exemplis*, c. 1: "Sicut quilibet evomere venenum, ne moriatur, recipiens aliquod amarum, sic per recordationem poenere aeternae debet homo venenum peccati evomere." (Margarinus de la Bigne, ed., *Bibliotheca maxima patrum*, 28 vols. [Lyons, 1677], XXV, 801).

66. A. Lecoy de la Marche, *La chaire français au moyen âge* (Paris, 1886); Th.-M. Charlond, *Artes praedicandi, contribution à l'histoire de la rhétorique au moyen âge* (Ottawa, 1936).

67. On the penitential orders, see G.G. Meersseman, *Le dossier de l'ordre de la pénitence au xiiie siècle* (Fribourg, 1961); G. Hallack and P. Anson, *These Made Peace* (Paterson, N.J., 1957). A general survey may be found in André Vauchez, "Pénitents," *Dictionnaire de spiritualité*, ed. M. Viller, et al., 13 vols. to date (Paris, 1937-1987), 1010-1023; A.G. Matanic, "Penitenti," *Dizionario degli istituti di perfezione*, ed. G. Pelliccia, et al., 7 vols. to date (Rome, 1974-1983), VI, 1359-1966.

68. André Vauchez, *La sainteté en occident aux derniers siècles du moyen âge d'après les procès de canonisation et les documents hagiographiques* (Rome, 1981) contains a great deal on lay piety. Gilles-Gerard Meersseman, "Storiografie delle confraternite laicali nell'alto medio evo," in *Storiografia e storia: Studi in onore di Eugenio Dupré Theseider*, 2 vols. (Rome, 1974), I, 39-64 attempts to disentangle the history of the confraternities. A wealth of material on the penitents is found in Mariano d'Alatri, ed., *I frati penitenti di San Francesco nella società del due e trecento* (Rome, 1977); idem, *Il movimento francescano della penitenza nella società medievale* (Rome, 1980); O. Schmücki, ed., *L'ordine della penitenza di san Francesco d'Assisi nel secolo xiii* (Rome, 1973).

69. James of Vitry, *Vita Mariae Oigniacensis*, in *ASS*, 23 June V: 547. A considerable bibliography has appeared recently on the beguine women. See e.g. Brenda Bolton, "Mulieres sanctae," *Studies in Church History*, 10 (1973), 77-95; idem, "*Vitae Matrum*. A Further Aspect of the Frauenfrage," *Medieval Women*, ed. Derek Baker (Oxford, 1978), 253-274; Jeanne Ancelet-Hustache, *Master Eckhart and the Rhineland Mystics*, trans. Hilda Graf (New York, 1957), 13 ff; Richard Kieckhefer, *Unquiet Souls, Fourteenth Century Saints and their Religious Milieu* (Chicago, 1984) deals extensively with Dorothy of Montau and Clare Cambacorta; the classic account remains Herbert Grundmann, *Religiöse Bewegungen im Mittelalter* (Hildesheim, 1961). Valerie M. Lagorio, "Medieval Continental Women Mystics," in Paul E. Szarmach, ed., *An Introduction to the Medieval Mystics of Europe*

(Albany, 1984), 161-194 attempts to distinguish between female piety, which is 'receptive', and male piety, which is 'active'. Visions represent an attempt by some women to intervene in the outside world. See also Peter Dinzelbacher, ed., *Frauenmystik im Mittelalter* (Ostfielden, 1985).

II. *Prolegomena to the Sources*

Given the many contexts in which speculation on the life cycle could be found, the present volume will concentrate on several discrete kinds of sources which have thus far received less attention, and through which a largely erudite tradition reached an ever-widening popular audience. Four sources will be examined: 1) hagiography; 2) autobiography; 3) the hortatory literature of advice; and, 4) encyclopedias. Much of this literature was influenced by the introduction of Aristotle and the greater acquaintance with Arabic learning in the schools, which reached its peak sometime after 1240. All indicate the powerful impact of the recently-founded mendicant orders, like the Franciscans and Dominicans, on the education of the laity, which sought to disseminate the fruits of scholastic speculation. The contributions of natural philosophers and moral theologians to discussion of the life cycle indicate a lively environment of optimistic intellectual debate which began to wind down about 1330, just prior to the gloomy crises of the fourteenth century. These turned men's attention away from life to death, away from the means of prolonging our stay in this world to the means of ensuring our place in the next.

While each of these sources deals with the various stages of life in either an episodic or more schematic fashion, each one belongs to a particular tradition of intellectual discourse which sometimes subordinated empirical observation to a pre-ordained framework dependent on long-cherished theological, moral or medical pre-suppositions. As a result, while discussions of child-rearing, the vagaries of aging, the selection of a suitable tutor, the crisis of adolescent sexuality, or the fickleness of youth, for example, were dealt with at great length, one often encounters a frustrating compartmentalization of knowledge. This was only occasionally breached by such figures as Engelbert of Admont or Bernard Gordon, who sought to shore up arguments drawn from Scripture with evidence from natural science in accordance with Bonaventure's remark that "the whole world is a reflection, a path, a vestige and a book with writing front and back."[1] It was a rare figure, such as Raymund Lull, author of a bestiary and a book of moral advice to his son, who could go beyond mere speculation to a recapitulation of his own spiritual development in the *Autobiography*.

Perhaps restrained by the forms which each tradition could impose, it is only the encyclopedic literature which undertook a comprehensive understanding of progressive human development; here, the physiological, psychological and spiritual changes we each undergo were linked to the essential laws governing the entire cosmos. The autobiographer dealt with an individual; the hagiographer with an idealized form of human behavior; the moralist or physician prescribed the therapeutic means of achieving such an ideal; while the encyclopedist linked the parts with the whole, the micro with the macrocosm, in order to explain how man's character reflects God's creation. A presentation of the sources exploited in this study will reveal a remarkable concern for the dynamic processes of human growth in the late thirteenth and early fourteenth centuries, accompanied by an attempt to situate the paradigmatic stages of life in a broader cosmic context.

Hagiography

The first group of sources which will be profitably examined are the lives of the saints, in which an idealized incarnation of the human life cycle found expression. Secular biography is uterly dwarfed by the sheer mass of hagiographical sources.[2] Several vernacular lives did appear, such as the biography of William the Marshal, Adam de la Halle's life of Robert of Sicily, and Gil Zamora's life of Alfonso VII. The Anglo-Saxon tradition of royal biography continued in the Latin lives of Edward II and Richard I; Walter Burley's *Liber de vita et moribus philosophorum* (1275/1337), on the other hand, was a completely derivative account of ancient philosophers. By and large, such secular biography never freed itself from its hagiographical roots.

David Herlihy has remarked concerning the considerable material found in medieval hagiography dealing with family, childhood, adolescence and marriage that "the evocation of motherhood, childhood and fatherhood contained in the lives of the saints must bear some correspondence with the way in which mothers, children and fathers were viewed in the real world... the sentiments expressed in a devotional context must have had parallels in feelings that prevailed in the natural family, for which we have no records."[3] This is particularly the case when one examines the ideology of marriage and child-rearing, the so-called "sentimental", rather than the demographic or economic aspects of family history.[4] Confirmatory evidence may be found in the saints' lives concerning the following developments: the greater acceptance of clerical celibacy and the suppression of oblation in the Gregorian age; the mediating role of the saintly mother between her martial husband and monastic son; and the centrality of women in the spiritual rearing of their children. The training of the child and adolescent, as presented in contemporary medical and encyclopedic guides to infant and child care, often found confirmation in the anecdotal tales of the child's formative years. Such observations were not, however, uniformly available, and must often be approached with caution and scepticism, given the didactic role these stories were meant to play.

The stereotypical and exemplary task of Christian biography had been enunciated quite early and remained the basis of later medieval hagiography. As Sulpicius Severus had noted in his oft-quoted prologue to the life of Martin of Tours, the function of sacred biography is to glorify the exemplary deeds of great men in order to arouse the reader to similar acts.[5] To Gregory the Great the lives of the saints are more effective than mere instruction in inspiring us to love heaven as our home. We learn that if we compare ourselves to those who preceded us, we may be filled with a longing for the future life; and if we have too high an opinion of ourselves, we are humbled by hearing of those who have done better.[6] For the utility of the saint's life lies in the examples of piety which it may provide the believer as he passes through the parallel stages of development from childhood, through middle age and senescence.

Medieval biography thus rarely freed itself from the organizational structure laid down by Gregory the Great (540-604), Sulpicius Severus (ca. 363-ca. 420), Athanasius (296-373) or Jerome (ca. 342-420), whose lives of the saints were to serve as a paradigmatic basis for all later hagiographers.[7] Much hagiography is therefore characterized by a uniformity in which the virtues of the saints, their struggles on the path to sanctity and the miracles they have performed follow a set pattern. The medieval biographer was often enslaved to the requirements of a literary form -- enshrined as it was with the canonical blessing of orthodoxy -- which allowed little room for originality. Only the needs of a public which sought to identify with its heroes occasionally demanded the inclusion of more precise data concerning the subject's family background and ministry, although in the case of purely monastic saints, such details were often minimized. The precedent for this type of biography can be found in the lives of Biblical figures such as Elijah (a kind of paradigm for the eremitical saint) or David (the royal ideal), or even pagan heroes.[8] The classical tradition of eulogy likewise served as an antecedent to much hagiographical literature. The stereotypical character of such sources has therefore remained a feature of such biography up until our own time, in which the Catholic saint may have been replaced by the politician or screen idol. At the same time, the very repetitiveness of certain themes indicates a wide cultural consensus, and the divisions of the saint's life reflected a generally accepted view of the critical stages of the human life span. A work such as James of Voragine's widely-read *Legenda aurea* (1255/66), for example, tended to follow its sources rather closely in stressing the stages of life described in the original biography.[9]

In the broadest terms, hagiographers were nearly unanimous in enumerating the following scheme of human development: 1) a prenatal life during which the subject's parents experienced visions or visitations by heavenly guests portending the birth of a saint; as Peter the Venerable said, "The visions experienced during sleep are not always foolish";[10] 2) a childhood often characterized by early signs of piety in the face of the immature puerility of one's peers; 3) an adolescence in which the fires of nascent sexuality vied with the urges of the spirit; 4) an adulthood of religious fulfillment; and 5) a *post mortem* life of miracles.

The overall stylistic structure of the saint's life did not always conform entirely to this neat chronological arrangement. Some were organized in accordance with the seven cardinal virtues, such as the lives of Hedwig of Silesia (1174-1243) or Mary of Oigniès (1214);[11] or the stages on the path to spiritual perfection, as in the cases of Angela of Foligno (1243-1309) or Lutgard of Aywières (1207-1246).[12] James of Voragine structured the *Vita* of Elizabeth of Thuringia (1207-1231) according to the seven spiritual stages of her life, in accordance with the words of *Daniel* 4.25 to Nebuchadnezzar: "Seven times will pass over you until you have learned that the Most High is sovereign..."[13] The miracles were often recorded in haphazard fashion, or arranged according to genre, which often requires external evidence to establish chronological limits.

Rules governing the life-cycle in hagiography were laid down during the patristic period. The prefatory chapter to Gregory's life of Benedict of Nursia, which was based on the reports of four of the saint's acquaintances, served to summarize the major elements of Benedict's life, and indicated the accepted chronology of spiritual development: "He was a man of venerable life, blessed (*Benedictus*) by his grace and by his name. From infancy (*infantia*) his heart was like that of an old man (*cor gerens senile*). Despite his age, in all his behavior he did not give his soul over to sensuous pleasures. While on this earth, although he could have freely devoted himself to the world, he despised as dry the world in its bloom".[14] Gregory reported that Benedict had in his youth been sent to Rome to study, but he rejected the vice displayed by his fellow students; abandoning his studies, he left his home and parental wealth behind, and sought the holy life. As Gregory noted, the separation from one's family, friends, fortune or country was a necessary turning point in the Christian pilgrimage of life, for "sometimes parents close the gates of heaven against their own children by not giving them a proper upbringing."[15] Childhood was thus recognized as the formative period, a theme which was to be strengthened with reference to Augustine's *Confessions.*[16] As Odo II of Cluny (d. 943) in his life of Gerald of Aurillac (d. 903) had said, "for at an early age, as we often see, children through the incitements of their corrupt nature are accustomed to be angry and envious and wish to be revenged, or attempt other things of this sort." Nevertheless, a sign of his future sanctity was Gerald's sweet and modest nature, and his avoidance of secular pursuits.[17] In such pious biography, whether the saint was a celibate cleric or a married female, the sexual strains of adolescence remained the focus, and a kind of spiritual symmetry characterized the stages of life. Childhood and adulthood were kept in delicate balance, separated by the wavering fulcrum of adolescence, when the soul was buffeted by the temptations of sexuality.[18]

But the graphic illustration of the stages of the human life span or the interest in childhood which are depicted in hagiography, must not blind the reader to the primarily exemplary, pedagogical role of the saint's life as a means of encouraging the adoption of a model worthy of emulation. As Caroline Bynum has noted, "twelfth century people tended to write about themselves and about others as types".[19] This could apply almost equally to the later middle ages. And even the saints themselves were praised for conforming to an established role; Gerald of Salles (d. 1120), for example, was compared to Hilary, Anthony, Christ, John, Benedict and Paul; Richard of Chichester (d. 1257) to Moses, Joseph, Esdras, Zerubbabel, Daniel, Ezechiel and Thomas Becket in his skill at confronting royal tyranny; and Engelbert of Cologne (d. 1225) to Judah the Maccabee and Solomon in his wise counsel and to a series of martyrs for his self-sacrifice; all the deeds and virtues of Louis of Toulouse (d. 1274-1294) found a suitable Biblical parallel.[20] The saint differed from others insofar as his outer and inner selves were in conformity, and he lacked the contradictions of the divided self to which man is prey. The humoral equilibrium espoused by physicians to achieve physical and mental health may not be discussed by hagiographers. Nevertheless, the same kind of balance of moral virtues to achieve spiritual health was displayed by the saints who had submitted to the medicinal balm of divine grace; for the illness of the body is paralleled by the corruption of the soul.[21]

As a result of the intervention of Rome in the canonization process beginning in the twelfth century, hagiography lost some of its paradigmatic character and was increasingly based on eye-witness testimony. Hearsay evidence was no longer admissible. All possible grounds for suspicion concerning the testimony of the saint's life were carefully scrutinized by boards of qualified examiners trained in law and theology, substantially increasing the reliability of hagiographical accounts.[22] These more exacting judicial standards prevalent in the thirteenth and fourteenth centuries allow us to observe with greater certitude the critical choices faced by the later saints. The saint's life, although taken to represent a stereotypical pattern of human development, now gained historical credibility as a consequence of the stricter rules of accuracy. The simple pattern of childhood, adolescence and adulthood remained, but an increasing emphasis on the formative role of infancy and childhood, and the catalytic character of adolescence were now observable in hagiography.

A new, direct source of testimony concerning the saints were the trials investigating candidates for sainthood, during which hundreds of witnesses drawn from every social class appeared and reported the virtuous lives and miraculous deeds of both contemporary and long-dead cult figures. Such testimony might be quite extensive, although somewhat episodic, concentrating on certain key incidents in the putative saint's ministry. While the aim was to focus on the life and miracles of candidates for canonization themselves, such sources nevertheless confirm the universality of certain themes found in learned biography. Each miracle might require the testimony of five or six eyewitnesses whose circumstantial evidence could assist in the reconstruction of the values and daily concerns of otherwise obscure folk. Indirectly, these trials also often provided purportedly direct quotations from the saints themselves, since a key witness was often the saint's own confessor, like John of Marienwerder in the case of Dorothy of Montau (1403), or the Dominican Marcel in the case of Margaret of Hungary (1276).[23] The cause of Dauphine of Languedoc (1363), for example, noted that "she often and frequently confessed... said Dauphine's confessions were so very pure, true and humble, that these same confessors, when hearing her confession, considered their own lives; they were astonished and edified to improve their own lives."[24] Such frequent confession may have encouraged the examination of one's own spiritual and intellectual development as a manifestation of the paradigmatic life cycle. In any case, it assists the scholar to more accurately reconstruct the contours of the saint's life.

Autobiography

At the same time, other kinds of evidence concerning the life span from birth to death, and the turning points in one's life, were to become available. This included personal confessions as reported by the subject's confessor, visions, and other kinds of autobiographical literature through which both laymen and clergy reflected on their own emotional, spiritual and physical development over a longer period of time. In Dilthey's words, "autobiographies are the most direct expression of reflection about life", permitting us to perceive most closely the underlying mentality and premises of the age.²⁵ The considerable body of confessional literature dating from the late thirteenth and early fourteenth centuries completely belies Paul Lehmann's contention that little of outstanding merit was produced in the field of autobiography in the middle ages.²⁶ A plethora of testimony concerning individual psychic and physical development was produced, not merely by theologians and philosophers, but also by laymen. These works did not concentrate merely on one episode, but reflected on a significant segment of the speaker's life, recounting not simply external facts (as do memoirs), but also inner experiences; such as the lives of Pope Celestine V (ca. 1300), Raymund Lull (1311), the Kabbalist Abraham Abulafia (1285), the chronicler Salimbene de Adam (ca. 1284), and even the autobiographical confession of a heretic such as Beatrice of Planissoles (1323).²⁷

In one important respect, medieval confessions differ from modern autobiography: they were invariably composed from a religious point of view which, rather than revelling in individuality, praised conformity to a paradigmatic model of spiritual conversion. This allowed the witness to rearrange and interpret his life in the framework of a given theology, most often centering around the conversion experience observable in much contemporary hagiography. The medieval autobiographer thus invariably subordinated his life to some transcendent purpose and after some reflection, saw himself as a creature of God's will, lacking the 'romantic' sense of wayward liberation which has so often characterized autobiography since the nineteenth century. And because the autobiography was partly an apologetic polemic, it may not convey a sense of contemporary development and change in the person's character throughout the life cycle.²⁸

It may well be, as Roy Pascal has said, that the stages of life from birth to death in such sources still remained more exemplary than individual, in keeping with tried and true hagiographical traditions. Selective memory remained directed toward the goal of illustrating the workings of God's grace in one's life.²⁹ Margery Kempe, for example, saw herself as a mirror reflecting God's will, despite the considerable twists and turns between impiety and religiosity which her early life displayed.³⁰ For the medieval autobiography was the necessary concomitant of the doctrine of conversion and personal salvation as understood by the early church fathers, who had themselves often experienced the cathartic spiritual transformation which often appears in autobiography.³¹

Medieval autobiography had characteristically appeared in several discrete periods, although at all times the 'conversion' crisis remained a significant turning point in the life cycle. The first age had produced the classic confessions of Patrick and Augustine, whose adolescent conversion crises were to become paradigms for the experiences of others.³² The second age of autobiography was associated with the spiritual and intellectual ferment of the early twelfth century and produced such works as Guibert of Nogent's *De vita sua*, Abelard's *Libellus de calamitatibus suis*, the life of Ovadia the Convert, Hermann of Scheda's *De conversione sua*, and Samau'al al-Maghribi's *The Silencing of the Jews*.³³ The conflict of Church and State, the Crusades, the rise of the city, and the introduction of Arabic and ancient wisdom in the schools were some of the factors which wrenched Europe out of its pastoral, "barbarian" slumber as an intellectual and political backwater. While apologetic and polemical in tone, the new autobiography provided greater historical detail than its predecessors and successfully blended the inner life of its central character with the observation of those external conditions which often encouraged his spiritual conversion. As Robert Hanning has noted, a new tension in the twelfth century between the public and personal world was reflected in the quest of the single hero in chivalric romance and greater emphasis on the inner life in contemporary biography. This stress on the individual in conflict with a hostile environment was to remain a feature of medieval biography in the thirteenth century. Both sacred and profane literature were to be characterized by personal awareness of the central figure and the use of the individual *ingenium* to confirm his/her personal autonomy.[34] The same elements informed contemporary autobiography.

The third great wave of autobiography appeared in the late thirteenth century, which witnessed an unprecedented rise in self-revelatory literature of all kinds. Georg Misch's magisterial *Geschichte der Autobiographie* would encompass all literary forms, including tomb inscriptions, in the annals of autobiography, insofar as their authors recorded instances of personal experience.[35] Such a definition would thus include the many epistolary collections (such as the letters of Angelo of Clareno), travel literature (like the immensely popular *Milione* of Marco Polo, and other largely Franciscan accounts of missionary activity in the East), and the revelatory visions (such as those of the Dominican Robert of Uzès or the Franciscan John of Rupescissa) which were produced in the late thirteenth and early fourteenth centuries.

Some such sources, of course, contain only incidental data and barely include a continuous narrative account of personal development, particularly the many contemporary collections of visions and revelations, which sometimes sought to voice concern about political issues through the language of vision. John of Rupescissa's *Liber secretorum eventum*, for example, described the circumstances of his visions, which dealt with the perils to the Church and anticipated great turmoil to commence in 1366. In his *Liber ostensorum* (1356) he appended a letter about his own origins.[36] Angela of Foligno's *Book of Divine Consolation* (1285/91) likewise contained some autobiography interspersed with an account of her mystical revelations.[37] In both cases the aim was to warn and instruct, rather than to provide any personal details. Even the chronicle of King James I of Aragon (1208-1276) was more an account of wars and political intrigue than of personal development. Only the first chapter, which deals with his childhood and the years prior to the consummation of his marriage, goes into some details about the rearing of a contemporary nobleman.[38] The tradition of testamentary advice represented by this document was to remain an important subgenre of autobiography, which was to grow vastly in the thirteenth century, and may include such diverse works as the *Dicta* attributed to Francis and his early disciples, the Jewish ethical wills, and the *Libre de saviesa o doctrina* (1246) by James of Aragon.

A more limited definition of autobiography, however, which includes only those narrative works which combine both a confessional account of the author's spiritual odyssey with particulars concerning family, birth and career, reduces the list to more manageable proportions. The apologetic element, of course, remained common. Angelo of Clareno's *Apologia pro sua vita* (ca.1330), for example, was intended as a theological refutation of charges that he had disobeyed ecclesiastical authority and as a treatise in support of apostolic poverty. He recounted the tribulations of the Franciscan Spirituals from 1294 to 1317, when he endured exile, imprisonment and house arrest at the home of James Colonna (1311-1318). Angelo recorded a venerable list of predecessors from Abraham to Anthony of Padua who fled the world and suffered exile rather than suffer at the hands of their enemies.[39]

The proliferation of autobiographies such as those attributed to Pope Celestine V (d. 1294) and Raymund Lull (d. 1315) was a natural consequence of the decree *Omnis utriusque sexus* passed by the Fourth Lateran Council of 1215 requiring believers over the age of discretion to undergo confession of sins yearly before competent persons.[40] Such confession was to be accompanied by a sense of sincere, heartfelt remorse, in heart, mouth and action, in order to achieve forgiveness of one's sins. While this measure may have had the partial aim of flushing out heretics like the Waldensians, who rejected the Catholic doctrine of confession and penance, the demand for a yearly avowal of sin had its precedents in twelfth century theology, particularly in the circle surrounding the Paris theologian Peter Cantor, who clearly saw this 'medicine of the soul' as an important instrument for the social control of non-conformists.[41]

Much of the new biographical material characteristic of the late thirteenth century was composed by confessors or spiritual advisors to such penitents, who recorded the trials or temptations their charges experienced. The spirit of penance which animated such persons was later voiced by Pope Celestine V, who on several occasions said, "I am a sinner who because of my sins am unworthy to appear before God."[42] In such circles, the public exposure of one's sins entailed enough embarrassment to ensure the satisfaction which God demands. Margaret of Cortona's (1247-1297) confessor Juncta thus reported that God had instructed her to report her scandalous early life and penitential conversion publicly; her confession was later checked by the local inquisitor, various officials of the Franciscan order, and Cardinal Napoleone Orsini before its publication.[43]

Concerning the central theme of the precise divisions of life, these autobiographical sources differed little from contemporary biography. In some respects, because it was based on either notarized statements intended to support a canonization trial, on testimony elicited at such a trial, or on the combined observations of several witnesses, biography -- despite its hagiographical intent -- may indeed be more precise.[44] A stated awareness of the more sophisticated scientific theories of the spiritual, physical and moral contents of the various stages of life barely made its appearance. Even such well-educated autobiographical informants as Abraham Abulafia (1240-1292) and Raymund Lull, schooled in the medical tradition, displayed a divorce between the life of the spirit and the mind, and were peculiarly non-observant in analyzing the passages in their lives. Lull *never* specified his age at any stage of his narrative account of a long, fruitful career; others spoke vaguely of "youth" as a time of spiritual and fleshly turmoil and experimentation. Among the Jewish subjects, age thirteen or fourteen, and twenty, the traditional ages of bar mitzvah and marriage, were decisive. But in all instances, the 'conversion' crisis most often occurring in late adolescence, remained the centerpiece of contemporary autobiography, thus effectively dividing life into three great stages: childhood, adolescence and adulthood. Thus, autobiography, like hagiography, was largely wedded to the Christian conception of sin and salvation, which required conformity to a long cherished division of life into three phases which reflect the Trinitariansim of Christian theology. Just as God revealed himself in three stages, so each of us, a microcosmic reflection of the Creator and His Creation, reaches spiritual fulfillment through a three-stage chronological development.

Hortatory treatises

In addition to the hagiographical and autobiographical sources, a vast body of more speculative and instructional literature appeared in the late thirteenth and early fourteenth centuries, which bears directly on the life cycle theory. It was often generated in the schools and was a consequence of the renewed acquaintance with such Aristotelian or pseudo-Aristotelian treatises as the *Politics, Economics, Ethics, Parva naturalia* or the *Secretum secretorum*. Because philosophy was considered a major component of medical studies, the assimilation of Aristotle was often championed by physicians; an intimate relationship thus developed between natural philosophy and logic and, through the arts faculty at Paris, theology.[45] This Aristotelian influence was strongly reflected in the secularized moral treatises, composed generally by princely commission, and dealing with the just governance of the State, catalogued in Wilhelm Berges' *Die Fürstenspiegel der hohen und späten Mittelalters*.[46] Some, like Thomas Aquinas' *De regimine principum* (1265/6), dealt entirely with the art of government. Others, directed often at a wider audience, were composed in the vernacular and stressed child-rearing and the inculcation of moral and religious virtues in childhood as the surest means of insuring just governance by the prince in adulthood; many dealt with other ages *in extenso*.

These didactic treatises often attempted to wed Christian morality to Aristotelian political economy and achieved wide currency after about 1260. William Peraldus' *De eruditione principum* (ca. 1265), for example, was largely a work of moral theology, divided into seven books dealing with the prince in general, his obligations to the church, to himself, his counsellors, his family, his subjects and his enemies. The section on child-rearing took as its cornerstone the Biblical condemnation of child neglect, berating those who show more care for their pigs than for their offspring.[47] Just as in nature the tree trunk feeds its branches, and the brute beasts nourish their young, so men should care for their children. The sovereign ought to be especially solicitous of his offspring, because the virtues acquired in childhood will later assist the future prince to rule justly. Just as animals are more effectively trained, reared and domesticated in youth, so also among humankind one more readily bears the yoke of God in adolescence than in old age.

Another such "mirror for princes", Giles of Rome's *De regimine principum libri III* (1277/9), composed for King Philip III of France, illustrates the degree to which Aristotelianism had penetrated the educational theory espoused in such manuals.[48] Giles followed very closely the relevant chapters in Aristotle's *Economics, Politics, Ethics* and *Rhetoric*, which formed the core of the curriculum in moral philosophy at Paris and Oxford, while at the same time espousing the more medieval view that moral characteristics are paralleled by physiological change. Giles described the strengths and foibles of infancy, childhood, adolescence, middle age and old age, although he did not discuss the *topos* of the ages of man. The fourth tractate of Dante's unfinished *Convivio* (1304/7), couched as a commentary on an allegorical poem, may be included among the hortatory treatises. It likewise contained an extended discussion of the four ages of man (*adolescenza, gioventute, senettute* and *senio*) and attempted to bring the fruits of contemporary philosophy to a wider audience, by expounding the properties of nobility peculiar to each age.[49]

The Christian didactic treatise was paralleled somewhat in Judaism by the 'ethical will' addressed by a learned rabbi to his son.[50] Lying somewhere between autobiography and the moral hortatory treatise, it often contained more personal detail that its Christian counterparts. The structure of life paralleled hagiography: childhood -- adolescence -- adulthood. While in Christianity the decision for celibacy was the turning point, in Judaism it was marriage and the acceptance of the responsibilities of both family and community. The element of wandering was a common motif, although not so much caused by a spiritual search as by the vicissitudes of the Jewish condition and the pressing need to find employment.

The scholastic educational manual or mirror for princes was soon supplemented by a diverse range of popular treatises concerned with personal development, dealing with the ages, household management, the rearing of women, and the insurance of good health. Such works may be likened to present-day guides to pop psychology and self-improvement. Discussions of the various stages of life and the process of degeneration were to be found largely in three contexts: 1) the pseudo-Aristotelian *Secretum secretorum* and commentaries on it; 2) treatises entitled *Regimen sanitatis*; and 3) commentaries on the Aristotelian *Parva naturalia*. The tenth century *Secretum secretorum* was an epistle which had purportedly been sent by Aristotle to Alexander the Great during the Persian campaign in response to a query concerning the best way to govern the peoples recently included in Alexander's empire.[51] According to the legend, the *Secretum* had been discovered in a temple repository of philosophical works and was translated into Arabic by its founder. It was twice translated from the Arabic by John of Spain or Seville (ca. 1135/42) in shortened form, and more completely by Philip of Tripoli (ca. 1240) for Guy Vere of Valence, bishop of Tripoli; it survives in hundreds of manuscripts and various versions, including vernacular translations and a 1257 edition by Roger Bacon with commentary. Thomas of Cantimpré, for example, in his *De natura rerum* (1228/1242) included a long citation from the chapters dealing with the daily regimen of health; Engelbert of Admont used it as a primary source for his *De regimine principum* (ca.

1290). In its simplest form, the *Secretum* is a mirror for princes, but was transformed into a veritable encyclopedia of health and conduct by its later commentators. This spurious letter may well have served as the nucleus for the *Regimen sanitatis Salernitani*, deriving its authority from the alleged Aristotelian authorship.

In his preface to the *Secretum* Roger Bacon listed the three elements which are required to insure a long reign: 1) the maintenance of justice; 2) the observation of the proper rules of health; and, 3) the knowledge of the means of preserving youth, known to the Greeks and Chaldeans.[52] Many of the themes which were to be found in contemporary encyclopedias and advice literature are found in the *Secretum*, such as the use of images drawn from natural history; the king, for example, is likened to a heavy rain or wind, which may bring both the benefits of nature and its dangers.[53] Much of the treatise is a guide to a prince concerned with insuring justice and the ordering of his realm, containing suitable preventive measures to guarantee good health; the correct equilibrium of the humors, accomplished through attention to diet, rest, evacuation, bloodletting, etc., is regarded as the key to health. The changing proportions of the humors, (blood, red bile, yellow bile, and phlegm) were linked to the four seasons, so that one's diet should depend on seasonal changes. While dryness is the natural cause of corruption and the destruction of the body, the accidental causes may include military attack or ill-counsel. The treatise included the kind of moral advice which was to become commonplace in many contemporary *Fürstenspiegel*: moderation in the pursuit of one's foes; loyal adherence to treaty obligations; the encouragement of learning; consultation with wise counselors and astrologers; the maintenance of adequate food supplies; and the conservation of health through proper hygiene. The author further hinted at the existence of certain wonder drugs which can cure all ills and prolong life.

The single most widely distributed source of medical speculation concerning the ages of man and the means of extending life was the *Regimen sanitatis Salternitani* or the *De conservatione sanitatis*, couched in the form of a letter to an unidentified king of England, which appeared in both prose and poetic versions, but which reached its final form of about 360 verses by the mid-thirteenth century.[54] The *aetates* were generally here classified as seven -- *infans, puer, adolescens, juvenis, vir, senex* and *decrepitus* -- each with its own unique character, depending on the condition of the humors. Stress was laid on good humor, moderate diet, rest and exercise as the keys to health, containing dietary regulations, lists of herbal medicines and other kinds of advice. Much of this material bore a close resemblance to the advice proffered by Averroes (d. 1202) in his *Colliget*.[55]

Apparently relying on the Salernitan framework, many leading physicians composed a *Regimen sanitatis*, either as part of a larger work or as an individual treatise. Most seem to have been composed by commission, and bear a marked similarity, suggesting either extensive borrowing or even plagiarism. Guy of Vigevano's (ca. 1280-1345) work, for example, was directed at older men planning a journey to the East, and formed part of a longer treatise on the conquest of the Holy Land prepared for King Philip IV of France.[56] It included chapters dealing with diet, rest, evacuation, good air, the care of the senses, poisons and the maintenance of sound spirits, in addition to tactical advice on the conduct of war in the East. *Le régime du corps* (ca. 1256/7) by Aldobrandino of Siena, composed in the Picard-Walloon dialect, was written at the request of Countess Beatrice of Provence on the occasion of her journey to visit four well-married daughters, and was a practical guide concerned with both general hygiene and particular problems of diet and disease, making wide use of Avicenna and Constantine the African.[57] The widely circulated *De regimine sanitatis* by Arnold of Villanova (1234/50 - 1311), composed for James of Aragon in 1307, is perhaps a translation of an earlier work by the twelfth century physician Avenzoar (d. 1162). Arnold was also the presumed author of a *Commentum super regimen sanitatis Salternitanum* and a *De conservanda iuventute et retardanda senectute* (largely dietary), in which he suggested that the ability to maintain a healthful regimen may depend on one's occupation and status in life.[58] The largely dietary *De regimine vite et sanitatis* by Bellino Bissolo may have been intended for the author's son and was based on personal experience.[59]

Bernard Gordon's (d. ca. 1320) *De conservatione vitae* was divided into four parts, containing an extensive *Regimen sanitatis* (1307/8) which is one of the most complete such works. Integrating medical, Scriptural and moral sources, and indicating the scholastic sophistication which could be achieved, Bernard made use of Aristotle's division of human nature found in the *Ethics* into the passionate, political and contemplative as the basis for a tripartite division of life into *pueritia* (til age 14), *adolescentia* or *iuventus* (til 35) and *senectus* (til death).[60] This classification found confirmation in the Augustinian trio of birth, labor and death as the chief concerns of life. Even if we were to prolong life with a proper regimen of health and God's help, said Bernard, this sequence of ages is inevitable, and in the end we all must face the divine tribunal. Following these moral injunctions, in accordance with the formulary structure of the *Regimen sanitatis*, Bernard discussed exercise, massage, bathing, diet, rest, sexuality, evacuation, the symptoms of disease and convalescence.

Within this medical tradition one might also include various editions and translations of the neo-Pythagorean *Oeconomicus* or *Oeconomicus Galeni* attributed to a certain "Bryson".[61] It was translated into Latin by Pierre Gallego, bishop of Carthagena (1250-1267) and by Armengaud Blasius (ca. 1284/1302) and contained a combination of moral and hygenic advice for the proper maintenance of one's home, servants, wife and children.

A further source of speculation concerning 'developmental psychology' was the Aristotelian corpus grouped under the title *Parva naturalia* (a sixteenth century designation), particularly the *De longitudine et brevitate vitae* and the *De morte et vita*, which were commented upon by such figures as Albertus Magnus, Giles of Rome, Peter of Spain and Siger of Brabant. These treatises were probably read in conjunction with the paraphrase by Averroes, which could also draw on such sources as Aristotle's *Meteorology*; although some difficulty remains concerning the precise form in which these two treatises appeared, whether individually or as one unit.[62] While much of this material had been translated into Latin by James of Venice (fl. 1136-1148) in the twelfth century, the papal prohibition of the study of Aristotle's *libri naturales* at Paris in 1210 may have inhibited their study. After the retranslation of the corpus in about 1230 by Michael Scot, however, these treatises were discussed in learned circles. An anonymous study guide of the period 1230/40 at Paris included the *Parva naturalia* among the works studied; commentaries were produced largely after 1240.[63]

The commentaries on Aristotle rarely strayed from the familiar view that the retention of warmth and moisture will prolong life. Some speculated further on life's stages. Giles of Rome in his commentary on *De iuventute et senectute* spoke of seven rather than the traditional six ages: *infantia* til age seven, *pueritia* til fourteen, *adolescentia* til twenty-five, *iuventus* til thirty-five, *virilitas* til fifty, *senectus* til sixty, and *decrepitus* til death. He added a second tripartite division based upon the continuing reduction of natural warmth in the body: *iuventus* til thirty-five, when such warmth reaches its peak; *status* til fifty, a time of stabilization; and *senectus* til death, when warmth is rapidly reduced.[64]

Encyclopedias

The thirteenth century had witnessed a vast increase in the number of encyclopedias directed at a more popular audience, expressing cultural values attractive to a wider circle than the noble and clerical consumers of earlier such works.[65] Some, composed in the vernacular, may be rather specialized, dealing with geography, or rather spare in their content.[66] A considerable number of lavishly illustrated encyclopedias were to appear, for example those of Bandini (ca. 1409/15) and Pastrengo (ca. 1350), but their distribution was more limited and they displayed the same penchant for plagiarism and redundancy found in their better-known predecessors. Others touched only fleetingly on the theme of the ages of man, such as Raffaelo Maffei's *Commentariorum urbanorum*.[67]

In order to gain a comprehensive consensus of opinion concerning the ages of man the following works have been examined at greater length, all of which treat the *aetates* and were relatively widely distributed:
1. The *De proprietatibus rerum* (ca. 1230/40) by Bartholomaeus Anglicus,[68] produced at Magdeburg by a Franciscan master of Paris, served as a nucleus for many of its successors. His stated aim was to assist the reader to understand Scripture which, he says, cannot be interpreted without knowledge of the "character and property of all things, not only material, but also artificial" accomplished through the citation of ancient and modern philosophers.[69] In his treatment of the ages of man, Bartholomaeus relied heavily on Aristotle's *Historia animalium* and *De generatione animalium*, along with Constantine the African's *Liber medicus* (ca. 1087), Augustine's *Confessions* and *City of God*, Isidore's *Etymologies* and Avicenna's *Canon of Medicine*.[70]
2. Thomas of Cantimpré's (1186/1210-1274/94) *Liber de natura rerum* (ca. 1228-1244)[71] produced by a leading hagiographer and exemplarist over a fifteen-year period, dealt with man in those sections handling the body, the soul and the strange races of mankind. His stated aim was to assist the reader to study things heavenly through knowledge of matters earthly, although he placed less emphasis on theological sources than do other

Dominican encyclopedists. This work may be profitably read in conjunction with his *Bonum universale de apibus* (1263), which described the similarity between the hierarchy of the bees and the Church.

3. The Dominican Vincent of Beauvais' *Speculum maius* (1244/54)[72] was the most ambitious such project, a veritable compendium of knowledge available in the thirteenth century, undertaken with material aid from King Louis IX of France. Vincent is also the presumed author of the more didactic mirrors for princes, the *De eruditione filiorum nobilium*, the *De morali principiis institutione* and the *De eruditione principum* (probably offshoots of the *Speculum*), which lay stress on ethical and pedagogical questions, and contained little of the natural science found in the *Speculum*. The overall structure may have owed something to the *Imago mundi* of Honorius Inclusus (ca. 1080) or Rabanus Maurus' (d. 856) *De universo*, and represented, according to Vincent, a mirror of all that is worthy of admiration or imitation in the visible or invisible worlds. Although not particularly original, Vincent was a reliable reporter of received wisdom, and occasionally even ventured an opinion. His treatment of the *aetates* fell under a lengthy discussion of the physical characteristics of mankind and the factors which affect human nature, namely the elements, complexions, humors, members, virtues, actions, spirit, colors, figures, the differences between the sexes, and the ages.[73]

4. The alphabetical *Lumen animae* (1318/30) is attributed to the Dominican Berengar of Landorre (1262-1330), Archbishop of Compostella.[74] Although perhaps begun at the instigation of either Pope Nicholas IV (1288-1292) or Boniface VIII (1294-1303), it was after 1316 that Pope John XXII provided three assistants to help translate Berengar's Greek material. Berengar himself had studied at the medical university of Montpellier and had served as *lector naturalium* at Brives, when he presumably began collecting *exempla*, in keeping with the growing practice of drawing examples from natural sources. The work is by no means comprehensive and all too often relies on second-hand knowledge. There is a frustrating lack of conformity between the many sources cited by Berengar and the original texts to which they are attributed; although he cited rarely mentioned works by Arnold of Villanova (d. 1316), Peter of Abano (d. 1316) and Raymund Lull (d. 1315), and the recently translated *Problemata* assigned to Aristotle, along with a host of Jewish and Moslem natural philosophers.

5. The *Summa de exemplis et rerum similitudinibus* (1300/10)[75] by the Dominican hagiographer and moral theologian John Gori of San Gemignano (ca. 1260 - ca. 1323) likewise attempted to derive moral principles from the natural world with the aid of Scripture. John saw example as the pedagogical tool par excellence and attempted to arrive at Christian principles through the observation of human biology and behavior drawn from pagan or Arabic natural philosophers.

6. The *Omnebonum* (ca. 1360/75)[76] by "Jacobus" is an unfinished illustrated encyclopedia, of English, perhaps Cistercian and anti-mendicant origin. While the text is largely derivative, the illustrations often contain domestic and educational themes of interest. The author listed one hundred and fifteen sources.

7. The *Reductorium moralis* and the *Reportorium* (or *Dictionarium moralis*) by the Benedictine prior of Nantes and Paris, Pierre Bersuire (1300-1362)[77] were apparently first published in 1340, and appeared in revised form in 1359. Long resident at Avignon, a holder of several ecclesiastical positions and an acquaintance of Petrarch, Bersuire composed his *Reportorium* as a preaching aid at the request of Cardinal Pierre des Prés, Bishop of Palestrina. At Paris in 1350 he was accused of heresy (although apparently more because of his personality than for doctrinal reasons) and briefly languished in an episcopal prison until, for unknown reasons, he found favor with King John II of France, and was included in a group commissioned to translate Livy's *Roman History*, probably in 1353.[78] His *Reductorium* is essentially an expanded *De rerum proprietatibus*, utilizing many of Bartholomaeus' sources, with considerable Scriptural additions. The *Reportorium*, an alphabetical moral dictionary of Biblical terms, relied very heavily on Scripture in attempting to parallel the natural and spiritual worlds, and enjoyed wide currency. Bersuire remained very much a Biblical exegete who undertook to explain the literal, allegorical, moral and anagogical meaning of each term.[79] Each word is interpreted in its natural (*naturalis*), moral (*virtualis*), and criminal (*criminalis*) sense.

These encyclopedias were typically organized into several books according to some overall scheme, usually the hexamerous order of Creation, or alphabetically, treating historical, scientific, ethical and moral subjects.[80] In his preface, Vincent of Beauvais specifically cited Isidore of Seville and Richard and Hugh of St. Victor as his predecessors. Thomas of Cantimpré, in addition to these and other sources, noted the *Hexameron* of both Ambrose and Basil.[81] Pierre Bersuire singled out Pliny's *Natural History*, Seneca's *On Natural Questions*, Solinus' *De mirabilibus mundi* and the *De Otiis imperialibus* by Gervase of Tillbury.[82] His considerable knowledge of classical belles-lettres (Bersuire composed a commentary on Ovid's *Metamorphoses*) is evident in the large number of examples drawn from ancient mythology.

The early encyclopedists in the group, like Bartholomaeus, Thomas and Vincent, typically strung together a series of citations on each theme, drawn from classical, Christian or Arabic sources, adding an occasional editorial comment, although they were often not above slavish imitation of their predecessors without any attempt at analysis. It would appear that much use was made of the widely circulated *florilegia* of citations from classical authors; like the *Florilegium gallicum* which, it has been shown, was a major source for Vincent's *Speculum*.[83] By the fourteenth century such works were arranged alphabetically for easy reference. Other tools for scholarly exegesis included the *distinctiones*, which contain words and definitions drawn from Biblical sources with their figurative meanings; verbal concordances to Scripture, such as Conrad of Halberstadt's *Concordantia veteris et novi testamenti* (1342/50) which might also serve as sources of reference for preachers; and compendia of philosophical wisdom such as the eleventh century *Liber philosophorum moralium antiquorum* and William of Conches' *Moralium dogma philosophorum*, which contain epigrammatic selections from classical sources.[84] Such treasuries of familiar quotations indicate the common base of received wisdom which permeated medieval culture. The encylopedists were not so much the creators of a culture as they were its communicators and popularizers, who made it more readily available to an audience of small gentry and urban dwellers.

These encyclopedias were unanimous in attempting to prove the essential agreement of secular and sacred literature, both ancient and modern, through the citation of pagan, Christian, Arab and Jewish sources. Some sources are remarkably absent, such as Nemesius of Emesa's *De natura hominis* (390/400), or the medical corpus of Maimonides.[85] There are, however, differences of emphasis, caused by the kinds of education each encyclopedist had received. Bartholomaeus Anglicus and Thomas of Cantimpré, strongly influenced by the nearly subversive influx of the Aristotelian and Arab philosophical traditions at Paris, stressed the biology of human development. Pierre Bersuire and John of San Gemignano were primarily Biblical exegetes who clearly viewed natural philosophy as the so-called "handmaiden of theology". Berengar of Landorre was determinedly naturalistic and included the largest number of references to both Arabic and more contemporary sources; while John of San Gemignano did not hesitate to stress the role of the stars in determining each person's destiny, perhaps reflecting the relative tolerance of astrology in the early fourteenth century.[86]

The ages of man were generally dealt with in two ways: either as a summary account of the ages as defined by Isidore or Avicenna; or each age was handled individually by a series of relevant selections from the sources. The transition to the alphabetical encyclopedia in the fourteenth century afforded the author an opportunity to select his own entries. At the same time, the systematic treatment of the ages of man found in the hexamerous structure may be found imbedded in the discussion of a particular term such as *pueritia* or *adolescentia*.

The relevant material found in the growing Aristotelian corpus, along with citations from Constantine the African, Razi and Halys in particular, formed the kernel of the scientific data. The role of the four elements as the constituents of the body was indisputable. The changing proportions, quality and quantity of the four humors, termed by Constantine the African "the children of the elements", were universally regarded (generally following Galen) as the dominant factors in the human constitution, accounting for differences in health and temperament. The four qualities of warmth, coldness, dryness and wetness, acting in conjunction with the humors, allegedly had a decisive impact on the aging process.

Popularization of Learned Theory

Although the present work concentrates on the biographical, pedagogical and encyclopaedic traditions, the speculations of the learned reached a wider circle through many channels. The belletristic tradition and the plastic arts, which tended to bemoan the vanities associated with each age, brought many of the commonplaces of the theologian and natural scientist before a popular audience.[87] Such poems as Marbod of Rennes' (ca. 1035-1123) *De senectute, Le Regret du Maximian* (13th century), *An Old Man's Prayer* (ca. 1310) and *God Send Patience in Our Old Age* (15th century) bewailed the physical weakness, illness, gluttony and lechery of old age and urged the cultivation of patience as an antidote, in accordance with an older classical tradition.[88] Elsewhere, the poet emphasized the springtime of youth, a time of vain pursuit of pleasure and wantonness, heedless of the perils of death. Several poems also attempted a more comprehensive survey of the ages, and betrayed perhaps some acquaintance with the medical tradition. Marbod of Rennes in his *De tempore et aevo* listed five ages, and defined the possession of natural warmth (*calor*) as the determining factor in the quality of each period.[89] The anonymous fifteenth century "The Day of Life -- Night Comes Soon" likened the ages to the times of the day, each personified by a particular figure: midday is the youthful knight; nones the robust king.[90] The balladeer Eustace Deschamps (1384) used seasonal imagery: youth is the spring; old age is winter.[91]

Such works were often rather formulary in their approach, although embellished with poetic metaphors.[92] Antonio Alemanni's "Trionfo dell'età dell'uomo", for example, made use of a quadripartite scheme introduced by the image of the wheel of fortune and ending with a lament on the vain transience of life; the sweet innocence of childhood, the amorous pleasure of youth, the glory and honor of adulthood and the declining fortunes of old age make their appearance. The Middle English *The Parlement of Thre Ages*, a debate between youth, middle age, and old age appears to have no analog.[93] Other such sources, however, were more episodic, and merely illustrated anecdotally a particular age and its foibles, and can be exploited for a more precise picture of the contemporary view of one age or another; the tenderness and protectiveness of a mother for her child were described in *La chanson du chevalier du Cynge et de Godfrid de Bouillon* and *Le Roman du Comte d'Anjou*; the playful games of children were found in *Charroi de Nîmes*.[94]

The audience for the medieval encyclopedia went far beyond the narrow confines to which earlier monastic treatises had been directed, to encompass a sizeable non-specialized intellectual elite, some of whom had been trained in the episcopal schools, monasteries and the university faculty of the arts, somewhat equivalent to the modern secondary school.[95] Along with the literate clerical and noble elite, this would include royal and seigneurial agents of justice, persons involved in financial and public administration, rich merchants, physicians and other skilled professionals. Edgar Boutaric described the late medieval encyclopedias as "tentative faites pour ouvrir à tous les portes du sanctuaire."[96] Bartholomaeus Anglicus, for example, himself referred to "rudes... et simplices" as the chief audience for his work.[97]

In order to achieve this wider distribution, some encyclopedias, such as Goswin of Metz's *Image du monde* (1245/6), Fazio degli Uberti's *Dittamondo*, and Brunetto Latini's *Li livres dou trésor* (1260/7), had been composed in the vernacular. Within about two hundred years, Bartholomaeus' work was translated into French, English, Dutch, Provençal, Italian and Spanish; while Thomas of Cantimpré was translated into French and German; Goswin of Metz even achieved a Hebrew translation. Glorieux in his study of the masters of arts at Paris in the thirteenth century listed seventy-one manuscripts for Brunetto Latini, and close to seventy for various parts of Vincent of Beauvais. Thomas of

Cantimpré's *De natura rerum* survived in nearly one hundred and fifty manuscripts, the *Lumen animae* in its various versions, close to two hundred.[98] The hortatory literature fared no less well. The *Secretum secretorum*, probably the ancestor of many of the advice books and the regimens of health, survives in perhaps over five hundred manuscripts, including many translations. Giles of Rome's *De regimine principorum* (1277/9) was soon translated into French, Catalan, Castilian Spanish, Portuguese, German, Italian, German, English, Swedish and Hebrew. Other *Fürstenspiegel* were originally composed in Italian, German, Norwegian, Catalan, French and German, presumably insuring a wider audience.[99]

The general principles discussed in the learned literature were exemplified and individualized in contemporary hagiography and autobiography, much of which was either written in the vernacular or translated soon thereafter. Here, a graphic picture of the crises which accompanied the passage from one age to another was provided. It has, however, been pointed out that the paradigm nature of much autobiographical and hagiographical literature casts doubt upon its reliability as a universal reflection of the patterns of life cycle. The almost monotonous recurrence of such standard themes as prenatal portents, childhood piety, sexual crisis, abandonment of family, wandering, persecution, penance and dream in such purportedly individual accounts of spiritual development often encourages the suspicion that the biographer attempted to force his subject into a pre-ordained framework; this framework, however, was widely acknowledged.

II. *Notes*

1. Bonaventure, *Collectiones, Hexaemeron*, XII, 14, in *Opera omnia*, 10 vols., ed. Patres Collegii S. Bonaventurae (Quaracchi, 1882-1902), V, 386.

2. D. Briesmeiser, "Biographie," in R. Auty, ed., *Lexikon des Mittelalters*, 3 vols. + 3 fasc. to date (Munich, 1977-1988), I, 202 notes: "Est ist fraglich, ob es eine Geschichte du B., d.h. du nicht hagiograph." This view is also voiced by Joachim Ehlers, "Historiographische Literatur," in *Neues Handbuch der Literaturwissenschaft. Europäisches Hochmittelalter, VII*, ed. Henning Krauss (Wiesbaden, 1981), 451. See also Antonia Gransden, *Historical Writing in England*, 2 vols, (London and Ithaca, 1974, 1984).

3. David Herlihy, *Medieval Households* (Cambridge, Mass., 1985). 115. For the saint's family and upbringing, see Donald Weinstein and Rudolph Bell, *Saints and Society* (Chicago, 1982), 19-72 and *passim*. A great deal is to be found in André Vauchez, *La sainteté en occident aux derniers siècles du Moyen Âge d'après les procès de canonisation et les documents hagiographiques* (Rome, 1981), *passim*. For a bibliography see Stephen Wilson, ed., *Saints and their Cults: Studies in Religious Sociology, Folklore and History* (Cambridge, 1983), 304-417.

4. A good survey of the various approaches is Michael Anderson, *Approaches to the History of the Western Family, 1500-1914* (London, 1980). On infancy in hagiographical sources, see Shulamith Shahar, "Infants, Infant Care and Attitudes toward Infancy in the Medieval Lives of Saints," *Journal of Psychohistory*, 10 (1983), 281-309; on adolescence, Michael Goodich, *Vita perfecta. The Ideal of Sainthood in the Thirteenth Century*, in *Monographien zur Geschichte des Mittelalters*, 25 (Stuttgart, 1982), 100-123; Pierre Riché, "L'Enfant dans la société monastique au xiie siècle ," in *Pierre Abélard. Pierre la Vénérable* (Paris, 1975), 692-700.

5. Sulpicius Severus, *Vita S. Martini*, ed. Jacques Fontaine, 3 vols. (Paris, 1967-1969), I.6. See Christopher Donaldson, *Martin of Tours, Parish Priest, Mystic and Exorcist* (London, 1980) on his early life. On the exemplary role of the saint see Peter Brown, "The Saint as Exemplar in Late Antiquity," *Representations*, 1.2 (Spring, 1983), 1-25.

6. Gregory the Great, *Dialogi*, ed. Adalbert de Vögué and Paul Antin, 2 vols. (Paris, 1978-1980), 1.2. Eustace of Faversham. *Vita sancti Edmundi*, ed. C.H. Lawrence, *St. Edmund of Canterbury* (Oxford, 1960), 203 quotes an Oxford letter supporting the case of Edmund Rich, Archbishop of Canterbury (d. 1242): "Crescente vero aetate crevit in virtute."

7. Strong dependence on Sulpicius Severus' life of Martin of Tours has been demonstrated in Gino Sigismondi. "La, Legenda Beati Raynaldi'. Le sue fonti e il suo valore storico," *Bolletino della società umbra di storia patria*, 59 (1959), 5-111. Several examples of hagiographical *topoi* are to be found in the essays of Baudouin de Gaiffier, *Études critiques d'hagiographie et d'iconologie* (Brussels, 1967).

8. On the parallel between the Christian saint and Greek hero see A.-J. Festugière, *La Sainteté* (Paris, 1949). The typology of hagiographical themes and their continuity with the Old Testament is well-illustrated in Ebenezer C. Brewer, *A Dictionary of Miracles* (London, 1966); on the Bible see Baudouin de Gaiffier, "Miracles bibliques et vie des saints," in *Études, op. cit.*, 50-61; J. Leclercq, "L'Écriture sainte dans l'hagiographie monastique du haut moyen âge," in *La Bibbia nell'Alto Medioevo. Centro italiano di studi sull'Alto Medioevo. Settimane di studio*, 10 (Spoleto, 1963), 103-128; a fascinating study of one particular genre of saint after 1200 is Rudolph Bell, *Holy Anorexia* (Chicago, 1985); see also Caroline Walker Bynum, *Holy Feast and Holy Fast. The Religious Significance of Food to Medieval Women* (Berkeley, 1987).

9. Sherry, L. Reames, *The Legenda aurea. A Reexamination of its Paradoxical History* (Madison, Wisconsin, 1985); James of Voragine, *Legenda aurea*, ed. Th. Graesse, 3rd ed. (Leipzig, 1890).

10. Peter the Venerable, *De miraculis*, II.25, in *MPL*, 189: 938, citing the life of Gerald of Aurillac by Odo of Cluny: "somniorum visiones non semper sunt inanes." For a typology of pre-natal visions, see Francesco Lanzoni, "Il sogno presago della madre incinta nella letteratura medievale e antica," *AB*, 45 (1927), 225-261.

11. The life of Mary of Oigniès by James of Vitry is organized in accordance with the seven cardinal virtues (fear, piety, knowledge, fortitude, prudence, understanding and wisdom), *ASS*, 23 June V: 557. The Biblical source is *Isaiah* 11.2: "The spirit of the Lord shall rest upon him, a spirit of wisdom and counsel and power, a spirit of knowledge and fear of the Lord."; see also Arnold of Foligno, *Vita Angelae de Fulgineo*, in *ASS*, 4 January I, 186-234.

12. The life of Lutgard of Aywières by Thomas of Cantimpré is divided into the *vita inchoantium, vita proficientium*, and *vita perfectorum*, in *ASS*, 16 June IV: 189; also Simon of Trebnitz, *Legenda major S. Hedwigis*, in *ASS*, 17 October VIII: 12. 225 ff.

13. James of Voragine, *Legenda aurea*, 752. The number seven is discovered by James embedded in Elizabeth's Christian name; the seven works of mercy play a role here. The *Sermo de translatione beate Elyzabeth* by Caesarius of Heisterbach likened the seven gates of Jerusalem to the seven cardinal virtues displayed by Elizabeth; see Albert Huyskens, ed., *Die Schriften des Cäsarius von Heisterbach über*

heilige Elisabeth von Thüringen, in *Publikationen des Gesellschaft für Geschichtskunde*, 43, pt. 3 (1937), 281-290.

14. Gregory, *Dialogi*, II.1.1.

15. Gregory, *Dialogi*, IV. 19; on the need to be free of one's family, see Gregory the Great, *Moralium libri*, VII.29 (in *MPL*, 75: 790c) commenting on *Luke* 14.26. Other Biblical citations justifying a break with one's kin include *Matthew* 4.22, *Matthew* 10.35-7, *Matthew* 23.9. See also the lives of Bernard of Clairvaux (*MPL*, 185: 225) and Romuald (*MPL*, 146: 768).

16. Thomas of Celano, *Vita prima S. Francisci*, in *AF*, 10 (Quaracchi, 1926-1941), fasc. 1.

17. Odo II of Cluny, *Vita Geraldi Aurilacensis*, in *MPL*, 133:644.

18. The *Processus* of Yves of Trécors, *ASS*, 19 May IV: 540 speaks of a struggle between *ratio* and *sensualitas*.

19. Caroline Bynum, *Jesus as Mother. Studies in the Spirituality of the Middle Ages* (Berkeley, 1982), 93.

20. *Vita B. Geraldi de Salis*, II.18, in *ASS*, 23 October X: 258; this is a late thirteenth century life; Ralph Bocking, *Vita Ricardi episcopi Cicestrensis*, in *ASS*, 3 April I: 288; Caesarius of Heisterbach, *Vita, Passio et Miracula S. Engelberti*, in *ASS*, 7 November III: 623-84; A. Heysse, ed., "Documenta de vita S. Ludovici episcopi Tolosani," *Archivum franciscanum historicum*, 40 (1947), 127-8.

21. Peter of Celle, *De puritate anime*, in Jean Leclercq, *La spiritualité du Pierre de Celle (1115-1183)* (Paris, 1946), 190-1: "Sicut in corpore omnia membra regit sanitas, sic in anima omnes motus componit puritas, et sicut aegritudo corruptio est sanitatis, sic corruptio privatio est puritatis. Sicut vero vita sine sanitate et cum insanabili languore est longa protractio deficientis naturae, sic propositum religionis sine puritate umbra sine veritate, species sine pulchritudine, membra sine vegetatione, ut itaque cadaver exangue et emortuum est corpus sine anima, sic religio sine munditia. Virtus virtutum, vita membrorum, sanitas complexionum est religio sine maculo [*James* I. 27], propositum bonum cum sanctimonia."

22. Stephan Kuttner, "Le réserve papale du droit de canonisation," *Revue historique de droit français et étranger*, 4th ser., 17 (1938), 172-228; Eric W. Kemp, *Canonisation and Authority in the Western Church* (London, 1948).

23. Johannes of Marienwerder, *Vita prima B. Dorothee*, in *ASS*, 30 October XIII: 493-499; Richard Stachnik, ed., *Die Akten des Kanonisationsprozess Dorotheas von Montau von 1394 bis 1521*, in *Forschungen und Quellen zur Kirchen- und Kulturgeschichte Ostdeutschlands*, 15 (Cologne, 1878); G. Franknoi, ed., *Inquisitio super*

vita, conversatione et miraculis beatae Margarethae virginis, in *Monumenta romana episcopatus Vesprimiensis*, 6 vols. (Budapest, 1896), I, 275 ff.

24. Jacques Cambell, ed., *Enquête pour le procès de canonisation de Dauphine de Puimichel comtesse d'Ariano (+ 26.XI.1360)* (Turin, 1978), 51.

25. Wilhelm Dilthey, *Selected Writings*, ed. and trans. H.P. Rickman (Cambridge, 1976), 212. For the value of autobiography as a guide to the history of consciousness, see Hans Müchow, "Über der Quellenwert der Autobiographie für die Zeitgeistforschung," *Zeitschrift für Religions- und Geistesgeschichte*, 17 (1966), 297-310.

26. Paul Lehmann, "Autobiographies of the Middle Ages," *Transactions of the Royal Historical Society*, ser. 5, 3 (1953), 51.

27. The most thorough study of autobiography is Georg Misch, *Geschichte der Autobiographie*, 4 vols. (Bern, 1949-1969); see William G. Spengemann, *The Forms of Autobiography* (New Haven, 1980), 170-245; F. Vernet, "Autobiographies spirituelles," in M. Viller et al., eds., *Dictionnaire de spiritualité*, 13 vols. to date (1937-1987), I, 1141-1159 for bibliography.

28. Karl Joachim Weintraub, "Autobiography and Historical Consciousness," *Critical Inquiry*, 1 (1975), 821-848. See his survey in *The Value of the Individual. Self and Circumstance in Autobiography* (Chicago, 1978); Miles F. Shore, "Biography in the 1980s. A Psychoanalytic Perspective," in Theodore K. Rabb and Robert I. Rotberg, eds., *The New History. The 1980s and Beyond* (Princeton, 1982), 89-113.

29. For some of the problems in defining autobiography as a literary genre, see Roy Pascal, *Design and Truth in Autobiography* (London, 1960); and James Olney, ed., *Autobiography: Essays Theoretical and Critical* (Princeton, 1980).

30. See William Butler Bowden, ed. and trans., *The Book of Margery Kempe* (New York, 1944); Sanford Meech and Hope Emily Allen, eds., *The Book of Margery Kemp*, in *EETS.*, *O.S.*, 212 (1940) for middle English version. Clarissa Atkinson, *Mystic and Pilgrim, the Book and the World of Margery Kemp* (Ithaca, 1983), 21 ff. confronts the issue of whether Margery's work represents true autobiography. Drew Hinderer, "On Rehabilitating Margery Kempe," *Studia mystica*, 5, no. 3 (1982), 27-43 argues that Margery's work is rather trite in spiritual content compared to Julian of Norwich; cf. Janel M. Mueller, "Autobiography of a New 'Creatur'. Female Spirituality, Selfhood, and Authorship in *The Book of Margery Kemp*," in Mary Beth Rose, ed., *Women in the Middle Ages and the Renaissance* (Syracuse, N.Y., 1986), 155-172; cf. also Karma Lochrie, "*The Book* of Margery Kemp: the marginal woman's quest for literary authority," *Journal of Medieval and Renaissance Studies*, 16.1 (1986), 33-55.

31. A.D. Nock, *Conversion* (Oxford, 1933); and Gerhart B. Ladner, *The Idea of Reform*, rev., ed. (New York, 1967) are two classic accounts. Some valuable remarks and bibliography are to be found in Giles Constable, "Renewal and Reform in Religious Life, Concepts and Realities," in *Renaissance and Renewal in the Twelfth Century*, ed. Robert Benson and Giles Constable (Cambridge, Mass., 1982), 37-67.

32. Ludwig Bieler, ed., "Libri Episolarum sancti Patricii episcopi. I. Introduction, Text and Commentary," *Classica et mediaevalia*, 1 (1951), 1-150. See also R.P.C. Hanson, *Saint Patrick, His Origins and Career* (Oxford, 1968); Margaret R. Miles, "Infancy, Parenting and Nourishment in Augustine's *Confessions*," *Journal of the American Academy of Religion*, 50 (1982), 349-364 notes the therapeutic function of the autobiography.

33. Mary McLaughlin, "Abelard as Autobiographer: the Motives and Meaning of his 'Story of Calamities'," *Speculum*, 42 (1967), 463-488. Some trenchant remarks are to be found in Richard Southern, "The Letters of Abelard and Heloise," in *Medieval Humanism* (New York, 1970), 88-90. Robert Hanning, *The Individual in Twelfth Century Romance* (New Haven, 1977), 15 sees Abelard's work as a turning-point in the depiction of the inner life: "Abelard's touchstone of repentance is no longer the public performance of prescribed penitential deeds... but the inner contrition of the sinner." See also Petrus Alfonsi, *Dialogi*, in *MPL*, 157: 535-7; Bernhard Blumenkranz, "Jüdische und christliche Konvertiten," in *Miscellanea mediaevalia. Jüdentum im Mittelalter*, ed. Paul Wilpert (Berlin, 1966), 264-80 for examples of conversion apologetica; Nahum Golb, "Megillat Ovadia ha-Ger," *Mehkarei Adoth ve-Genizah*, ed. Shlomo Morag (Jerusalem, 1981), 78 ff. [Hebrew]; see also Joshua Prawer, "The Autobiograhy of Obadyah the Norman, a Convert to Judaism at the Time of the First Crusade," in *Studies in Medieval Jewish History and Literature*, ed. I. Twersky (Cambridge, 1979), 110-134. Some Jewish autobiographical sources are listed in Martin Buber, *Ecstatic Confessions*, ed. Paul Mendes-Flohr (New York, 1985), xxx; Joseph Dan, "Autobiography," *Encyclopedia Judaica*, ed. C. Roth, 16 vols. (Jerusalem, 1972), IV, 1010-1015; Joseph Dan, "Wills, Ethical," *ibid.*, XVI, 530-2; Hermannus Judaeus, *De conversione sua*, ed. Gerlinde Niemeyer, *Monumenta germaniae historica. Quellen zur Geistesgeschichte des Mittelalters*, 2 (Weimar, 1963); Arnaldo Momigliano, "A Medieval Jewish Autobiography," *History and Imagination. Essays in Honour of H.R. Trever-Roper*, ed. H. Lloyd-Jones, et al. (London, 1981), 30-36; Samau'al al-Maghribi Ifham al-Yahud, *Silencing the Jews*, ed. and trans. Moshe Perlman (New York, 1964).

34. Hanning, *op. cit.*, 3-50.

35. Misch, *op. cit.*, vols. 2-4 on the middle ages.

36. Jeanne Begnami-Odier, *Études sur Jean de Roquetaillade (Johannes de Rupescissa)* (Paris, 1952), 16, 114.

37. Paul Doncoeur, ed., *Le livre de la bienheureuse Angèle de Foligno* (Toulouse, 1925).

38. Jaime I, King of Aragon, *Chronicle*, 2 vols., trans. John Forster (London, 1883), cc. 1-19, 426-497.

39. Angelo of Clareno, "Apologia pro sua vita," ed. V. Doucet, *Archivum franciscanum historicum*, 39 (1948), 63-100. For a recent study see Lydia von Auw, *Angelo Clareno et les spirituels italiens* (Rome, 1979).

40. Joseph Alberigo, et al., eds., *Conciliorum oecumenicorum decreta* (Bologna, 1972), 245: "Omnis utriusque sexus fidelis postquam ad annos discretionis pervenerit, omnia sua solus peccata confiteatur fideliter, saltem semel in anno proprio sacerdoti, et iunctam sibi poenitentiam studeat pro viribus adimplere."

41. Nicole Beriou, "Autour de Latran IV (1215): la naissance de la confession moderne et sa diffusion," in Groupe de la Bussière, *Pratiques de la confession* (Paris, 1983), 73-93; Hervé Martin, "Confession et contrôle sociale à la fin du moyen âge," in *ibid.*, 117-134.

42. Franz Xaver Seppelt, ed., *Akten des Kanonisationsprozess...*, in *Monumenta Coelestiniana. Quellen zur Geschichte des Papstes Coelestin V* (Paderborn, 1921), 278.

43. Juncta of Bevagna, *Vita Margaritae*, in *ASS*, 22 February III: 302-363. Other works which have an 'autobiographical' aspect, since they were written by confessors and were at least partly dictated by the subjects themselves, include L. Reypens, ed., *Vita Beatricis. De Autobiografie van de Z. Beatrijs van Tienen O. Cist. 1200-1268* (Antwerp, 1964); Peter of Florence, *Vita Margaritae de Faventia*, in *ASS*, 10 June II: 847-851; Michele Faloci-Pulignani, ed., *L'Autobiografia e gli scritti della B. Angela da Foligno* (Città di Castello, 1932).

44. Conrad of Castellario's life of Benvenuta Bojano, *ASS*, 29 October XII: 152-185 gives the exact age at which each new austerity was introduced; John of Marienwerder's biography of Dorothy of Montau likewise provides precise dating, see Hans Westpfahl, ed., *Vita Dorotheae Montoviensis magistri Johannis Marienwerder* (Cologne, 1964).

45. Charles B. Schmitt, "Aristotle among the Physicians," in A. Wear et al., eds., *The Medical Renaissance of the Sixteenth Century* (Cambridge, 1985) 1-15; F. van Steenberghen, *Aristotle in the West*, trans. Leonard Johnson (Louvain, 1955). For the role of Aristotle's works in the arts curriculum see James A. Weisheipl, "Curriculum of the Faculty of Arts at Oxford in the Early Fourteenth Century,"

Mediaeval Studies, 26 (1964), 175; James Murphy, "Aristotle's Rhetoric in the Middle Ages," *The Quarterly Journal of Speech*, 52 (1966), 109-115. For contemporary translations, see Aristotle, *Politica*, trans. William of Moerbeke, ed. Pierre Michaud-Quantin, in *Aristoteles latinus*, 19.1 (Bruges, 1961); and F. Süsemihl, ed., *Aristotelis Politicorum libri octo cum translatione Guillelmi de Moerbeke* (Leipzig, 1872); Aristotle, *Ethica Nicomichea*, trans. Robert Grosseteste, ed. Renatus Antonius Gauthier, 3 vols., in *Aristoteles latinus*, 26, 1-3 (Leiden, 1972-3); Aristotle, *Ars rhetorica*, ed. Leonard Spengel, 2 vols. (Leipzig, 1867), 178-342 for an anonymous early thirteenth century translation. See also Pseudo-Aristotle, *Oeconomica*, ed. F. Süsemihl (Leipzig, 1887), for a translation ca. 1270/95,; see also Pseudo-Aristotle, *Oeconomica*, ed. B.A. van Groningen and André Wartelle (Paris, 1968), xxi-xxvi on translations; R.A. Gauthier, "Deux témoignages sur la date de la première traduction latine des 'Économiques'," *Revue philosophique de Louvain*, 50 (1952), 273-83. A list of Aristotelian translations, which has been the object of much scholarly controversy, is found in Martin Grabmann, *Guglielmo di Moerbeke O.P. il traduttore delle opere di Aristotele* (Rome, 1946); and Heinrich Schipperges, *Die Assimilation der arabischen Medizin durch das lateinische Mittelalter* (Weisbaden, 1964), 59-60.

46. Wilhelm Berges, *Die Fürstenspiegel des hohen und späten Mittelalters* (Stuttgart, 1938), 191-356, contains a comprehensive list of texts; cf. also J. Batany, "Regards sur l'enfance dans la littérature moralisante," *ADH*, 8 (1973), 123-132, who summarizes several sources.

47. William Peraldus, *De eruditione principum*, published in Thomas Aquinas, *Opera omnia*, ed. S.E. Fretté, 28 vols. (Paris, 1875), XVII, 604 ff. on childhood; on William, see A. Dondaine, "Guillaume Péyraut, vie et oeuvres," *Archivum fratrum praedicatorum*, 18 (1948), 162-236. A similar treatise is the *De regimine principorum* by Engelbert of Admont.

48. Giles of Rome, *De regimine principum* (Rome, 1607), I.iv. 1-3; III.i. 16; II.ii. 1-17; III.iii. 3. This is based largely on Aristotle, *Politics*, VIII. 3; VII. 15, 16, 17; V. 8; *Rhetoric*, II. 12, 13, 14; I. 14; *Ethics*, VIII. 12. For a 1285 French translation by Henri de Gauchy see S.P. Molenaer, ed., *Li Livres de Gouvernement des Rois* (Paris, 1899).

49. Dante Alighieri, *Il Convivio*, ed. G. Busnelli and G. Vandelli, 2nd ed. (Florence, 1964), IV. 23-28. *Les quatres âges de l'homme* (ca. 1265) by Philippe de Navarre, ed. Marcel de Fréville (Paris, 1887), is rather similar in its four-fold structure.

50. Israel Abrahams, ed., *Hebrew Ethical Wills*, 2 vols. (Philadelphia, 1926).

51. M. Grignaschi, "La diffusion du *Secretum secretorum* (Sirr al-'asrar) dans l'Europe occidentale," *AHDLMA*, 47 (1980), 7-69; R.A. Pack,

"Pseudo-Aristotelis Epistola ad Alexandrum de regimine santitatis a quodam Nicolao versificata," *AHDLMA*, 45 (1979), 307-325 for textual history; cf. also M. Grignaschi, "L'origine et les métamorphoses du 'Sirr-al-asrār'," *AHDLMA*, 43 (1976), 7-112.

52. Roger Bacon, *Secretum secretorum cum glossis et notulis*, ed. Robert Steele, in *Opera hactenus inedita Rogeri Baconi*, fasc. 5 (Oxford, 1920).

53. The unglossed thirteenth century Latin translation appears in Hiltgart von Hurnheim, *Mitteldeutsche Prosaübersetzung des Secretum Secretorum*, ed. Reinhold Möller (Berlin, 1963), along with German translation. Further translations are found in M.A. Manzalaoui, ed., *Secretum secretorum, nine English versions*, in *EETS*, 276 (Oxford, 1977).

54. I have used the edition in Salvatore di Rienzi, ed., *Flos medicinae scholae Salerni*, 2nd ed. (Naples, 1856); a partial translation of 1607 is found in John Harrington, trans., *The School of Salernum, Regimen sanitatis Salerni* (Salerno, 1959). The work has appeared under many different names. See Karl Sudhoff, "Zum Regimen sanitatis Salternitanum," *Archiv für Geschichte der Medizin*, 7 (1914), 360-62; 8 (1915), 29, 352-373; 9 (1916), 221-249; 10 (1917), 91-101; 12 (1919), 149-180.

55. Averroes, *Colliget*, VI, 1-17 in *Aristotelis Opera cum Averroes commentariis*, 10 vols. + 3 Suppl. (Venice, 1562-1574), Suppl. 2: 133-142 contains references to Galen, Aristotle, Razi and Avenzoar, and bears a marked similarity to the other guidebooks to health.

56. Sarton, III.1, 746 ff., *passim* contains the names of many who composed glosses on texts bearing a similar name, such as Niccolo Bertruccio, Manno di Manieri, Magnino, Albino di Montecaliero, Peter of Spain, William of Saliceto and Simon of Genoa. For Guy, see *Paris, B.N. Lat.*, 11015, 32r-54v.

57. Louis Landouzy and Roger Pepin, eds., *Le régime du corps de maître Aldobrandin de Sienne* (Paris, 1911).

58. Arnold of Villanova, *Opera* (Lyons, 1511), 15r; Sarton, III.i, 893-900 and Michael McVaugh, "Arnald of Villanova," *DSB*, I, 289-91 suggests that much of Arnold's opus is either apocryphal or heavily plagiarized.

59. Vincenzo Licitra, ed., "Il *Liber legum moralium* e il *De regimine vite et sanitatis* di Bellino Bissolo," *Studi medievali*, Ser. 3, 6 (1965), 450-454.

60. Bernard Gordon, *De conservatione vitae* (Leipzig, 1570); see Luke E. Demaitre, *Doctor Bernard de Gordon: Professor and Practitioner* (Toronto, 1980), 62 ff.

61. Martin Plessner, ed., "Der OIKONOMIKOC des Neuphythagorers 'Bryson' und sein Einfluss auf die islamische Wissenschaft," *Orient und*

Antike, 5 (Heidelberg, 1928), contains Latin, Hebrew and German versions of the thirteenth and fourteenth centuries. See also A. Pelzer, "Un traducteur inconnu, Pierre Gallego," *Miscellanea Francesco Ehrle*, 2 vols. (Rome, 1924), I, 407-56. For evidence of the influence of "Bryson" on the treatment of children in al-Ghazzali, see Avner Gil'adi, *Makhshevet ha-Hinukh shel al-Ghazzali* (Hebrew University of Jerusalem unpublished doctoral dissertation, 1983), 48 [Hebrew].

62. For English translation of *Parva naturalia*, see W.S. Hett, ed. and trans., Aristotle, *On the Soul. Parva naturalia. On Breath* (Cambridge, Mass., 1935), 387-426; the treatise *De vita et morte* deals almost entirely with respiration. Latin paraphrase by Averroes in *Aristotelis Opera*, VI, 144v-148v and in Aemilia Ledyard Shields, ed., in *Corpus commentariorum Averrois in Aristotelem*, VII.1 (Cambridge, Mass, 1949); also Harry Blumberg, ed., *Averroes' Epitome of the Parva Naturalia* (Cambridge, Mass., 1961); For commentaries, Charles Lohr, "Medieval Latin Aristotle Commentaries, " *Traditio*, 23 (1967), 313-413; 26 (1970), 135-216; 27 (1971), 251-352; 28 (1972), 281-396; 29 (1973), 93-198; 30 (1974), 119-144; idem., "Medieval Latin Aristotle Commentaries. Addenda and Corrigenda," *Bulletin de philosophie médiévale*, 14 (1972), 116-126.

63. Lynn Thorndike, *Michael Scot* (London, 1965), 27-29; for translations, see G. Lacombe, "Medieval Latin Versions of the *Parva Naturalia*," *New Scholasticism*, 5 (1931), 389-411; Lorenzo Minio-Palluelo, "Iacobus Veneticus Grecus: Canonist and Translator of Aristotle," *Traditio*, 8 (1952), 265-304; Grabmann, *op. cit.*, 96; Schipperges, *op. cit.*, 59-60. Translations were also made by Hermannus Alemannus (fl. mid-13th century) and Guillelmus de Lunis (fl. 13th century).

64. Giles of Rome, *Commentationes physicae et metaphysicae* (Rome, 1582), 861-4.

65. On medieval encyclopedias, see Ch. V. Langlois, *La vie en France au moyen âge*, 4 vols. (Paris, 1926-1928), III, xvi ff; Robert Collison, *Encyclopedias, their History throughout the Ages* (New York, 1966), 59 ff.; Bernhard Wendt, *Idee und Entwicklungsgeschichte der enzyklopedischen Literatur* (Wurzburg, 1941); Pierre Michaud-Quantin, "Les petites encyclopédies du xiiie siècle ," *Cahiers d'histoire mondiale*, 9 (1965/6), 580-595; Maurice de Gandillac, "Encyclopédies premédiévales et médiévales," *Cahiers d'histoire mondiale*, 9 (1965/6), 483-518; Maria Teresa Beoneo-Crocchieri Fumagalli, *Le enciclopedie dell'occidente medievale* (Turin, 1981), 49-54 for a good bibliography; Maurice de Gandillac et al., *La pensée encyclopédique au moyen âge* (Neuchatel, 1966); Traugott Lawlor, "Encyclopedias and Dictionaries, European," *Dictionary of the Middle Ages*, ed. Joseph Strayer (New York, 1984), IV, 447-50. The publication of encyclopedias must be seen in the context of a vast proliferation of reference guides published between 1230 and 1280. See Richard Rouse, "La diffusion en occident au XIIIe siècle des outils

de travail facilitant l'accès aux textes autoritatifs," in George Makdisi, et al., eds., *L'Enseignement en Islam et en Occident au moyen âge* (Paris, 1976), 114-147. See also Richard McKeon, "The Organization of of Science and the Relations of Cultures in the Twelfth and Thirteenth Centuries," in *The Cultural Context of Medieval Learning*, ed. J.E. Murdoch and E.D. Sylla, *Boston Studies in the Philosophy of Science*, 26 (Boston, 1975), 151-192.

66. Pierre d'Ailly, *Imago mundi*, ed. Edmond Buron, 2 vols, (Paris, 1930); for English translation, see Edwin Keever, *Imago Mundi by Petrus Alliacus* (Wilmington, N.C., 1948); Brunetto Latini, *Li livres dou trésor*, ed. Francis J. Carmody (Berkeley, 1948); Fazio degli Uberti, *Dittamondo*, ed. Silvestri (Milan, 1926); Gautier of Metz, *Mirour of the World*, ed. Oliver H. Prior, *EETS*, 110 (1913) was even translated into Hebrew in the sixteenth century; Iacopo di Dante Alighieri, *Il Dottrinale*, ed. G. Crocioni (Città di Castello, 1895); Cecco d'Ascoli, *Acerba*, ed. P. Rosario (Lanciano, 1913); Michel de Boüard, *Une encyclopédie médiévale: le Compendium philosophiae* (Paris, 1936) contain little on the ages of man. A useful discussion of some later Jewish texts is Abraham Melamed, "Hebrew Italian Renaissance and Early Modern Encyclopedias," *Rivista di storia della filosofia*, 1 (1985), 93-112.

67. Raffaelo Maffei, *Commentariorum urbanorum* (Venice, 1515), fol. 331v merely quotes Jerome's commentary on Amos to the effect that old age has the advantage of freeing one from enslavement to the passions. Domenico de Bandino's (d. 1418), *Fons memorabilium universi*, in *Oxford, Baillol*, 238 E. f. 425 quotes Cicero, and notes the presence of vice in every age.

68. The edition here used is Bartholomaeus Anglicus, *De rerum proprietatibus*, ed. Georg Barthold (Frankfurt, 1601). On the author see Gerald E. De Boyar, "Bartholomaeus Anglicus and his Encyclopedia," *Journal of English and Germanic Philology*, 19 (1920), 168-189; T.B. Plassman, "Bartholomaeus Anglicus," *Archivum franciscanum historicum*, 12 (1919), 68-109; J. Goyens, "Barthelémy l'Anglais," *DHGE*, 6: 975-7; Lynn Thorndike, *A History of Magic and Experimental Science*, 8 vols. (New York, 1959-1964), II, 401-435.

69. Bartholomaeus, *op. cit.*, 1: "ad intelligenda aenigmata scripturarum, quae sub symbolis & figuris proprietatum rerum naturalium & artificialium a Spiritu sancto sunt traditae & velatae..."

70. *Ibid.*, VI, cc. 1-14 *passim*. For a partial translation of these chapters see Michael Goodich, "Bartholomaeus Anglicus on Child-Rearing," *Journal of Psychohistory*, 3(1975), 75-84.

71. Thomas Cantimpratensis, *Liber de natura rerum. Text.*, ed. H. Boese (Berlin, 1973) for the first part; also Alfons Hilka, ed., *Liber de monstruosis hominibus orientis* (Berlin, 1933); an Old French partial translation appeared ca. 1300. There are many manuscripts, e.g.,

B.M., Royal 12.E.XVII; *Royal* 12.F.VI; see Pearl Kibre, "Thomas of Cantimpré," *DSB*, 13: 347-9; Thorndike, *op. cit.*, II, 372-98; Pauline Aiken, "The Animal History of Albertus Magnus and Thomas of Cantimpré," *Speculum*, 22 (1947), 205-225; G.J.J. Walstra, "Thomas de Cantimpré. *De naturis rerum.* État de la question," *Vivarium* 5.2 (1967), 146-71; 6.2 (1968), 46-71; L. Thorndike, "More Manuscripts of Thomas of Cantimpré's *De natura rerum*," *Isis*, 54 (1963), 269-77 for a history of this work.

72. Vincent of Beauvais, *Speculum maius*, 4 vols. (Douai, 1624) is divided into a *Speculum historiale, Speculum doctinale, Speculum naturale* and *Speculum morale* (probably spurious, added about 1300). On Vincent, see Henri Peltier, "Vincent de Beauvais," *DTC*, XV.2: 3026-3033; Michel Lemoine, "L'oeuvre encyclopédique de Vincent de Beauvais," in de Gandillac, *op. cit.*, 77-85; Joseph McCarthy, *Humanistic Emphasis in the Educational Thought of Vincent of Beauvais* (Leiden, 1976); Astrik L. Gabriel, *The Educational Ideas of Vincent of Beauvais* (Notre Dame, Ind., 1962); Astrik L. Gabriel and Edward G. Rytko, *L'educazione nel medio evo e l'educazione d'oggi* (Rome, 1962). The *Speculum doctrinale* contains much also found in his *De eruditione...*

73. Idem, *Speculum naturale*, XXXI. 57 ff.

74. M.A. Rouse and R.H. Rouse, "The Texts called 'Lumen animae'," *Archivum fratrum praedicatorum*, 41 (1971), 5-113; the edition here used is Berengar of Landorre, *Lumen animae*, ed. Matthias Farinato (Augsburg, 1477). On Berengar, see *DHGE*, VIII: 372-4.

75. John of San Gemignano, *Summa de exemplis et rerum similitudinibus* (Venice, 1584); on John, see Antoine Dondaine, "La vie et les oeuvres de Jean de San Gemignano," *Archivum fratrum praedicatorum*, 9 (1939), 128-183.

76. *B.M., Royal* 6.E.VI; *Royal* 6.E.VII; for mss. description see G. Warner and J. Gilson, *British Museum Catalogue of Western Manuscripts in the Old Royal and King's Collections* (London, 1921), I, 157-9. Lucy Freeman Sandler is preparing a major critical study of this work.

77. Pierre Bersuire, *Opera omnia*, 6 vols. (Cologne, 1731), vol. 2 for *Reductorium*; vols. 3-6 for *Dictionarium*; Marijke vander Bijl, "Petrus Berchorius - les Sermons de Bersuire," *Vivarium*, 22.2 (1984), 113-20; *DHGE*, VIII: 914-6.

78. Bersuire apparently did not complete a projected collation from different authors.

79. Bersuire's method paralleled Nicholas of Lyra's well-known versified approach to Biblical exegesis, "the literal teaches facts, the allegorical what you ought to believe, the moral what you ought to do, and the anagogical what you ought to strive for." He also appears to owe

much to Rabanus Maurus, *De universo libri XXII*, vii.i, in *MPL*, 111: 179-85.

80. Ambrose, *Hexameron*, in *Opera amnia de Sant' Ambrogio. I sei giorni della creazione*, ed. Gabriele Banterle (Milan, 1979) is perhaps the most important precedent, in which he provides a Christian cosmology and an anthropomorphic treatment of the natural world, dealing systematically with the human body. For a list of commentaries on the six days of Creation, some of which were 'encyclopedic' in character, such as Lactantius' *Institutiones*, see E. Mangenot, "Hexaméron," *DTC*, VI.2: 2325-3254; Gian Carlo Garfagnini, *Cosmologie medievali* (Turin, 1978) contains selections from the commentaries on *Genesis*; pp. 40-45 for bibliography.

81. Vincent of Beauvais, *Speculum maius*, I, *prologus*, c. 7; Thomas of Cantimpré, *prologus*.

82. Pierre Bersuire, *Reductorium moralis*, pp. 1-2.

83. Richard H. Rouse and Mary A. Rouse, *Preachers, Florilegia and Sermons: Studies in the Manipulus florum of Thomas of Ireland* (Toronto, 1979), 7 ff. on the kinds of derivative thesauri available; Rosemary Burton, *Classical Poets in the "Florilegium Gallicum"* (Frankfurt, 1983) for some such texts; also R. Rouse, "Florilegia and Latin Classical Authors in Twelfth and Thirteenth Century France," *Viator*, 10 (1979), 131-160; B.L. Ullman, "Classical Authors in Medieval *Florilegia*," *Classical Philology*, 27 (1932), 1-42 has shown that Vincent made use of the *Florilegium gallicum* at *Paris, B.N. Lat.* 17903; see also Franz Brunholzl, "Florilegium Treverense," *Mittellateinische Jahrbuch*, 1 (1964), 65-77; 3 (1966), 129-217. The *Manipulus florum, B.M. Royal* 7. C. III, 100v on *iuventus* cites Ambrose, Bernard, Cyprian, Cassian and Seneca. *Senectus* (f. 170v-171v) cites Ambrose, Augustine, Seneca, Jerome and Cassian.

84. William of Conches, *Das Moralium dogma philosophorum des Guillaume de Conches*, ed. John Holmberg (Uppsala, 1929); Ezio Franceschini, ed., "Il ,Liber philosophorum moralium antiquorum'," *Atti del Reale Istituto veneto di scienze, lettere ed arti*, 91, pt. 2 (1931), 393-597. This work is attributed to the eleventh century Cairene philosopher and physician Abu 'l Wefa Mubeschschir ben Fatik. A Spanish translation entitled *Bocados de Oro* appeared at the court of Alfonso the Wise, and a Latin translation followed.

85. Nemesius of Emesa, *De natura hominis*, ed. G. Verbeke and J.R. Moncho (Leiden, 1975), written ca. 390/400, long attributed to Gregory of Nyssa, was translated into Armenian, Arabic and Georgian, and twice into Latin, by Alfano of Salerno (d. 1085) and Burgundio of Pisa (d. 1193). The work deals with the humoral constitution of the body and provides a regimen for health.

86. John of San Gemignano, *op. cit.*, iv: "Hinc est quod actus humani (praecipue qui per corpus explentur) ex variis impressionibus siderum

disponuntur: ac etiam ex constellationum virtutibus (quae hominum corporali conceptui vel ortui dominantur) ipsi homines ad diversa officia & mores inclinantur."

87. This is covered at greater length in J.A. Burrow, *The Ages of Man: A Study in Medieval Writing and Thought* (Oxford, 1986), Elizabeth Langford Sears, *The Ages of Man in Medieval Interpretations of the Life Cycle* (Princeton, 1986).

88. Marbod of Rennes, *De senectute*, in *Liber Marbodi episcopi decem capitulum*, c.5, in *MPL*, 171: 1702-4; Carleton Brown, ed., *English Lyrics of the XIIIth Century* (Oxford, 1932), 92-100; idem, *Religious Lyrics of the XIVth Century*, 2nd rev. ed. (Oxford, 1957), 3-7; idem. *Religious Lyrics of the XVth Century* (Oxford, 1939), 233-6.

89. *MPL*, 171: 1695.

90. Brown, *XVth Century*, 230.233; for a long account of the seven ages, see R. Girvan, ed., *Ratis Raving and Other Early Scots Poems on Morals*, in *Scottish Texts Society*, 3rd series, 11 (Edinburgh, 1937), 32 ff.

91. Eustache Deschamps, *Oeuvres complètes*, ed. Marquis de Queux de Saint-Hilaire, 11 vols. (Paris, 1878), I, 250-1.

92. Charles Singleton, ed., *Canti carnascialeschi del Rinascimento* (Bari, 1936), 240-1.

93. M.Y. Offard, ed., *The Parlement of the Thre Ages*, in *EETS*, 246 (London, 1959).

94. Celestin Hippeau, ed., *Chevalier du cynge et Godefroid de Bouillon*, 2 vols. (Geneva, 1969), II, 26; Jehan Maillart, *Le Roman du Comte d'Anjou*, ed. Mario Roques (Paris, 1931), 128-131; Jacques Le Goff, "Petits enfants dans la littérature des xiie - xiiie siècles," *ADH*, 8 (1973), 129-132.

95. Michel de Boüard, "Encyclopédies médiévales. Sur la connaissance de la nature et du monde au moyen âge," *Revue des questions historiques*, 112 (1930), 258-304; Henri Pirenne, "L'Instruction des marchands au moyen âge," *Annales d'histoire économique et sociale*, 1 (1929), 20-28.

96. Quoted in de Boüard, *op. cit.*, 272.

97. Bartholomaeus Anglicus, *De rerum proprietatibus, prologus*.

98. R. Glorieux, *La faculté des arts et ses maîtres au XIIIe siècle* (Paris, 1971), *passim*; T.B. Plassman, "Bartholomaeus Anglicus," *Archivum franciscanum historicum*, 12 (1919), 68-109; H. Boese, "Zur Textüberliefung von Thomas Cantimpratensis' Liber de naturis rerum," *Archivum fratrum praedicatorum*, 39 (1969), 53-68, M.

Grignaschi, "La diffusion du *Secretum secretorum* (Sirr al-'asrar) dans l'Europe occidentale," *AHDLMA*, 47 (1980), 7-69.

99. Berges, *op. cit.*

III. *Common Themes of Life Cycle Theory*

In attempting to understand the medieval periodization of life one is struck by the often imprecise use of age-related terms. Joseph Kett, discussing age distinctions in pre-industrial America, noted that "the language of age had a nebulous quality"; childhood might often extend to twenty-one and rarely referred to chronological age.[1] This tendency was also evident in medieval judicial sources, in which a witness might be described as a child (*puer*), or "about twenty".[2] Kett therefore preferred to divide the life-cycle into three stages of dependency, semi-dependency and independence. In many medieval biographies, this scheme might be more useful; for despite the classical divisions of age-reckoning found in Isidore of Seville or Avicenna, hagiographers preferred a simple three-part division of childhood, adolescence and adulthood: such terms as *iuvenis* and *adolescens* might be used interchangeably.[3]

Age-Oriented Terminology

As a mere perusal of Ducange's *Glossarium* indicates, particular circumstances rather than traditional definitions might determine the connotations of a term.[4] *Infans* might refer to a new-born child, a neophyte Christian, an oblate, or anyone still under the legal care of parents, guardian, or tutor, at whatever age. A *puer* may be a servant, young soldier, oblate, student, or someone of a lower ecclesiastical rank. In Frankish charters, *adolescentulus* could imply anyone between eleven and thirty. In early fourteenth century Aragonese charters, the lower social orders were described as *iuvenes* as opposed to the high-born *seniores*. The term *iunior* may refer to anyone in a subordinate position, regardless of chronological age; while a *senior* may be simply a married man, an abbot or lord.

Remarkably, as René Metz has pointed out, there is no canonical text which clearly defines the various stages of human life and the religious responsibilities and liabilities attached to each.[5] Such terms as *puer*, *infans*, *adolescens*, etc. were used with great imprecision, apparently because it was assumed that the reader would understand their meaning, although a clarifying explanation might be provided in a particular context. Thus, Hostiensis (ca. 1250) noted three "ages of discretion", pertaining to penitence, marriage and clerical rank. Despite the large amount of legislation governing a sacrament such as matrimony, the precise ages required for each stage of the process from betrothal to marriage ceremony remained fluid, and in any case dispensations were possible. Thus, engagement was permitted after the age of seven (although among the nobility we often hear of promises exacted with regard to two-year-old children); the marriage ceremony could be performed at the legal age of puberty, twelve for girls and fourteen for boys, although the *actual* age of puberty might come later, and had to be medically determined. Again, although twenty-five was the minimum age for priestly rank, and thirty for episcopal, many clerical offices precede the priesthood, and children were allowed to hold minor offices and benefices. Perhaps the most controversial date concerned the licit age for admission to the monastic life; child-oblation was not abolished until 1439, although after Gratian's *Decretum* (ca. 1150) children of fourteen were permitted to reject the promises made by their parents, and in the thirteenth century one year of probation was usually required for admission. Less uncertainty surrounds baptism, which was to occur without delay, especially in light of the reluctance of heretics to present their offspring at the baptismal font. The minimal age for the performance of confession, confirmation and communion was regarded as the age of "reason" or "discretion"; although no fixed rule appears to have existed, by the fourteenth century fourteen for boys and twelve for girls became the generally recognized ages suitable for the performance of these sacraments.

The only 'theological' context which allowed some speculation on the ages as a *topos* was a text included in Peter Lombard's *Summa Sententiarum* IV.40 (1148-50) containing remarks from Isidore's *Etymologiae* concerning the grades of consanguinity. Some glosses here referred to the ages of man; Bonaventure, for example, simply listed the ages without comment. Innocent V admitted the wide differences concerning the duration of old age, which runs between fifty and eighty.[6]

While the classical sources had suggested a multiplicity of terms and schemes for the ages of man, the definitions provided by Isidore of Seville (d. 636) in his *Etymologiae* or *Origines* XI.2 were to become the *locus classicus* for all discussions of the *topos* of the ages of man. Isidore's work was to lay down the conceptual terms of reference for the next eight hundred years. Isidore's definitions enunciated the principle that the word is an adequate representation of the virtue of that which it designates. Six ages, their etymology, and characteristics were listed, and were paralleled by six ages of history.[7] *Infantia* was derived from *non fari* (incapable of speech), a time of ignorance which extends to seven. *Pueritia* comes from pure (*purus*), the period just before puberty which ends at fourteen. Adolescence (*adulescentia*) is a time of growth and concupiscence which extends to twenty-one. *Iuventus* derives from *iuvare* (to help), because one has become independent, and ends at forty-nine. The fifth age is *aetas senioris* or *gravitas*, a time of decline ending at seventy, when the blood grows cold. *Senectus* occupies the period before death; the very end of life may be termed *senium*, thus expanding the original six into seven ages. These definitions appeared with minor changes in Isidore's *Differentiarum, sive de proprietate sermonum libri duo* II.74.[8] Here, Isidore further noted the increasing strength of the soul, the body and the intellect during the first stages of life. Isidore's definitions were adopted by Rabanus Maurus (d. 856), who provided a positive and negative "mystical" definition of each term with citations from Scripture.[9] Thus, for example, the term *infans* may refer either to a person who zealously pursues the Gospel, or to a foolish child. The *senex* may be either a man of consummate justice and upright wisdom free of domination by others, or one possessing dulled senses, foolish error, and physical weakness.

The Isidorean definitions were adopted with little change by subsequent lexicographers, such as Papias (ca. 1053), Osburn of Gloucester (ca. 1150), Eberhard of Bethune (13th century), Huguccio of Pisa (1210) and Joannes Balbi of Genoa (1286).[10] Theological dictionaries such as

Alan of Lille's (d. 1202) *Liber in distinctionibus dictionarium theologicalium*, and William Brito's (d. 1356) *Summa, sive Expositiones vocabulum Biblii* emphasized the Biblical context of each term.[11] Joannes Balbi also noted the quadripartite division of life, indicating the growing influence of natural science by characterizing *pueritia* as a springlike time of warmth and humidity; *iuventus* is summery, warm and dry; *senectus* is like the fall, cold and dry; and *senium* is like the winter, wet and cold, caused by the accumulation of phlegmatic humors in old age.[12] By the later period, the seven-age system hinted at by Isidore had become more widespread, as in the fifteenth century *Promptuarium parvulorum, sive clericorum* (ca. 1440).[13] Reacquaintance with some classical sources could lead to a revival of older schemes. Relying on Gellius and Quintillian, for example, Matteo Palmieri (1405-1475) again spoke of six ages: *infantia, pueritia, adolescenzia, viridità* (28-56), *vechezia* (til 70), and *decrepità* (til 120).[14] John of Wales' (d. 1285) *Communiloquium*, while retaining the Isidorean scheme, is notable for the anecdotes drawn from other sources to illustrate his moral strictures concerning each age.[15] For example, he berated modern parents for busying themselves too much with the honors of this world rather than of the next in the rearing of their offspring, citing the example of Edmund of Canterbury's mother, who paid special attention to her son's spiritual welfare. He cited Cicero concerning the pedagogical beatings meted out to Spartan youth; the decisive significance of adolescence in the development of the mind is illustrated with the story of Barlaam and Josaphat.

In addition to Isidore, a second source which increasingly influenced speculation on the life cycle was Avicenna's (ca. 980-1037) *Liber canonis*, translated in 1127 by Gerard of Cremona. Avicenna listed four ages: *aetas adolescendi* (til 30), *aetas consistendi* (til 35 or 40), *aetas minuendi* (til 60), and *aetas senium* (til death).[16] He did however subdivide the first age into three periods corresponding to infancy, childhood and adolescence, thus yielding a total of six ages. Avicenna further provided a more detailed description of the humoral transformations which accompany the passage from one period to another, which bring about emotional, physiological and intellectual changes. The influence of astrological speculation could further expand the ramifications of the divisions of life to include the four parts of the Zodiac, the four seasons, the humors and the ages of man.[17]

Despite the existence of various contending approaches to the ages, the seven-fold structure tended to take precedence in the late medieval encyclopedia. In Vincent of Beauvais,[18] for example, the rubric *aetates* began with the definitional remarks of Isidore of Seville in the *Etymologiae*, which had proposed six ages (i.e., *infantia, pueritia, adolescentia, iuventus, gravitas, senectus*), in which a seventh phase, *senium*, forms a part of *senectus*. This was followed by Avicenna's remarks, which at base propose a four-part scheme in which the first period was likewise subdivided into three periods, namely infancy, childhood and adolescence, thus resulting in six ages. Bersuire referred to the seven-age scheme, which allowed him to exploit the parallelism with the seven spiritual virtues to which the believer should gradually succumb throughout life--namely humility, charity, piety, fortitude, honesty, prudence and fear of God--all of which correspond to the needs of each specific age. On the other hand, in order to make use of the metaphor of the bee as an example to man, following Aristotle and Ambrose, Bersuire also suggested a three-age structure of adolescence, middle age and old age, reflecting the three sets of legs with which the bee transfers the honey (i.e., virtue) from period to period.[19]

In the Jewish homiletical tradition, *Ecclesiastes Rabbah* I.2 (ca. 640-900) had likewise posited a seven-part framework, perhaps taken from Hippocrates who, according to Arab sources, suggested such a division.[20] Here, the seven ages were likened to animals; three is a pig rolling in the mud; ten is a kid jumping about; twenty is a lustful wild horse; in marriage one is a dull, lazy ass; as a parent, a dog protecting its litter; in old age one is furrowed like an ape. Elsewhere, apparently relying on Isidore, as in Shemtov ibn Falaquera (ca. 1225-1295), a six-part scheme was suggested. The ten-age division was found in poems by Samuel ibn Naghrillah (993-1056) and Judah Halevy (1075-1141), although not derived from the *Pirqe Avoth*, which does not appear to have been known in Spanish circles before the thirteenth century (although such a scheme appeared in the ninth century Muslim Thabit b. Abi Thabit).

The most widely-known Jewish treatment of the ages was found in the *Pirqe Avoth* 5.25 (5.24 in some editions), a collection of moral statements by Midrashic figures. It apparently became a part of the Midrash after the eleventh century, and was included in the *Mahzor Vitry* by Simhah b. Samuel of Vitry (d. before 1105).[21] The text on the ten ages of man is attributed to one Ben Bag Bag (in the Vitry version to Samuel Hakatan) and states that at five one studies the Bible, at ten the Midrash, at thirteen Mitzvoth, at fifteen the Talmud, at eighteen one marries, at twenty one displays ambition, at thirty strength, at forty wisdom, at fifty counsel, at sixty old age, at seventy white hair, at eighty survival, at ninety one is stoop-shouldered, at one hundred one dies.[22] This verse provided a graded summary of the learning and responsibilities of the Jewish male, and was commented upon many times, although with varying degrees of originality. To cite one example, the Kabbalistic exegete Bahya ben Asher ben Hlava of Saragossa (late 13th century)[23] provided dietary advice for little children in his commentary, and likened the male child to the fruit of a tree or plant which one is prohibited from eating for three years after planting (*Leviticus* 19.23). In its fourth year such fruit is considered whole and may be consecrated to God; and in the fifth year, one may partake of the fruit, just as the child begins to study at five. Making use of the hermeneutical technique of Gematria (numerology), Bahya referred the reader to other Scriptural sources which may further illuminate the ages of man. At thirteen, he said, the child becomes a man in earthly law and is responsible for his acts, like Levi, son of Jacob (*Genesis* 34) who avenged the dishonor done to his sister Dinah by Shechem. He was termed a man, although in the heavenly court complete punishment is not exacted until age twenty. Bahya said that at forty a man reaches the fullness of his wisdom (like Moses who, according to Menachem ben Hameiri, knew his Creator)[24] and his body starts to decay, just as the Children of Israel travelled in the desert forty years until they achieved understanding and nationhood. At fifty one can give advice, for the ancient Levites (*Numbers* 8.25) retired from regular service at this age, and thus could provide counsel. At sixty one's age shows because of the drying out of one's members; for some, like David, death comes at seventy; those who reach eighty are termed survivors for having lasted so long.

Natural History

The contemporary treatment of progressive human development from birth to death was based upon a number of assumptions which, while present in medieval theology and philosophy from the beginning, reached a wider audience in the thirteenth century. A synthesis was achieved between those schools of learning which had flourished in the twelfth century, i.e. the philosophical (based largely on Arabic and pagan sources), and the theological.[25] While the twelfth century philosophers had often suffered from poorly translated or incomplete sources, and the conflict between philosophy and theology, such thirteenth century figures as Thomas of Cantimpré, Robert Grosseteste or Albertus Magnus moved easily between the worlds of natural philosophy and theology. A theme such as the ages of man, for example, had been present in some earlier encyclopedias, like those of William of Conches, Honorius of Autun and William of St. Thierry; it was absent in others, such as Hildegard of Bingen, Alexander Neckham and Herrad of Landsberg. On the other hand, all of the thirteenth century encyclopedias deal with the subject, combining both Christian and non-Christian sources.

The theme of the ages was most often dealt with in the framework of a discussion of man as a microcosmic reflection of the earthly and heavenly realms. The justification for an examination of the physical world and man's place in it was traced to Basil (ca. 333 - 379), who in his *Homilies on the Hexameron* had proposed to describe the organization and principles which govern the visible world, not as the result of the spontaneous gathering of the elements, but of God's action in the universe (I.1)[26] The authors of commentaries on the six days of Creation or of sermons on this theme, often dealt, albeit sometimes fleetingly, with man's genesis, character and development as a microcosmic reflection of God's image. Such investigation of the physical world was, however, invariably undertaken as a means of illustrating moral truths with the assistance of examples drawn from nature. Thus, Peter Damian (1007-1072), for example, in his *De bona religiosi status* had likened the monastery to a zoological garden (*vivarium*) peopled by a variety of beasts who provide allegorical examples of human behavior. "The beasts of nature," he said, "are discovered with the aid of spiritual understanding in the conduct of men: just as in many things one discovers what pertains to men." In the bestiary tradition, Peter provided a list of animals and the salvific lessons to be learned from them.[27] To the bestiarist, the eagle, for example, who may live a hundred years and rejuvenates itself by flying high and swooping down into cold water, may represent the spiritual man burdened with sin who rejuvenates himself through penance aided by the Holy Spirit. The life of the bee in particular was often taken to symbolize the human condition. Thomas of Argentina (d. 1357) suggested that man's concupiscence is similar to that of the pig, his anger to a dog's and his fierceness to a lion's, for his emotions are animalistic and his wisdom angelic.[28]

In accordance with the exploitation of nature as a source of moral *exempla*, Bartholomaeus Anglicus justified his concern for matters earthly by saying that "it is not possible for the soul to achieve contemplation of the invisible unless it has achieved understanding of the visible."[29] He noted the conformity of the earthly and celestial and suggested that the enigmas of the spirit may be illuminated , with the aid of Scripture, by the signs and figures of natural phenomena. Both Berengar of Landorre and John of San Gemignano argued that basic theological principles could be derived from the observation of nature. In his prologue, Berengar wrote "since theology is solidly planted in all the works of nature, because it is known through the presentation of examples, no one is deprived or bereft of the [knowledge of] it by any forgetfulness whatever."[30] We thus all possess inherent understanding of the secrets of the Creator if we care to open our eyes to His Creation. John of San Gemignano lay stress on the exemplary function of nature, taking as his model the artisan who maintains in his mind's eye an image of what he seeks to attain, and the child who learns to write with the aid of examples produced by his master. He likened human life variously to a shadow, flower, flax, ashes, vapor, a river, yarn, and the wind, whose genesis and characteristics share much in common with human nature.[31] Thus, the specific examples drawn from nature help us to perceive greater Christian principles.

The exploitation of the entire world of nature as a source for moral principles became more widespread in the thirteenth century as a feature of mendicant preaching, which sought to supply more dynamic, concrete images to the public it sought to convert. The alphabetical *Tabula exemplorum* (late 13th century),[32] in order to demonstrate the foulness of wealth, noted that just as excrement is generated in human viscera by a superfluity of matter, and metals and gems are extracted from the bowels of the earth, so also temporal goods and wealth were designated by the apostles as *stercora*. And while a tree which bears fruit will have stones cast upon it, so, on the other hand, one who posesses wealth will be bothered by thieves, princes and bailiffs who wish to seize his goods. The well-known image of the journey of life likewise called forth comparisons from the realm of navigation. Those undertaking a journey across the sea of this life may construct a ship which can be boarded by the devil, and may store away as nourishment the biscuits of envy, the wine of drunkenness, the water of greed and the salted meat of lust. And just as tiny rivulets may become vast rivers or small drops of water can fill a cistern or lake; in the same way venial sins can multiply and turn into mortal ones. One's journey through life may likewise be undertaken by horse rather than ship. Just as the body may be likened to a packhorse which relays the soul through this world, the exemplarist argued that in its reluctance the horse's soul must be pricked by the spurs of penance and fear. But just as the spurs of countryfolk are fashioned of iron, so deeds of penance should be iron-like in order to withstand the sufferings of hell. In another equestrian image, the evil horse who had consumed enough to feed three others, although he wouldn't labor for more than one, was compared to those clerics who devour many prebends but only serve at one.

Dignity of Man

The theme of the dignity of man and his supernatural character underlay all treatments of the ages of man, and was found in the earliest commentaries on *Genesis*, which were later strengthened by citations drawn from Aristotle concerning man's boundless potential.[33] Created in God's image, his eyes turned heavenward, man serves as a mediator between the visible and invisible worlds; and despite his wretched condition, can attain eternal life. He is a microcosmic combination of the four elements: his body derives from the earth, his blood from water, his breath from the air and his warmth from fire. Capable of reaching the heights of God, and reducing himself to the depths of the beast, he can rule the world. The *Secretum secretorum* likewise described man as the noblest of creatures whose body is a city, his mind a king, properly situated in the highest and noblest part of the body, his head; and like a city under seige, he is protected by five lines of defense: sight, hearing, smell, taste and touch.[34] The familiar theme of man as the microcosm of the universe -- a *minor mundus* -- possessing the vices and virtues of all the beasts, minerals, herbs and even planets, was detailed. The limitless possibilities which inform man's character had been well-summarized in the *Sacramentarium* of William of Conches (ca. 1090-ca. 1160):[35]

> "Man is called a microcosm in Greek, namely a small world, for his head is in the round form of a sphere, in which his two eyes shine like the sun and the moon. His chest is like the air, in which he coughs and breathes, just as in the air there are winds and rains. His stomach which receives food and drink, may be likened to the sea, just as the sea receives rivers. His feet, which hold up his body, are similar to the earth, just as the earth sustains all things. From the earth he receives his flesh, from the water his blood, from the air his spirit, from the fire his soul. There are four seasons; spring is childhood (*pueritia*), summer is youth (*juventus*), autumn is old age (*senectus*), winter is senescence (*aetas decrepita*); knowledge illumines like the day; ignorance darkens like the night. Sight comes from fire, hearing from the ether, odor from the air, taste from water, touch from the earth, bones from stones, nails from trees, hair from plants, sweat from dew, thoughts from the clouds. In the mind one possesses sense, and the seat of wisdom is situated there, disposing of all as in a court of law; in the face resides shame, or rather confusion (*confusio*); in the eyebrows one finds pride; in the

temples sleep; in the knees the rudeness of shame; in the heart one's thoughts and will; in the liver cupidity; in the lungs elation (*elatio*); fortitude in the stomach, laughter in the spleen; anger in the gallbladder; in the kidneys pleasure; titillation in the loins; procreation in the genitals. Like the birds, fish and beasts [man] possesses five senses and like them is mortal. Like the angels he possesses reason, making him immortal. Because of this man is a small world; therefore it is not unworthy to compare the wheel of human birth to the movement of time."

In his *Elementorum philosophiae libri quattuor* William of Conches had paralleled the four humors, seasons of the year, elements and ages of man, and made use of this image to discuss the learning process.[36] The first age is not conducive to learning because of the body's warmth and wetness; the child consumes a great deal, creating a constant turmoil of flux within the body. The vapor and smoke rise to the brain, causing the child to be confused and incapable of learning. But in the second age, *iuventus*, the natural humors which have been drawn from the womb begin to dry up, and stability allows learning to proceed. In *senectus*, one becomes cold and dry; natural warmth disappears; nevertheless, one's memory may remain strong, although bodily strength is dissipated. In *senium*, a cold and damp period, lacking natural warmth, one is overwhelmed by cold phlegm. One loses one's memory and becomes puerile. William cited Plato's *Timaeus*, the source of much contemporary cosmological speculation; he compared the ages of man to wax which, if too soft or too hard (as in childhood and old age), cannot accept the impression made upon it. He warned his readers to respect their teachers more then their parents; from parents one may acquire bad habits; from teachers one gains wisdom. And this knowledge will yield good acts. William's *Dragmaticon* (1144/51),[37] an expanded version of his *De philosophia mundi* (1130) in the form of a dialogue with the duke of Normandy and count of Anjou, probably Geoffrey Plantagenet, may be regarded as a close predecessor of such encyclopedists as Vincent of Beauvais. It contained chapters devoted to the development of the foetus, the five senses, the virtues, complexions, colors, etc., thereby placing the ages in a wider context of human development and citing both secular and sacred sources.

The relatively mechanistic philosophy and the search for causality, the desire to find "legitimate cause and reason" for every physical event, exemplified by William of Conches, was a direct result of the rapid assimilation of Arabic sources, not only among physicians, but also among the natural philosophers, most of whom were active at Paris.[38] William's views showed a marked similarity to those found in a work of physiological psychology, the *De differentia spiritus animae* by the Melchite Christian Qosta ibn Luqa (d. 912), which had been translated into Latin and included in the corpus attributed to Constantine the African (ca. 1080) and widely known in the thirteenth century.[39] Qosta's stated aim was to demonstrate the causes of the differences between people's characters, conduct, passions and penchants. Beginning with an invocation to the Trinity (which proved his orthodoxy), he listed twenty main areas in which men's characters differ, including intelligence, capacity for cruelty, pity, sexual orientation, food tastes, etc. These differences may be attributed to men's differing nature, temperaments and habits, and their attitudes toward good and evil. Some children are innately good, compassionate, friendly, generous, obedient, and modest; while others are evil, greedy, gluttonous, cruel, impudent, intractable, disobedient and foul-mouthed (a catalog oft-repeated by the thirteenth century encyclopedists in their discussions of childhood). The differences between children are caused by innate natural differences, some being naturally noble. Similar differences occur among the animals, some being solitary in character, others more sociable; some store away food for the future, others collect it anew each day; while some steal from others. In fact, all the facets of human character have their parallel in the animal world. Thus, while some human beings, like domesticated animals, may be amenable to training, others, like snakes and scorpions, are intractable.

Human differences are also, according to Qosta, a function of the domination of the organs of the body -- the brain, heart, liver and testicles -- and their constitutions. Each organ differs in size, function, and the kind of fluid it contains, causing character differences. As an example, the cavities of the brain control discernment, locomotion, aesthetic sense, memory, vision, imagination, presumption, thought, illusion, etc., and the relative development of each cavity will affect these faculties in each human. The qualities which reside in the heart, for example, include courage, irritability, hardness, pusillanimity, cowardice, anger and the other passions; because the brain dominates the heart, however, these emotions may be restrained. The stomach controls the digestive functions, and desires food in accordance with its own constitution, unless one is ill.

A poetic rendering of the approach found in the natural philosophers appeared in Dante's *Convivio* (1304/7). In accordance with Albertus Magnus' commentary on the Aristotelian *Parva naturalia*, the four complexions and humors were regarded as the constituent elements which effect change from period to period, and the qualities of heat and moisture determine the different cycles of life through which we pass. These four ages parallel the four seasons and the four parts of the day, comparable to the "carro del sol" of the pagans, drawn by four horses.[40] Although the four periods conclude at roughly twenty-five, forty-five, seventy and eighty, the precise length of each is dependent on the individual's constitution. The ratio of these stages in every life is proportionate to the full length of one's life. Since all life is controlled by Heaven, which is in the form of an arc, life itself is likened to a rising and descending arc, the high point being reached between thirty and forty for most people. The perfection achieved at age thirty-five is proven by the example of Jesus who possessed the most perfect constitution, and died at this age, since it would not have been fitting if his divine character had declined like that of other mortals. *Luke* 23.44 testified that Jesus died at midday, the sixth hour of daylight, which is the noblest and most virtuous time of day; the church offices are for this reason concentrated near this time. Each age is endowed with its own weapons of defense; the child, for example, defends himself with his skin and arms; the adolescent with the virtues of obedience, suavity, shame and beauty, tempered by adult guidance. Each period in the *Convivio* was personified by a different figure drawn from classical literature. Following Aristotle, Dante equated the prolongation of life with the preservation of bodily warmth. A figure such as Plato who was certainly nearly perfect and quite handsome (which is why Socrates was enamored of him), retained his natural youth (and bodily warmth) until the age of eighty-one.

Analogical Thinking

The earlier encyclopedists had merely copied out the leading authorities without attempting their integration within a unified theory of human biological and moral development. By the early thirteenth century, more sophisticated schemes for the structure of knowledge, replete with illustrative diagrams, exemplified by Raoul Ardent, placed man's character and development within a broad conceptual framework.[41] The later authors, notably Berengar of Landorre, John of San Gemignano and Pierre Bersuire in their attempt to derive moral, pedagogical and theological principles from natural phenomena, linked the ages of man to the unifying laws which govern the universe. The principles of analogical thinking were often applied to create a series of parallel metaphoric structures in the material, moral and spiritual worlds. While preserving their own integrity as logical, fully explicable closed systems, one structure assimilated the other so as to enhance, expand and illuminate its parallel on a one to one basis.[42] The physical characteristics of youth and old age were thus assimilated into the moral features of aging in such a way as to provide a multifaceted picture of the aging process which took into account the physiological, moral, and spiritual. Human development and senescence for example, may be likened to the aging of the world itself. Thus, the link between the ages of man and the ages of history was established.

The same organic maturing process allegedly evident in the cultivation of the virtues, the sacrament of penance, or the ascent of the soul to perfection was reflected in the ages of man; and through analogy, each process shed light on the other, creating a kind of all encompassing theory of developmental psychology. The literal text taken from Avicenna or Razi, in the absence of an empirical methodology, might generate an awareness of parallel systems which sometimes treated the factual data rather cavalierly in the service of theological truth. This approach may be observed in the linguistic method adopted by Isidore, who had made use of sometimes fanciful etymologies (as did the hagiographers) in order to derive the moral and physical characteristics inherent in each age from the term which denotes it. A further antecedent of the analogical method may perhaps be found in the earliest Christian allegory, the *Psychomachia* (fourth century) by Prudentius, in which the moral struggle between good and evil which engages every mortal soul was likened to a battle. Later allegories, such as the anonymous morality play *Everyman*, made use of the journey or pilgrimage as a metaphor for the path of the soul to virtue.[43]

The late medieval encyclopedist whose work largely summarized the contributions of others, stressed the microcosmic character of man. Thus an organic theory of human development from childhood to old age appeared, which could draw upon the entire natural world as a source of inspiration, and which placed man in the context of the natural laws which governed the universe. The principle of assimilation permitted the metaphorical application of this theory to the history of salvation whereby theology, biology and psychology work in tandem, endowing the entire cosmos with an ethical significance. As Judson Boyce Allen noted: "facts are mythologized, revised and allegorized to make their descriptions convenient to the faith."[44] The physical attributes of each age could thus be assimilated to their supposed moral features. These comprehensive encyclopedias, which encompassed both medicine and theology, were closely allied to such sources as Bernard Gordon's *De regimine sanitatis*, which indicated a concern for all aspects of health, both physical and mental, through the integration of several formerly diverse traditions.

The principle of analogy and assimilation did not remain the sole property of the learned. Perhaps the most widely known and exploited context in which the periods of life as an organic whole could be discussed was Biblical exegesis, whether in the form of learned Scriptural commentary, or tracts on specific themes.[45] Such expositions of Scripture reached a popular audience through the agency of sermon, a flourishing art form in the thirteenth and fourteenth centuries, largely due to the evangelical efforts of the mendicant orders. The 'ages of man' could represent to the preacher a useful illustration of how the entire universe had been endowed at Creation by God with the same laws governing birth, growth and death. Scripture could thus be inexhaustibly mined as a guide to the secrets of nature and history, in which man is an active participant. This theme was often characterized by a search for numerical symmetry, as when Ambrose (340?-397) speculated about the number four: the four books of the Evangel, the mystical beasts, the corners of the world and the ages of man (*pueritia, adulescentia, iuventus* and *maturitas*). In his commentary on *Genesis*, Ambrose described man as a microcosm of the universe whose anatomical perfection essentially mirrored the perfection of all Creation.[46] Victorinus of Pettau (d. 303?) paralleled the four elements, seasons, beasts of the Apocalypse, Evangelists, rivers of Paradise, creatures before the Throne, and the ages of man. He also provided a list of sevens, including the seven cardinal virtues and the seven heavens, although the ages do not appear here.[47]

The subject of the ages tended to be discussed in connection with certain Scriptural passages either in Biblical exegesis or in the extensive sermon literature.[48] The *Sermones de tempore* were delivered on a particular feast day or on Sundays, and used selected Biblical passages as the means of conveying a moral message. The *Sermones ad status*, an increasingly common homiletical genre in the thirteenth century, were addressed to particular classes or professional groups, including noblemen, clergy, merchants, tavernkeepers, etc. Many were also directed at age or sex-defined groups - children, parents, widows, married persons, etc. - such as James of Voragine's *Sermones* - and summarized the conduct demanded of each group. The *Sermones de sanctis* were delivered on a saint's day, and conveyed the message of his/her ministry. In this way both the details of the saint's life and the stereotypical life patterns became part of a wider popular culture. These sermons were probably the chief means whereby not merely the hagiographical and hortatory traditions reached the ears of the unlettered, but learned figures such as John of San Gemignano or Albertus Magnus also included references from natural history as a means of illustrating the essential unity of the secular and the sacred.

In *Genesis* 2 the days of Creation were taken to represent both the ages of history and of man. While several patristic commentaries on the Hexameron such as those of Basil (330-379) and Ambrose were sometimes cited, the *locus classicus* appears to have been Augustine's (354-430) *De genesi contra Manichaeos*, which paralleled the course of God's plan for salvation with the human life cycle.[49] *Matthew* 20.1-16, the parable of the laborers in the vineyard of the Lord, was used to compare the hours of the day when the landlord hired out workers with the possibilities for repentance during the different ages; here the interpretations of Gregory the Great and Jerome appear decisive. *John* 2.2 concerning the miracle of the six jugs of wine at the marriage of Cana-in-Galilee was understood to represent the six ages of man and history. A variety of other Biblical citations, such as *Matthew* 2.2 on the three Magi, *Luke* 12.35-8 on the vigils of the night, *Revelations* 21.13 on the twelve gates to the city of Jerusalem, and *Luke* 1.24 on the pregnancy of Elizabeth, were less frequently used to provide a framework for human development.

The days of Creation as a reflection of the ages of man and history, interpreted by Augustine, was to become standard fare in the medieval philosophy of history; and just as the days of the week are divided into night and day, so also the ages of man and of history witness a dawn and a sunset.[50] On the first day of Creation God brought forth light, a kind of infancy for the human race parallel to the exit of man from the womb into the light of day. In history, this period lasted for ten generations from Adam to Noah. But just as the flood destroyed all recollection of the infancy of humanity, so we are oblivious to our early years of life. The second age, *pueritia*, which lasted from Noah to Abraham, is comparable to the second day of Creation, when the firmament separating the waters was created. In history, this age reached its apogee with the confusion of tongues at Babel. Like our own *pueritia*, mankind retains a memory of this time, although the Children of Israel did not yet exist, since in childhood we are not yet capable of generation. The third age, which lasted from Abraham to David, akin to our *adolescentia*, parallels the third day of Creation, when the earth was separated from the waters; for in this age the Chosen People were distinguished from the idol-worshipping Gentiles. For the Jews are similar to the irrigated earth which bears fruit. The aridity of the earth before the coming of Abraham is replaced by the fertility brought by Holy Scripture and the prophets, says Augustine, when the earth thirsts for the shower of divine commands.

The third age had witnessed the birth of the people of God, for in adolescence mankind can bear children. This age drew to a close when the people disregarded the divine commands and allowed the evil King Saul to rule over them. The fourth age, which lasted until the Babylonian Captivity, is *iuventus*, the youth of humanity, the brightest of all the ages of man, comparable to the fourth day of Creation, when the stars appeared in Heaven. The two brightest stars, the sun and the moon, were indeed the Synagogue and the Kingdom (later identified as the *sacerdotium* and the *regnum*) created in the Davidic period. The fifth age, which lasted from the Captivity in Babylon to the Advent of Christ, is comparable to the decline of youth (*iuventus*) into old age (*senectus*), called the *aetas senioris*. The strength (*robur*) of the Jewish kingdom was broken just as in this stage of life a man's vigor declines. It is comparable to the fifth day of Creation when the birds of the air and the fish of the sea were created akin to mankind, which occupies an unstable place in the world. The sea-monsters described in *Genesis* are like those great men who can dominate the winds of history, and are not depraved by the cult of idols. Through them, as the living creatures were admonished to increase and multiply, the Children of Israel were dispersed among the peoples of the earth; although in this age the Jews were so befouled with sinfulness they could not perceive the Savior. The sixth age, corresponding to *senectus*, commenced with the preaching of the Evangel by Jesus, when the carnal kingdom (as in a man's development) has wasted away, the Temple thrown down, and sacrifices have ceased. At this time a new man is born who will live in the Spirit, comparable to the last age of life when one prepares for the carnal death which precedes eternal life. The seventh day of Creation does not find a complete parallel in the ages of man on this earth, but is deferred to the time of rest, the heavenly life after death.

The persistence of schemes paralleling the *aetates* of history and of man was evident in many later interpretations of the Creation myth, which was viewed as a blueprint for the subsequent fate of man and his world, particularly after the twelfth century. Among those who made use of this program were Abelard and Bonaventure (who employed three-part, six-part and seven-part divisions).[51] Godfrey of St. Victor (1125/40-1194), while essentially adopting this framework in his *Microcosmus*, appended a discussion concerning the winds of change by which man is buffeted from birth to death (*John* 14.1-2, 4). He thus described the progress of the soul undergoing a series of trials consonant with the vicissitudes of age, a theme likewise adopted by Absalom of St. Victor (d.1203).[52] The Pseudo-Bede *De sex dierum creatione liber*, suggested that the receipt of the seven gifts of the Holy Spirit parallels the order of the seven days of Creation.[53] Each event of the Hexameron thus possesses characteristics similar to these gifts, which one should acquire in the same order.

This multilevel interpretation of Scripture permitted the application of the ages of man and history to the interpretation of *Matthew* 20 derived from Jerome (342?-420), i.e. the parable of those selected by a wealthy landowner at different hours of the day to labor in his vineyard, and yet receive the same wages regardless of their length of service. It was used by Honorius of Autun in his *Gemma animae* to reflect the liturgical hours, the stages of history and man, and the ecclesiastical orders (although employing slightly different terminologies).[54] Matins was likened to *infantia*, when we are born into the light of day, and to the rite of baptism which brings us to the truth. Prime recalled *pueritia*, when we begin to study and may undertake the service of God. Tierce recalled adolescence, when we may undertake clerical orders, and are associated with the ministers of God. Sext paralleled *iuventus*, when we are permitted promotion to the priesthood and deaconate, and may be selected as rulers and teachers of men. Nones was identified with *senectus*, a time when higher ecclesiastical office may be conferred. Vespers was the time of *decrepita*; some may still convert to a better life at this age, like those in the parable who malingered idly in the marketplace, leading lives of vanity and who may yet be chosen to achieve eternal life. Complines referred to the end of one's life, when we hope to be saved through confession and penance. The parallel ages of history cited by Honorius were represented by the just men such as Abel and Enoch of the first age, followed by Noah and his brood, the Jewish patriarchs, the prophets, the apostles, and the honorable men in the days of the Antichrist. In the *Mitrale, sive summa de officiis ecclesiasticis* by Sicard of Cremona (1155-1255?), the seven canonical hours served as a metaphor for the forms of grace imparted by the Holy Spirit, the mysteries whereby Jesus is revealed, the periods of history (totalling seven thousand years), and the ages of man.[55]

Bruno of Segni (1049-1123) added four gates to this vineyard, through which admission grows progressively more arduous, although the adolescent suffers the severest impediment because of the snares of lust.[56] William Peraldus, citing Gregory, spoke of the various kinds of wisdom acquired in the course of the four ages, which permit more complete understanding of God.[57] Nicholas of Lyra's (1270-1340) interpretation related man's life to the circuit of the sun, whose warmth is greatest at midday.[58] James of Voragine (1230?-1298) spoke of four periods, a time of erring, of renewal, of reconciliation and of pilgrimage, which are paralleled by the four parts of the liturgical year, four periods of history, the four seasons, and four parts of the day.[59] Richard of St. Victor (d. 1173), citing the historical/human chronology employed by Augustine, made use of the six stone water jars at the marriage of Cana-in Galilee (*John* 2.1-2) as an image representing the ages of the world and man, laying stress on the parallels between the rearing of the children of God and the disciplining of man. The six empty jugs are likened to the emptiness of sensual pleasures; history and the individual in the course of time are filled with the wine of new revelations, grace and divine consolation.[60] To Albertus Magnus (1206?-1280), the six jugs symbolized the six virtues of innocence, justice, obedience, patience, penance, charity and benevolence, each of which is apotheosized by a particular historical figure.[61]

Despite the many schemes for the ages of man which may be found in medieval exegesis, one must be wary of the central role which numbers play in cosmology and of the many didactic purposes to which numerological programs could be adapted. As Russell Peck has noted, "Number and its eternal language underlies not only such basic medieval concepts as macrocosm and microcosm, form and image, and the explaining through analogy of the relationships of the correspondent parts; it also correlates morality and mental states with external realities."[62] Thus, the formal division of life into ages may be seen as a kind of symmetrical esthetic structure which provided the commentator with a framework in which the more substantive issues of biological development, the acquisition of virtue, the path to salvation, and the process of learning, could be expounded. The many uses to which the concept of number in the study of the human life cycle could be adapted are illustrated in Robert Grosseteste's *Hexaemeron* (1228/35). After recounting the ramifications of the six days of Creation as a framework for the Augustinian six historical ages, Grosseteste described the mental development of man: in infancy the light of consciousness enters the newborn's body; in childhood, intelligence; in adolescence, learning; in youth (*iuventus* or *virilitas*), a combination of learning, doctrine and moral action dominate; in old age, internal virtue presides; and in senescence one achieves divine wisdom.[63] In another allegorical interpretation of the Creation myth, Grosseteste spoke of six stages in the process of learning: the simple examples of history, reason, the control of one's appetite, the pursuit of virtues, the wisdom of old age and eternal life. In another six-stage scheme, one first achieves free will, then the recognition of truth, the conquest of concupiscence, good deeds, proper doctrine, and the contemplation of God.[64] Grosseteste further provided an extended discussion of the ramifications of the number seven: the life cycle is reckoned in periods of seven years; the senses are experienced through seven apertures; one moves in seven different directions.[65]

III. Notes

1. Joseph Kett, *Rites of Passage. Adolescence in America, 1790 to the Present* (New York, 1977), 11. Philippe Ariès, *Centuries of Childhood*, trans. Robert Baldick (New York, 1962), 25, cites a 1556 translation of Bartholomaeus Anglicus, *De proprietatibus rerum*: "It is more difficult in French than in Latin, for in Latin there are seven ages referred to by various names, of which there are only three in French; to wit, childhood, youth and old age." Perhaps the terminological confusion resulted from the difficulties of conceptualizing simultaneously in several languages, each of which possessed a different tradition. This problem presumably became more acute in the late thirteenth century, with the increasing use of the vernacular languages for the transmission of information.

2. In a lengthy protocol such as that of Yves of Trécors, held in 1330, *Monuments originaux de l'histoire de S. Yves*, ed. A. de la Borderie et al. (Saint-Brieuc, 1887), the ages stated are approximate. The far later *Livre des miracles de Sainte-Catherine-de-Fierbois (1375-1470)*, ed. Yves Chauvin (Poiters, 1976), provides no ages for the witnesses.

3. See e.g. Martino Bertagna, ed., "Note e documenti intorno a S. Lucchese." *Archivum fransciscanum historicum*, 62 (1969), 452: "Hic juventutis sue flore uxorem... duxit et [ex] ea filios procreavit." The *Chronica XXIV generalium ordinis minorum*, in *AF*, III (Quaracchi, 1897) contains many lives of Franciscan saints, few containing any terms of age.

4. C. de Fresne Ducange, *Glossarium mediae et infimae latinitatis*, 10 vols. (Paris, 1883-1887), I, 88; II. 765; III, 821-2, 956-7, 924-6; V. 506; VI, 185-5; cf. J.F. Niermeyer, *Mediae latinitatis lexicon minus* (Leiden, 1976), 531, 567, 870, 956-7.

5. René Metz, "L'Enfant dans le droit canonique médiéval. Orientation de recherche," in *L'Enfant. Recueils de la société Jean Bodin de l'histoire comparative des institutions*, 26.2 (Brussels, 1976), 9-96; see also J. Delmaille, "Âge," *DDC*, I: 315-347.

6. Isidore of Seville, *Etymologiarum sive originum libri II*, 2 vols., ed. W.H. Lindsay (Oxford, 1911), IX.6; Bonaventure, *In IV Sententiae*, Dist. 40, dub. 3 in *Opera omnia*, 10 vols., ed. Collegii S. Bonaventurae (Quaracchi, 1882-1902), IV. 854; Innocent V, *In IV Librum Sententiarum Commentaria*, 4 vols. (Toulouse, 1651), IV. Dist. 40; Thomas Aquinas, *Commentum in quattuor libros Sententiarum*, IV. Dist 42. *Exp. text.*, in *Opera omnia*, 26 vols. (Parma, 1852-1873), VII.2, p. 1035; Richard de Mediavilla, *Super quattuor libros Sententiarum*, 4 vols. (Brescia, 1591), IV. Dist. 40. *Conclusio*.

7. Isidore of Seville, *Etymologiae*. V.38, XI.2; for a recent assessment of Isidore's enormous influence, see J.N. Hillgarth, "The Position of

Isidorean Studies: A Critical Review of the Literature 1936-1975," *Studi medievali*, Ser. 3, 24.1 (1983), 816-905. An exhaustive list of the ancient and patristic sources concerning the *aetates* is found in *Thesaurus linguae latinitatis*, 10 vols. to date (Leipzig, 1900-1984), I, 1126 ff., in addition to entries under each age.

8. Isidore of Seville, *Differentiarum sive de proprietate sermonum libri duo*, in *MPL*, 83: 81-2.

9. Rabanus Maurus, *De universo libri xxii*, VII.1 in *MPL*, 111: 179-185.

10. Papias, *Elementarium doctrinae rudimentum* (Venice, 1496), *aetas decrepita, iuvenis, puer, vir, senex*; Joannes Balbi, *Catholicon* (Strassbourg, 1483), *etas, infans, puer, senex*; Eberhard of Bethune, *Graecismus* ed. Johannes Wröbel (Bratislava, 1887), XII.36-49; Osburn of Gloucester, *Panorma*, ed. A. Mai, *Thesaurus novus latinitatis. Classicorum auctorum e vaticanis codicibus editorum*, 8 (Rome, 1836), 58; Paget Toynbee, *Dante Studies and Researches* (London, 1902), 97-114 on Huguccio of Pisa as a source for Dante; on dictionaries see Roswitha Klinck, *Die lateinische Etymologie des Mittelalters* (Munich, 1970); Louis L. Paetow, ed., *Morale scolarium of John of Garland (Johannes de Garlandia)* (Berkeley, 1927).

11. *MPL*, 210: 693, 914, 825-6, 940-1; William Brito, *Summa sive Expositio vocabulum Biblii*, ed. Lloyd Bernardine Daly, 2 vols. (Padua, 1975), II, 616; I, 18-19. A collection of *Distinctiones*, i.e. the meanings of words drawn from Scripture, written in a 13th century hand, *B.M. Royal* 7.C.V. fols. 41v-48v, *De homine* contains Biblical citations concerning childhood and infancy.

12. Balbi, *op. cit., Etas.*

13. Albert Way, ed., *Promptorium parvulorum sive clericorum*, in *EETS*, O.S., 89 (London, 1865), 7. This is a Latin-English dictionary.

14. Matteo Palmieri, *Vita civile*, ed. Gino Belloni (Florence, 1982), 22-30. This is an educational tract.

15. Johannes Gallensis, *Communiloquium sive Summa Collationum* (Strassbourg, 1489). II Dist. 4, c. 2; III. Dist. 2. c. 1-6.

16. Avicenna, *Liber canonis*, trans. Gerard of Cremona (Venice, 1506), Lib. I, Fen. I. Doct. III c. 3 (p. 3 v.); cf. also Avicenna, *De animalibus super de animalibus Aristotelis*, trans. Michael Scot (Venice, 1508), XII.3. *De etatibus et accidentibus etatum.*

17. P. Boffito, ed., "Il 'De principiis astrologiae, di Cecco d'Ascoli," *Giornale storico della letteratura italiana. Supplemento*, 6 (Turin, 1903), 10-11. This is essentially a commentary on Alcabitius.

18. Vincent of Beauvais, *Speculum naturale*, xxxi. 75 in *Speculum maius*, 4 vols. (Douai, 1624); Isidore of Seville, *Etymologiae*, 2 vols., ed. W.M. Lindsay (Oxford, 1911), xi.2; Avicenna, *Liber canonis*, I.fen.i.

doct.ii. c. 3. See also Avicenna, *De animalibus super de animalibus Aristotelis*, xii.3, in which four ages are listed, ending at 25, 35/40, 50, 60 + . He notes the difference of opinion among physicians concerning the quantity of warmth in *pueritia* and *iuventus*.

19. Pierre Bersuire, *Dictionarium*, vol. III, p. 74, in *Opera omnia*, 6 vols. (Cologne, 1731). Ambrose, *Hexameron, op. cit.*, V. 21, 67-72 in *Opera omnia de Sant' Ambrogio, I sei giorni della creazione*, ed. Gabriela Banterle (Milan, 1979), regarded the bees as a perfect society, made more so by the spontaneous generation which eliminated both lust and pain from procreation; cf. Aristotle, *Historia animalium*, IX.27, III.10, ed. A.L. Peck, 2 vols. (London, 1965-70) on bees; Pliny, *Naturalis historia*, XI, ed. L. Ian and C. Mayhoff, 6 vols. (Stuttgart, 1967). See vol. 6 under *apes* for many citations concerning the bees.

20. In addition to Leopold Löw, *Die Lebensalter in der jüdische Literatur* (Szegedin, 1875) on the treatment of the ages in Jewish sources cf., Norman Roth, "The 'Ages of Man' in Two Medieval Jewish Poems," *Hebrew Studies*, 24 (1983), 41-44: see Samuel Rappaport, trans., *A Treasury of the Midrash* (New York, 1968), 178.

21. Ben-Zion Dinur, ed., *Masekhet Avoth* (Jerusalem, 1974) for introductory remarks on textual history; p. 132 ff. for text with commentary. For a list of commentaries on this text see Menachem M. Kasher and Jacob B. Mandelbaum, eds., *Sarei ha-Elef*, 2 vols., 2nd ed. (Jerusalem, 1978-1979), I, 308-39.

22. I am indebted to Prof. B.Z. Kedar for the suggested preference of 'survival' over 'heroism' for the Hebrew *gevoorah*.

23. Bahya ben-Asher, *Perush Rabbenu Bahya al Masekhet Avoth* (Jerusalem, 1962), V.25; Yitzhak Ber Shlomo me-Toledo, *Perushim al-Masekhet Avoth* (Jerusalem, 1965) is quite similar, although more dependent on Gematria. The commentary found in the *Mahzor Vitry*, ed. S. Hurwitz (Nuremberg, 1923), and that attributed to Rashi, in *Perushei ha-Rishonim le-Masekhet Avoth*, ed. M. Kasher (Jerusalem, 1973), contain much of the commentary found in the thirteenth century, suggesting a decisive commentary prior to the eleventh century.

24. Menachem ben Shlomo ha-Meiri, *Beit ha-Bechira al-Masekhet Avoth*, 2nd ed. (Jerusalem, 1965). The commentary of Rabbenu Bahya suggests some medical knowledge, for he relates aging to the drying up of the body.

25. Fernand van Steenberghen, "La philosophie de la nature au xiiie siècle," in *La filosofia della natura nel medioevo. Atti del terzo congresso internazionale di filosofia medioevale* (Milan, 1966), 114-132; idem, *La philosophie au xiiie siècle* (Louvain, 1966), 123 ff. Domenico di Bandino (1415), quoting Avicenna, notes the conformity of sacred and secular literature concerning the ages of man. See Francesco

Novati, "Nuovi studi su Albertino Mussato II," *Giornale storico della letteratura italiana*, 7 (1886), 43, no. 2.

26. Basil of Caesarea, *Homélies sur l'Hexaeméron*, ed. Stanislas Giet (Paris, 1949), I.1; on three ages of life, see idem, *Sur l'origine de l'homme (Hom. X et XI de l'Hexaeméron)*, ed. Alexis Smets and Michel van Esbroeck (Paris, 1970), X.i. 13; Vincent of Beauvais, *Speculum maius*, 4 vols. (Douai, 1624), I, *prologus*, c. 6 sees the natural world as a reflection of the greatness of the Creator, since it was created in God's image.

27. Peter Damian, *De bono religiosi status*, in *MPL*, 145: 763-792: "Nam et naturales actus pecorum per spiritualem intelligentiam reperiuntur in moribus hominum; sicut et in hominibus aliquid invenitur, quod ad officia pertineat angelorum." (c.2, col. 767); also "Verumtamen in hujusmodi versutiis et fraudibus animalium aliquando salutaris allegoriae deprehenditur sacramentum." (c. 8, col. 771).

28. Thomas of Argentina, *Compendium theologice veritatis* (Strassbourg, 1489), II.61; *Physiologus*, ed. Consali Ponce de Leon (Rome, 1587) cites many authorities concerning the eagle and the bee.

29. Bartholomaeus Anglicus, *De rerum proprietatibus*, ed. Georg Barthold (Frankfurt, 1601), *praefatio*, pp. 1-2: "Non potest animus noster ad invisibilium contemplationem ascendere, nisi per visibilium considerationem dirigatur." Judson Boyce Allen, *The Ethical Poetic of the Later Middle Ages. A decorum of convenient distinction* (Toronto, 1982), 194 quotes Bernard Silvestris' commentary on Martianus Capella's *De nuptiis*...: "This sensible world is a certain book having divinity written intrinsically on it. The single creatures are letters and notes of something which is divinity. The immensity of the world is a note of the divine wisdom: the usefulness of the world, of the divine goodness." Bonaventure, *The Mind's Road to God*, trans. George Boas (New York, 1953), II. sec. 2 says that the elements of the sensible world are reflections, traces, pictures, echoes, shadows, *simulacra* of the First Principle, which will direct the believer from the visible to the invisible.

30. Berengar of Landorre, *Lumen animae*, ed. Matthias Farinato (Augsburg, 1477), *prologus*, pp. 1-2. See M.A. Rouse and R.H. Rouse, "The Texts called 'Lumen animae'," *Archivum fratrum praedicatorum*, 41 (1971), 5-113 for translation.

31. John of San Gemignano, *Summa de exemplis et rerum similitudinibus* (Venice, 1584), *prologus*: "Nam qui sunt in arte periti, interius habent exemplar, scilicet formam artis, secundum quam operantur... pueri qui scribere discuntur, tenent prae oculis exemplar magistri." See *ibid.*, I.86; IX. 85; IX. 84. Almost every animal in vol. V is likened in some way to man.

32. J. Welter, ed., *Tabula exemplorum de habundancia... secundum alphabeti ordinata* (Paris, 1926), 21, 53, 60, 62, 73 for examples of the application of moral qualities to the beasts for didactic purposes.

33. A treatment of this theme prior to the Renaissance is found in Eugenio Garin, "La 'dignitas hominis' e la letteratura patristica," *La Rinascità*, 1, pt. 4 (1938), 102-146; cf. Richard C. Dales, "The Medieval View of Human Dignity," *Journal of the History of Ideas*, 38 (1977), 557-572; E. Ruth Harvey, *The Inward Wits - Psychological Theory in the Middle Ages and Renaissance* (London, 1975), 3ff. The Aristotelian account of man's nobility notes that animals possess merely vegetative and sensitive power, while men possess intelligence. See Giles of Rome, *Hexameron, sive de mundo sex diebus condito*, in *Opera*, I (Rome, 1555), 56r.

34. See the unglossed 13th century Latin translation of the *Secretum Secretorum* in Hiltgart von Hurnheim, *Mitteldeutsche Prosaübersetzung des Secretum Secretorum*, ed. R. Müller (Berlin, 1963)

35. *MPL*, 172: 773-4; cf. Bede (?), *De mundi coelestis terrestrisque consuetudine liber*, in *MPL*, 90: 881-2 on the four humors, notes that blood is similar to the air, grows in the spring and rules in youth; the choleric humor is like fire, grows in summer, and rules in adolescence; melancholia is similar to the earth, grows in autumn, and rules in maturity; and phlegm is like water, grows in winter, and rules in old age; see also Honorius of Autun, *De imagine mundi libri tres*, II.49, in *MPL*, 176: 154 on the emotional character of each humoral personality; cf. Hugh of Foliot, *De medicina animae*, in *MPL*, 176: 1184-5; Thomas of Argentina, *Compendium...*, II.57; William of St. Thierry, *De natura corporis et animae libri duo*, in *MPL*, 180: 695-726. On man as a microcosm see Rudolph Allers, "Microcosmus: From Anaximandros to Paracelsus," *Traditio*, 2(1944), 319-407. A fine illustration is found in Herrad of Landsberg, *Hortus deliciarum*, ed. A. Straub and G. Keller (Strassbourg, 1879-1899), fol. 16. The microcosmic theme appears in all commentaries on the days of Creation, e.g. John of San Gemignano, *Opusculum de operibus sex dierum* (Paris, 1512), 2r.

36. *MPL*, 90: 1150, 1178.

37. William of Conches, *Dragmaticon*, Stanford University Ms. M412, 7r; for *De philosophia mundi*, IV. 9ff. see *MPL*, 172: 88-99. For the Latin translation by Calcidius of Plato's *Timaeus*, see Plato, *Timaeus*, ed. Raymund Klibansky, in *Corpus platonicum medii aevi*, 4 (London, 1962), 3-60.

38. Marie-Therèse d'Alverny, "Translation and Translators," in Robert L. Benson and Giles Constable, eds., *Renaissance and Renewal in the Twelfth Century* (Cambridge, Mass., 1982), 421-462; L.D. Reynolds, and N.G. Wilson, *Scribes and Scholars. A Guide to the Transmission*

of Greek and Latin Literature, 3rd rev. ed. (Oxford, 1974); David C. Lindberg, ed., *Science in the Middle Ages* (Chicago, 1978), 52-90; Heinrich Schipperges, *Die Assimilation der arabische Medizin durch das lateinische Mittelalter* (Wiesbaden, 1964).

39. Paul Sbath, ed., "Le livre des caractères de Qosta ibn Louqa," *Bulletin de l'Institut d'Egypte*, 23 (1940/1), 140-163: Sarton, III, 427; Schipperges, *op. cit.* The tenth century Latin translation appears in *Opera Constantini Africani*, 2 vols. (Basel, 1536-1539), I, 308-317 as *De animae et spiritus discrimine liber, ut quidadm volunt*, attributed to Constantine the African; elsewhere, the translation is attributed to John of Spain or a certain Constabulus; see also C.S. Barach, ed., *Costa-ben-Lucae: De differentia animae et spiritus liber*, in *Bibliotheca philosophorum mediae aetatis*, 3 (Innsbruck, 1878).

40. Dante Alighieri, *Il Convivio*, ed. G. Busnelli and G. Vandelli, 2nd ed. (Florence, 1964), IV. 23-28. The parallel of the seasons, humors and quarters of the Zodiac is found in Cecco d'Ascoli's *De principiis astrologiae*, ed. P. Boffito, *Giornale storico di lettere italiani*, Suppl. 6 (1903), 18; Ovid, *Metamorphoses*, I.2. vv. 153 ff., ed. O.E. Ribbeck, *Virgilii Maronis Opera* (Leipzig, 1894). Dante's notion of the arch of human life as paralleled in the four seasons, humors and qualities appears to be derived from Albertus Magnus' *De juventute et senectute* I. 2, a commentary on Aristotle. See Paget Toynbee, *Dante Studies and Researches* (London, 1902), 35-55.

41. See *B.N. Lat.* 3229, 2v for a scheme of the parts of *Scientia*.

42. A good account of the technique of parallel structures is found in Judson Boyce Allen, *op. cit.*, 182 ff. Sheila Delany, "Undoing Substantial Connection: The Late Medieval Attack on Analogical Thought," *Mosaic*, 5, no. 4 (Summer, 1972), 31-52, traces the working of analogical thinking in political theory and cosmology in the fourteenth century by such figures as Dante, Buridan, John Quidort, Marsiglio of Padua and William of Ockham.

43. On Prudentius' *Psychomachia* as an allegorical history of conversion, see Macklin Smith, *Prudentius' Psychomachia. A Reexamination* (Princeton, 1976), 109 ff.

44. Allen, *op. cit.*, 192.

45. Elizabeth L. Sears, *The Ages of Man, Medieval Interpretations of the Life Cycle* (Princeton, 1986), 54 ff. covers the subject of exegesis and sermons quite thoroughly. The possibilities which an investigation of Scriptural commentary open up are revealed through perusing Johannes-Baptist Schneyer, *Repertorium der lateinischen Sermones des Mittelalters für die Zeit von 1150-1350*, 9 vols., in *Beiträge*, 43 (Munich, 1969-1980); Friedrich Stegmüller, *Repertorium Biblicum medii aevi*, 11 vols. (Metriti, 1940-1980).

46. Ambrose, *Hexaemeron*, trans. John F. Savage (New York, 1961), VI.9; idem. *De Abraham*, II.9. 65, in *Opera*, ed. Carolus Schenkl, *CSEL*, 32.1 (Leipzig, 1897), 620.

47. Victorinus of Pettau, *Tractatus de fabrica mundi*, in *MPL*, 5: 304, 310-312.

48. A. Lecoy de la Marche, *La chaire française au moyen âge* (Paris, 1886); Jean Welter, *L'exemplum dans la littérature religieuse et didactique du moyen âge* (Paris, 1927); Th.-M. Charlond, *Artes praedicandi, contribution à l'histoire de la rhétorique au moyen âge*, in *Publications de l'Institut d'Études Médiévales d'Ottawa*, 7 (Ottawa, 1936).

49. An important predecessor was Firmicius Lactantius, *Divinae institutiones*, VII.3, ed. Samuel Brandt, in *Opera omnia, CSEL*, 19 (Leipzig, 1890), 633-4; VI. 14 in *ibid.*, 624, which divides Roman history into periods paralleling the five ages, *infantia, pueritia, adulta, adolescentia,* and *senectus*; cf. Franz Cumont, *Lux perpetua* (Paris, 1949), 278-82.

50. Augustine, *De genesi contra Manichaeos*, I, 23 ff. in *MPL*, 34: 190-194; *De diversis quaestionibus...*, II.58, in *MPL*, 40: 43; *Ennaratio in Psalmos*, 127.15, in *MPL*, 37: 1686.

51. Pseudo-Alcuin, *Disputatio puerorum*, 6, in *MPL*, 101: 1112-3; Peter Abelard, *Expositio in Hexaemeron:*, in *MPL*, 178: 771-3; Bonaventure, *Hexaemeron. Collatio XV*, in *Opera omnia*, V, 400, ed. Patres Collegii S. Bonaventurae, 10 vols. (Quaracchi, 1968), Bonaventure, *Breviloquium, prologus*, 4, in *Opera omnia*, V, 205; Bede, *De temporibus liber*, 6, ed. Charles W. Jones (Cambridge, 1943), 303; many others discuss the ages of history, but not of man, e.g. Isidore, the *Glossa ordinaria*, Remi of Auxerre and Wicbod.

52. Godefroy of St. Victor, *Microcosmus*, ed. Philippe Delhaye (Lille, 1951), I. 13-14; Absalom of Springiersbach, *Sermo IX in epiphania Domini*, in *MPL*, 211: 62.

53. Bede (?), *De sex dierum creatione*, in *MPL*, 93: 207-304.

54. Jerome, *Expositio Quattuor Evangelii, Matthew* 20, in *MPL*, 30: 574; Honorius of Autun, *Gemma animae*, II.53-4, in *MPL*, 172: 632-4.

55. Sicard of Cremona, *Mitrale, sive Summa de officiis ecclesiasticis*, IV.3, in *MPL*, 213: 159-62; VI.8, in *ibid.*, 272-5.

56. Bruno of Segni, *Homiliae XXII*, in *MPL*, 165: 771-2; *Commentaria in Matthaeum*, in *MPL*, 165: 237-8.

57. Gregory the Great, *XL Homilarum in Evangelia. I Hom. XIX.*, in *MPL*, 76; 1155; Guilelmus Alvernus, *Opera omnia*, 2 vols. (Paris, 1674), II, 201-2. This work is incorrectly ascribed to William of Auvergne.

58. Nicholas of Lyra, *Glossae seu postillae perpetua in Veterum et Novum Testamentum*, 3 vols. (Nuremberg, 1471-2), *Matthew* 20; cf. also Jerome, *Commentarium in Evangelium secundum Matthaeum*, in *MPL*, 26: 146; Rabanus Maurus, *Commentariorum in Matthaeum*, in *MPL*, 107: 1026; Haymo of Halberstadt, *Homiliae de tempore*, in *MPL*, 118: 156; Godfrid of Admont, *Homiliae dominicales*, in *MPL*, 174:74: 133-4; Albertus Magnus, *Sermo XXI in dominica Septuagesimae*, in *Opera omnia*, 38 vols., ed. August Borgnet (Paris, 1890-1898), XIII, 104; idem, *Ennarationes in Evangelium Matthaei*, in *Opera omnia*, XX, 699; idem, *Orationes supra Evangelia, Dom. in Quad.*, in *Opera omnia*, XIII; Absalom of Springiersbach, *Sermo IX in epiphania Domini*, in *MPL*, 211: 57-63.

59. James of Voragine, *Legenda aurea*, ed. Th. Graesse (Leipzig, 1890), prologus.

60. Richard of St. Victor, *Liber exceptionum*, ed. Jean Chatillon (Paris, 1958), 442; Guilelmus Alvernus, *Opera omnia*, II, 186-91; Augustine, *Tractatus in Joannis Evangelium*, XI.1.2.6, in *MPL*, 35: 1461: Bede, *Expositio in S. Joannis Evangelium*, in *MPL*, 92: 658 ff. contains a long historical account and a discussion of penance, but nothing on the ages of man.

61. Albertus Magnus, *Sermones de tempore*, ed. P. Jammy, new ed. (Toulouse, 1883), 65-71.

62. Russell A. Peck, "Number as Cosmic Language," in David A. Jeffrey, ed., *By Things Seen. Reference and Recognition in Medieval Thought* (Ottawa, 1979), 49.

63. Robert Grosseteste, *Hexaemeron*, ed. Richard C. Dales and Servis Gieben (London, 1982), Particula octava. XXXIII.1-6; cf. Bede, *Hexaemeron*, I, in *MPL*, 91: 20; Pseudo-Bede, *Commentaria in Pentateuchum, Genesis*, in *MPL*, 91: 195-6.

64. Grosseteste, *Hexaemeron*, Particula octava, XXXIII. 1-6; XXXIV. 1; cf. Augustine, *De vera religione*, XXXVI. 49, in *MPL*, 24: 143-4.

65. Grosseteste, *Hexaemeron*, Particula nona. X.9-10.

IV. Infancy and Childhood

The standard definition of infancy was taken from Isidore of Seville, who derived *infans* from *non fari*, since the infant is not yet able to speak and his teeth are not yet developed in order to form words clearly.[1] This formally ends at seven, when the child has reached the 'age of reason'.[2] From both the theological and biological points of view, however, the moment of conception was properly regarded as the commencement of life, and both the hagiographical and 'scientific' sources viewed prenatal life as the seed of all those principles which govern both the corporeal and spiritual components of human existence.

Pre-Natal Life

In the hagiographical tradition, much stress had been laid on the prenatal life of the saint, and a number of rhetorical devices were employed which foretold the saint's virtues. The most widely used was an etymological analysis of the saint's name as a premonition of future achievement, often based on Isidore's *Etymologiae* or Jerome's *Liber interpretationis nominum hebraicorum*.[3] It was argued that all things are named in accordance with the properties they possess. Examples abound. Albert of Trapani's (1240-1306) name was derived by his biographer from the Hebrew and Latin words for milky and sweet (*alab*), fountain (*ber*), and incense (*tus*), "Thus", he argued, "as the Philosopher [Aristotle?] says, the name of a thing is a consequence of the virtue it possesses."[4] Raymund of Capua in his *Vita* (1386) of Agnes of Montepulciano (1272-1317) said that "this virgin is similar to a ewe lamb [*agnus*] in all things, with the exception of one letter; otherwise both names are in concord."[5] Ralph Bocking in his *Vita* (ca. 1262) of Richard of Chichester (1197-1253) quoted a certain Peter of Ravenna to the effect that the names of the saints foretell their merits, deriving Richardus from *ridens* (smiling), *carus* (beloved) and *dulcis* (kind).[6] Caesarius of Heisterbach's *Vita, Passio et Miracula S. Engelberti* (1225) derived the martyred archibishop's name from *angelicus* and *libertas*.[7]

The most widely-distributed such source in which word-play made its appearance was James of Voragine's *Legenda aurea* (1255/66). Here Elizabeth of Thuringia's (1207-1231) name was derived from the Biblical Elisheva. Firstly, this may be translated as "my God knew", i.e. God knew her, watched over her, and approved of her; secondly, as "the seventh part of God", i.e. she displayed the seven deeds of mercy, and experienced the seven states of virginity, marriage, widowhood, the active life, the contemplative life, the religious life, and the state of glory; thirdly, as "the fullness of the Lord". In Caesarius of Heisterbach's *Vita* (1238) of Elizabeth of Thuringia, the seven cardinal virtues which are encapsulated in her name, formed the framework of her life.[8]

In the case of Francis of Assisi (1182-1226), James noted that his name had been changed from John to Francis for seven reasons.[9] Firstly, this denoted the fact that he miraculously acquired knowledge of French from God. As his legend reported, when filled with the Holy Spirit, Francis spoke French. Secondly, the French language served as a more efficient vehicle of conveying the mendicants' message to the world. Thirdly, as a consequence of Francis' ministry, many of his disciples who had been enslaved to the devil, were made free (*franci*). Fourthly, this was a sign of his open-heartedness, a virtue possessed by the French, who were also known to be as ferocious as beasts. Fifthly, as a result of Francis' ferocity, he also possessed verbal eloquence, with which sins were cast down; and sixthly, demons are driven away. Finally, the battle axes (*franciscae*) which preceded the Roman consuls were a sign of the awe, honor and strength which they, along with Francis, possessed.

A second prenatal hagiographical device often employed to herald the saint's greatness, based on Biblical and patristic sources, involved a heavenly guest (such as those who visited Abraham, Mary and Hannah) who prophesied the birth of a child whose life would be dedicated to the service of God. Such a heavenly portent may answer the prayers of infertile parents, as in the case of Nicholas of Tolentino (1245-1305), whose parents were visited by an angel, and who named their son Nicholas after the church they had visited; or Angelo of Furci (1246-1327), whose parents were visited by the Archangel Michael along with a bishop dressed in Augustinian garb, presumably St. Augustine himself.[10] Such miracles generally exacted a price, by requiring that the child be dedicated to a religious order with which he/she was connected; like Thomas Aquinas, who was given to the Benedictines of Montecassino; and Albert of Trapani, who became a Carmelite.[11] Such a prenatal guest also visited the mother of Judah ben Asher ben Yehiel (1290-2349) of Toledo who reported that his mother had dreamed that she would bear a son, expressing a preference for a wise over a rich one.[12]

A third such rhetorical device entailed some sign, either before or at birth, which presaged saintliness; in infancy, Thomas Aquinas stubbornly grasped a scrap of paper which had miraculously appeared inscribed with the *Ave Maria*, when taken by his nurse to church. At the birth of Agnes of Montpulciano, a great light filled the room in which her mother and the midwives were gathered; Pope Celestine V appeared at birth to be garbed in ecclesiatical dress and while conversing with his friends, sparks of fire issued from Bartolo Buonpedoni's mouth.[13]

Largely as a consequence of revived interest in Aristotle, along with the translation of Arabic sources, late thirteenth century theologians such as Giles of Rome and Peter of Palude sought to provide Christianized interpretations of sexuality and conception.[14] Likewise, Pierre Bersuire's encyclopedic article on infancy presented a moralized account of prenatal life through a gloss on Constantine the African.[15] He applied the principle that the natural world is imbued with symbolic transcendental messages which assist us to understand the Creator. The womb is likened to the Church or the Christian faith, the proper site for the nurturing of the penitent or believer. The semen is the word of God or the preacher's sermon, which animates the obedient soul germinating in the womb. The warmth which is the efficient cause of generation is likened to the grace of the Holy Spirit, while the afterbirth is akin to the charity which envelops all within the womb/matrix of Mother Church. The foetus feeds on menstrual blood, which is akin in this argument to the blood shed by Jesus.

Scriptural cover for this imagery is provided by the *Wisdom of Solomon* 7:2, "in my mother's womb I was wrought into flesh within a ten-month's space."[16]

In another rather fanciful image the womb represents the soul, and the foetus sin, which, in order to be expelled, must break through the afterbirth, which symbolizes the hindrances to salvation. Like the woman in childbirth whose sufferings are referred to in all the relevant sources, the soul will suffer danger. Bersuire quoted *Job* 38: 8-9: "Who watched the birth of the sea,/ when it burst in flood from the womb?/ when I wrapped it in a blanket of cloud/ and cradled it in fog." The sea here is taken to represent the bitter sin which during confession is expelled from the vulva of conscience beset by the clouds and fog of evil. The afterbirth may also represent original sin, which is washed away in baptism. Bersuire quoted Constantine the African's passage concerning the formation of the principle organs of the body, i.e., the heart, brain and liver, signifying the theological virtues -- charity, faith and hope -- which feed the outer limbs, namely the Church Militant (i.e., the prelates and ecclesiastics). Repeating a truism found in Galen, Augustine and Constantine,[17] Bersuire remarked that a longer period is required for the gestation of the female. The male signifies the good, strong and virtuous; the female the imperfect, carnal and sinful. Several sources are added to prove that the foetus is imbued with life by the forty-sixth day; this accords with *John* 2: 20 in which the forty-six years taken to build the Temple were likened to the forty-six days which elapsed from the conception of Jesus to his Nativity.[18]

The foetus is gradually formed out of the contrary seeds of male and female; only Christ was created in distinguishable form in the womb at conception. Birth occurs in the eighth, ninth, or tenth month, after the soul has entered the body, and skin covers all his members. The exit of the afterbirth is accompanied by great pain; because of the softness of the infant's limbs, it requires tender care.

Infancy

Hippocrates in *De anatomia* had observed that the infant cries out because he has no teeth; when he has two or three he will mumble; and when all have appeared he will talk.[19] Vincent's discussion of these tears shed at birth represented an opportunity to cite all of the major sources concerned with the wretchedness of the human condition, prefigured at birth, including Augustine, William of Conches, Solinus, Philo, Bernard of Clairvaux, Peter Comestor and Pliny.[20] The tenor of these remarks bolstered the words of *Ecclesiasticus* 40.1: "A heavy yoke is laid upon the children of Adam, from the day when they come from their mother's womb/ until the day of their return to the mother of all; troubled thoughts are theirs,/ and anxious expection of the day of their death." The commentators note that, regardless of our exalted station, whether we be a king like Solomon, or a pope like Eugenius III, addressed by Bernard of Clairvaux, once the accoutrements of office are taken away, we are all revealed in the grievous, guilt-laden, sorrowful condition of our birth, and the cry of the newborn is a portent of future suffering. Both Solinus and Augustine had pointed to Zoroaster as the only man who allegedly laughed at birth, mistakenly anticipating good fortune, but who was eventually conquered by King Ninus of Bactria. Peter Comestor had argued that Eva was so named by Adam because of "eiulatio" (wailing), and each cry of the child thus recalls man's sinfulness. The male child allegedly cries out "Ah...", for the letter A of Eva, and the girl child wails "Eh..." for the E of Eva, for both are born of woman.[21] In his *Physiognomia*, Michael Scot had suggested that the infant boy wails "Oa!" as if to say "Oh Adam, why have you sinned? Because of you I will suffer infinite misery." The infant girl cries out "Oe!", signifying "Oh Eve, why have you sinned? Because of you I will undergo a wretched life in this world."[22]

The defenseless condition of man at birth was proven by Vincent[23] with citations from William of Conches, Augustine, Hugh of St. Victor and Gregory of Nyssa. Following the medical tradition, William attributed this weakness to the corruption of menstrual blood and of the faculty of reason. The infant, Augustine argued, is ignorant and acts solely out of instinct, incapable of admonition. Hugh noted that although possessing reason, man's corporeal senses are inferior to those of the other beasts. The lynx possesses superior sight, the dog taste; Gregory pointed out that at birth man lacks even the most elementary means to defend himself, neither claws, teeth, talons, barbs, hair, horns, a strong mouth nor swiftness, and so on. Nevertheless, man eventually subdues all and makes use of the other beasts in order to overcome his own weakness.

The human infant (following Aristotle) is weakest of all because it is nurtured on menstrual blood, which was universally regarded as a source of putrefaction and degradation.[24] Innocent III, for example, in his *De contemptu mundi*,[25] pointed out that the poison of menstrual fluid allegedly kills all plant life with which it comes into contact. Dogs who consume it become rabid, while in the Mosaic law, a menstruating woman was regarded as unclean. The flesh of man was thus naturally weak, like his spirit, because of its genesis in the debasement of menstrual fluid. While the other creatures walk and labor immediately, because of the corruption of menstrual fluid, man is weak; only in his seventh year is he in full possession of his senses, although still lacking reason and intellectual power. But despite these liabilities, mankind eventually dominates all, and makes use of the creatures to overcome its inadequacies.

The sorrow of birth was often discussed with citations from such sources as William of Conches, who noted that the wail of the infant is caused by the discomfort of passage from the warm, humid pleasure of the womb into the inhospitable, cold, dry world.[26] Nurses customarily place their charges in tepid water, in order to return them to the kind of environment in which they were nourished. The first sound of the child is therefore one of grief. A sense of joy only appears on one's sixtieth day. While all the other beasts emerge armed with some natural defenses, man is born defenseless.

The tears of the infant, which bespeak the sorry condition of humanity, totally humbled, dependent, docile, naked, ill-formed and bound by swaddling clothes, symbolized both the inherent weakness of mankind, and its potential for perfection. To Bersuire this baby may personify *in bono* the so-called "spiritual child" lacking guile, who can yet reach complete virtue; and *in malo* the evil man, who thinks only of the present and is prone to the temptations of the devil.[27]

Although all observers agreed that mother's milk is superior to that of a nurse, beginning in the eleventh century we have increasing evidence of the use of wetnurses. Such a woman either lived at home with her employer, or in a village situated near town, in which she might care for several children, thereby neglecting her own.[28] Evidence from the early Renaissance suggests that the middle class child often suffered a series of traumatic crises; deprived of his mother at birth, he was nursed by a wet-nurse, occasionally a slave, at some distance from his family. At two or three he returned home, although direct contact with his biological parents remained limited. By seven, he might be shipped off to school, while girls might unwillingly find themselves either cloistered or married between ten and sixteen. As a result, while the hagiographical sources provided living illustrations of saints reared by nurses, the hortatory and encyclopedic material provided advice on her selection, character and physical condition.

Giles of Rome's remarks on the treatment of children til age seven, based largely on Aristotle's *Politics* VII.17, stressed the care of the child's health through the selection of a suitable nurse whose complexion conforms to that of the mother; he recommended moderate exercise and recreation and the avoidance of wine and excessive crying. In preparation for military pursuits, the infant's natural warmth should be reduced through exposure to the cold, since cold limbs are stronger than warm. Bissolo's treatise, apparently directed at a more bourgeois audience, praised the feeding of children by their mothers, and devoted much attention to the quality of milk fed the child, for it will determine his moral character.[29] Repeating the same injunctions concerning the health of the wetnurse, her constitution, appearance and moral character and the quality of the milk she provides found in Isidore and Avicenna,[30] Bersuire viewed her as a symbol of the preacher or educator who knows how to apply the redemptive balm of penitence; as the prelates who guide the Christian community; or as Christ who shows solicitude for the human race.

Razi and Avicenna,[31] cited by Vincent, had provided detailed directions on the feeding and care of the neonate. It should suck the breast so that the stomach is not distended, lest the infant suffer drowsiness or sluggishness. While it should get a lot of sleep, it should not be turned around a lot, and care should be taken that it doesn't vomit excessively. It's eyes ought to be covered with cloth so as to protect it from strong light, while colored pieces of glass and rags should be dangled on the crib, as it is lulled with the sound of sweet, restful music. When the time for speech draws near, the nurse ought to massage its gums and tongue, frequently talk to it, and begin to teach simple and easy words. Once the teeth have begun to appear, the gums should be rubbed with an ointment of butter, chicken fat and barley water.

John of San Gemignano (like Bersuire), made use of Constantine the African's[32] oft-repeated passage concerning infant care in order to expound on the means of directing the newly converted (*conversus*) to salvation. Each stage in the treatment of the newborn served as an example of the treatment to be accorded the convert. Just as infants require tender loving care since their limbs are weak and soft, and they are still bound in swaddling clothes, for example, so the convert must be treated with introspection. The water which removes the amniotic fluid and the redolent rose-water in which the infant is bathed were compared by John to the examples and virtues of the saints to which the convert is to be exposed. The moderately salty water in which he is then bathed recalls the selected examples which the convert must learn, lest he be driven away. Just as the interior of the infant's mouth is to be rubbed with honey, the convert should not at first be exposed to severe austerities and punishment, for the soothing comfort of the honey will hasten the acceptance of inner change. The child should afterwards be bathed in aromatic liquids and all its members massaged. These frequent baths to John were comparable to the tears of consolation to which the myrrh of temperance and the rose oil of patience are applied to soothe the penitent. Both Avicenna and Constantine had counseled putting the infant to sleep in a dark spot so that concentrated light will not damage his tender eyes. Likewise the newly converted should be taught the simple precepts of the Faith rather than be damaged by complex arguments. Concerning the child's nourishment, all authorities, including Avicenna, Razi and Haly Abbas urged the avoidance of tainted milk which can cause disease, and the supervision of the nurse's diet, for the infant can be either infected or cured by the milk it consumes.[33] The new convert should likewise not be fed on wrong or heretical opinions which will generate error. Proper doctrine is a kind of medicine which can be extracted from the lives of the saints.[34]

Just as infants are to be wrapped in swaddling clothes in order to straighten out their limbs, since they are easily malformed, John argued that so also converts, especially youths, must be controlled by laws and regulations lest they become deformed. Since infants eat a lot and require much sleep, in order to aid digestion, instill interior warmth in their bodies, and lull them to sleep, they ought to be gently rocked. This will encourage the slow movement of vapors in the brain and the child will derive pleasure from the gentle singing. In the same way, the convert, and especially youths who are ready for spiritual sustenance, will be excited by the divine love in them by means of contemplation and meditation. If they are laity they should lend their ears to the sweet music of divine praise; if clergy they should themselves give voice to such music. Augustine himself reported that at the time of his conversion he heard the sound of church music ringing in his ears. Much of John of San Gemignano's work was then taken up with a catalog of the physical diseases taken from the natural philosophers and physicians, and their moral equivalents. Each symptom of physical decay in old age, taken from the classic source by Cyprian, *De abusionibus saeculi*, was compared to the vagaries of sin.

John's precise comparison of the new believer to the neonate recalls a letter of Adam of Perseigne (ca. 1190)[35] in which the monastic novice was likened to an infant and the church to a mother whose breasts distill the milk of holy doctrine and allow the pure and innocent of heart to grow into manhood. Elsewhere the diapers in which Jesus was wrapped were akin to the controls of faith which keep away the filth of crime; the bands which tie Him to his cradle were the limits set by the faith; the creche symbolizes the altar in which Christ is offered as nourishment; the hay in which He rested at birth was like the flesh which is subject to the spirit. Adam's letter further envisioned Mary as Mother Church at whose breasts we all suckle.

Childhood

Infancy was succeeded by *pueritia*. According to Isidore,[36] the word child (*puer*) is derived from purity (*puritas*) which indicates the purity of the child's natural instincts and the fact that he is not covered with down. Seven was universally regarded as the beginning, and fourteen (usually twelve for girls) as the end of this stage. Youths may also be called *ephaebi* from the young and beardless Phoebus. For upon rising in the morning, the child appears fresh and new. The term *pueritia* may be understood, according to Isidore, to refer to the period of birth or nativity of Christ, as described in *Isaiah* 9.6: "He is born as a boy (*puer*) for us." It may refer to the youthful age of the child, i.e. eight or nine; or to his receptivity to the faith, as when God spoke to *Jeremiah* 1.7: "You are my boy, do not be afraid." The term *puberes* (young men), is derived from the sexual part of the body, the *pudenda*, for it is here that hair appears at puberty, a sign of the ability to bear children. Thomas of Cantimpré[37] in his treatment dated this stage from the period when the child can both walk and speak, which occurs after the *fonticulus* in the back of the cranium has dried up and the shell of the head has hardened, which may not occur at precisely the same time for all children. In infancy the intelligence and reason which distinguish man from the beasts are gradually implanted until the onset of childhood, once the child has been completely weaned away from the breast.

Ideally, as William of St. Thierry (ca. 1085-1188) had noted, childhood was to be a time of tears and sorrow.[38] An oft-repeated hagiographical *topos* concerned the child who possessed the soul of an old man and who might pursue virtue even in the face of parental dismay, sometimes hiding himself away in order to carry on religious exercises.[39] Juliana of Cornillon (1192-1258), sent to study at age five, avoided games and fasted without her teacher's permission, displaying strong emotions during the communion service, a harbinger of her championship of the cult of the Corpus Christi; and Elizabeth of Thuringia (d. 1231) supposedly transformed childish games into opportunities for pious exercises.[40]

Testimony concerning childhood in Vincent[41] was based on a string of quotations from Augustine's *Confessions* which describe his persistent efforts to express himself in infancy and childhood. He acquired the faculty of speech by imitating the sounds which had been applied to various objects which had been pointed out to him, from the gestures and glances which accompanied the utterance of certain words and implanted them in his memory. For, he argued, the natural language of all nations is spoken first through glances, gestures, facial expressions,etc. When Augustine went to school, he was beaten for idleness, although the so-called idleness of children often differs little from the "business" of adults, who nevertheless fail to commiserate with the brutalized child. His parents even laughed at the child's misery, and disregarded the torments he suffered at the hands of his masters, so that his sole recourse was to God. Augustine admitted to being a mediocre student, largely because he was forced to study, and his teachers failed to point out the utility of his studies. Nevertheless, he confessed to finding pleasure in the quest for truth, possessing a kind of inner Providence, although he sinned by seeking pleasure in God's creatures rather than in the Creator, thus falling into error. Nevertheless, mortal life is regarded as a continual trial, in which children are required to learn through the infliction of punishment. Adolescence by its nature is a time of folly and concupiscence; if left to our own devices, we would live lives of lawlessness and lust. But Providence is merciful, providing law in order to curb our human passions, and education in order to dispel our natural ignorance. These are inculcated by tutors through corporal punishment, thereby taming the naturally slothful and ignorant child, making him amenable to learning.

Vincent's chapter on the child's diet and training drew upon Arabic medical and pagan Latin sources.[42] Avicenna advised that the aim of education is to moderate the child's character and to permanently implant virtue, insuring that no single vice such as anger or sadness becomes overwhelming. For ire heats up the body while sadness dries one out; sluggishness relaxes the animal virtues, and creates a phlegmatic personality; mental and bodily health demand a temperate character, which can be guaranteed through proper training. While in infancy the child requires frequent washing, feeding and play; by about age six he may be handed over to a teacher and gradually introduced to learning, although a regular diet cannot be introduced until fourteen (although Halys suggested that by twelve the child has sufficient control to regulate his own diet). All of the authorities warned against giving wine to children, which generates red cholera. Razi provided details concerning the child's diet, suggesting the avoidance of fatty foods, such as milk and cheese, limitations on sweets and fruit, and the insistence upon moderate amounts.

The separation of the child from the breast causes grief, so that the disciplinary training of tutors becomes necessary in childhood.[43] Because of the narrowness of the veins and the warm and moist complexion of childhood, sexual movements do not occur until puberty. The flesh is soft and flexible; as a result children are nimble and amenable to training. Living without care, taking pleasure in jest, fearing little but the rod, children lack modesty and readily display their naked bodies, unable to distinguish praise from blame. The warmth and mobility of the humors within them encourage quick excitability, instability and a preference for easy pleasures. This warmth also stirs the appetite which may lead to overeating and a consequent tendency toward illness. The child is also easily offended and unable to suffer toil. In Horace's words, "The child, who but now can utter words and set firm step upon the ground, delights to play with its mates, flies into a passion, and as lightly puts it aside."[44]

Aristotle had noted that the voice and face distinguish the child from the adult, for a sign of puberty is the changing pitch which occurs when generation is possible in adolescence. Nevertheless, the influence of one's parents was regarded as decisive in childhood, for just as the corrupting humors of gout and leprosy were considered hereditary, so bad habits are readily learnt from one's parents. Much attention was therefore paid to the bad habits of small children, which demand correction. For children are present-minded, little concerned with the future, pursuing games and other vain occupations rather than what is useful and profitable. They cannot distinguish the trivial from the important, preferring for example an apple to gold or a castle, weeping over the loss of a pear or apple more than the loss of an inheritance. Highly emotional, children may appreciate pictures more than adults do; forgetful of favors done them, they demand everything with their voices and hands. They love to babble away, in turn laughing, shouting, crying and chattering, even when asleep. Preferring the company of other children to that of adults, they love to be filthy and unkempt and resist all correction. The child's greatest pleasure is in food and drink, which he demands when he has scarcely risen from bed.[45]

Bernard Gordon[46] noted that children lead a life of brute beasts without reason, subject to their passions and the satisfaction of corporeal pleasures. The first age is a time of growth and uncertainty, for we are all wretched, abandoned, deprived, filthy, agitated and changeable at birth. Citing Avicenna, Bernard noted that we are all created out of *limositas* and *humiditas*, which are gradually dissipated until death by the natural warmth of the body. Aristotle confirmed that at birth we are all *tabula rasa*, easily impressed by opinions, fantasies, laws and faith, so that in our youth we are like balls tossed about by a juggler, torn between good and evil, life and death.

On the other hand, despite all these apparent vices, Bersuire drew a distinction between those children who may be easily placated and are susceptible to education, and others who are incorrigible in vice.[47] The various virtues which pertain to children are a result of their physical attributes. The pure and unstained nature of childhood produces chastity, sanctity, and innocence. The softness implies piety; flexibility of the body permits obedience; warmth leads to charity; mobility entails both diligence and agility in the performance of good deeds. Docility leads to subtlety and intelligence, while beauty and affection are associated with attractive speech and honesty. At the same time, the explanation *in malo* noted the innumerable faults of the child, whose puerility and ignorance are shared with the sinner, whose insatiable appetite, akin to that of the child, is caused by greed, or whose concern for the present is a result of imprudence. All of the vices of the sinner -- vanity, insolence, foolhardiness, belligerence, immodesty -- are parallel to the sometimes intractable characteristics of childhood; although subjection to one's parents, prelates or teachers may correct such faults.

The interpretation *in bono* of the child allowed Bersuire to draw upon a host of Biblical citations, largely concerned with the child Jesus, and classical allusions largely recorded by Ovid and Livy. He adduced the examples of beautiful children who were so pleasing in character and appearance that, even after being nourished in childhood by beasts, retained their innocence, humility and kind-heartedness. Just as Providence may save the sinner, so also such children as Cyrus, Remus and Romulus, Henry III and Henry IV, who had been abandoned by men, may be saved by brute beasts. The purity of the child, he argued, is even recognized by the pagans, like the Mongols, who sacrificed innocent children in order to insure the salvation of the people.

The formative character of childhood was recognized by the biographers of both Louis of Toulouse and Edmund of Abingdon, who quoted *Proverbs* 22.6, "Start a boy on the right road, and even in old age he will not leave it"; and Guibert of Tournai said "one learns with difficulty in old age what one hasn't learned in childhood."[48] The standard life (1229) of St. Francis of Assisi (d. 1226) by Thomas of Celano which was to serve as the cornerstone of all future mendicant biography and which voiced the aspirations of a generation of disaffected youth, contained an extended discussion of the damage which may be wrought by unresponsive parents who are unwilling to cultivate their children's spiritual needs. While still nestling in their cribs, even before they have begun to speak or babble, infants may absorb the foul influence of those around them, which may damn them to corruption.[49]

Childhood Education

The passage from infancy to childhood at age seven, which was generally the onset of formal education and perhaps confirmation, represented a turning-point.[50] By seven one should have observed the child's natural capabilities and inclination, and a suitable occupation determined, in accordance with his social class, physical condition and intellectual potential;[51] although the period between weaning and schooling cannot always be determined with any accuracy in medieval biography.[52] For the combination of the fear of God inculcated at home and the learning provided at school, perhaps strengthened by a charismatic teacher, may ignite the sparks of childhood piety.[53] At this age, the child's handsome countenance, upright bearing and robust physique might be a portent of future greatness.[54] Spiritually, the putative saint overcomes the limitations of human nature.[55] Hugh of Lincoln (1140-1200) admitted that his initiation into learning was accompanied by the master's rod, which discouraged him from joining in the play of children.[56] Several hagiographers provided a detailed regimen of the austerities which began at this age: Ambrose of Siena (1220-1282) began to recite the office of the Virgin daily at age seven, and the vigils of the saints at age nine; from seven to twelve Benvenuta Bojano (1254-1292) recited one hundred Hail Marys and one hundred Paternosters daily during the week and two thousand on the Sabbath, in addition to donning a series of painful garments.[57]

As Honorius of Autun had noted in his *De vita claustrali*, the monastery functioned as a primary educational institution[58] As a consequence, an important source for knowledge of the formative years of childhood were the many manuals for novices and oblates which were intended to provide guidelines for the inculcation of monastic discipline. Both the Basilian and Benedictine rules had allowed child oblation, with the result that monastic constitutions contained regulations governing the education and behavior of oblates in particular and indicate the fear of physical and homerotic contact which the close, sexually segregated monastic environment could generate.[59] Less was said of the other periods of life, with the exception of the aged, who may require exceptions to the normal rigors of the rule. While the decisions of chapters-general tended to concern themselves largely with the condition, age, health and profession of novices, works such as the constitutions of Hirschau (ca. 1000 A.D.)[60] or the biographies of William of Volpiano (962-1031) and Stephen of Obazine (d. 1159) indicate the Spartan supervision and widespread use of the rod which characterized the rearing of novices in the central middle ages; this might lead to flight from the monastery for those unable to accept such harsh discipline.[61]

As a result of considerable criticism of such practices, most of the newer orders (with the exception of the Cluniacs) tended to prohibit admission before the age of fourteen. In order to mitigate abuses, a perceptive critic such as the master of novices Adam of Perseigne in a letter of 1190/96 to Osmund of Mortimer laid stress on imitation of the master's character as the cardinal educational tool; he therefore counselled the master to display fear of God, love of wisdom, proper comportment, and solicitude for those under his care, holding friendly dialogues with them on matters spiritual.[62]

By the thirteenth century those orders which maintained the practice of oblation had tended to require reconfirmation at the age of fourteen of the promise given by one's parents, and a one year trial before taking the vow, according to a rule of Honorius III (1220). A considerable polemical literature concerning the legality of the oblation imposed by one's parents appeared in the Parisian schools, engaging Thomas Aquinas, Nicholas of Lisieux, Peter of Palude and others; it was largely occasioned by the not entirely unfounded accusations of such secular masters as William of St. Amour that the mendicants had lured callow youths into their orders without parental approval. Despite the continuing controversy over the presence of children or adolescents in monasteries, it was not until 1430 that the friars completely abandoned the practice.[63] The dangers which might accompany oblation were expressed by the Francisan minister-general Bonaventure (1221-1274) in his rule for novices; he prohibited sleeping on one's back, or "any other lewd manner", e.g. naked, with hands touching the body, buttocks protruding, or insufficiently clothed. In order to further drive away temptation, Psalms should be recited at night, and an image of the crucified Christ borne in mind.[64]

Perhaps in response to the excesses of oblation in the Gregorian age, the twelfth century had witnessed a heightening of interest in childhood within monastic circles, and several figures sought the kernel of goodness hidden in the shell of indiscipline which allegedly surrounded the child. In the Gregorian epoch Anselm of Canterbury (1033-1109) in his *De similitudinibus* had taken note of the special concern exhibited by the saint for adolescents and youth under his care.[65] When asked why he displayed such interest, Anselm had replied that youth is like a piece of wax which must be the right consistency in order to receive a perfect impression, between hardness (*duritia*) and softness (*mollitie*) in order to accept a clear, whole image. This is comparable to the ages (*aetates*) of man, for if one is immersed in worldly affairs from infancy til old age, one will have difficulty understanding spiritual matters. A young boy will not be able to distinguish good from evil, and can only be guided though proper education. This image of the impressionable child as a waxen seal was later found in Hugh of St. Victor, who singled out humility as the virtue which is necessary in order to mold the waxen, callow child into shape, while obedience will establish his willingness to reform. The figures which stand out most graphically when the seal is pressed are those which have been most deeply sculpted in the wax.[66] The same image of the impressionable wax likewise appeared in Eva of St. Martin's *Vita* of Juliana of Cornillon (1192-1258), who argued that "just as wax receives its impression from the seal, so morality in life is a product of example."[67]

In response to a fellow abbot who beat incorrigible and disobedient youths in his charge, Anselm had compared such a child to a tree whose growth has been stunted.[68] He is likely to become resentful and crooked through ill-treatment. Sympathy, fatherly gentleness and encouragement are preferred. Just as an infant who is fed solid food, although not yet ready to digest it, is likely to strangle because his body is still weak, the fragile soul of the young monk likewise requires appropriate nourishment. The child (or oblate or novice) therefore demands gentleness, kindness, compassion, loving forebearance and encouragement. Unlike many of those who scorned the vices of children (even though he himself had faced conflict with his father over the turn to religion) Anselm often spoke affectionately of his childhood, and occasionally used the playfulness of childhood as an object lesson. It is reported that on the road he once witnessed a boy playing with a bird on a string. The bird tried to escape, but each time he was held in check by the child, who derived great pleasure from this game. Anselm rejoiced and used the episode to compare the bird to a man who is held in check by evil.

Another twelfth century figure who displayed special interest in the vagaries of childhood and adolescence had been Ailred of Rievaulx (1109-1167). His biographer Walter Daniel described Ailred's youth as a time when "the heat of the blood often obliterates the mind and clouds the affections and burns away energy".[69] Despite the childhood virtues allegedly displayed by Ailred, Walter was forced to admit that at the Scottish royal court his chastity had been compromised. In answering the charge that his subject was therefore not a true monk, Walter countered that the core of monastic purity is humility, for no one, even the infant who has spent one day of life on earth, is free of sin.

Another later saint whose solicitude for children received considerable attention was Hugh of Avalon (d. 1200), who derived pleasure from hearing the babbling of infants, played with and caressed them. Upon observing the frolicking child, he remarked, "Blessed are the pure in heart, for they shall see God." (*Matthew* 5.8) This contrasted sharply with his own sombre recollections of childhood: "I never learned children's games," he said, and recalled the master's rod which sorely tried him.[70]

By the later middle ages, greater concern was voiced for the rearing of children outside the monastery, although many of the monastic truisms remained. The impressionability of the child which the twelfth century monastic sources had stressed was later voiced by Conrad of Megenberg in his *Oeconomica* (1352). He noted that the training of the child after seven is based on imitation rather than the application of reason.[71] Thus, by observing a tanner curing a hide the callow child might just as readily grab the scissors and incautiously cut his hands. He told the story of a child in Nuremberg in the time of Louis IV of Bavaria (1314-1347) who, after watching his butcher father slaughter a lamb, took a stick and severed his friend's throat as they played, saying, "Thus my father slaughters lambs." One therefore ought to keep sharp tools away from children. Some children are so garrulous, imitative and lacking discretion, that they will repeat everything heard at home, so that caution should be exercized when in earshot of children.[72] Conrad recommended the use of little dolls, carvings, and mirrors to please the child, raise his blood and sharpen his wits, although play should be confined to the home because of the dangers which lurk without. As they grow, children should also be introduced to more strenuous games such as rolling hoops, javelin-throwing, wrestling, etc.

Conrad argued that by the age of seven it should be clear whether the child is dull-witted, average or clever, and an occupation suitable to his physical attributes should be found.[73] Between seven and fourteen he can then be directed toward his future profession, whether clerical, military or commercial. For his education should be geared to the skills he will need; the offspring of merchants should be taught to read and write in the vernacular; future artisans are to be provided the rudiments of the mechanical arts; soldiers should be given miniature horses, swords and arms; rural children ought to be brought periodically to the city to hear sermons and take part in prayers.

Giles of Rome noted that the period of *pueritia* which commences at seven is not fixed, but may end anytime between twelve and sixteen, depending on the child's strength. During this period, the body, the will and the intellect are to be developed through the cultivation of virtue and the accumulation of knowledge. The body requires the gradual introduction of more arduous chores and exercises; the will must be curbed through limitations on one's desires; the mind should be gradually exposed to grammar, logic, and music, followed by the other arts.

Thus, the discussion of infancy and childhood, while acknowledging the moral weakness which is the inherited bane of mankind, at the same time took note of the child's impressionability and accessibility to learning. Because of his physical constitution, the child may be subject to extremes of behavior, but can be controlled either by the application of persuasion or discipline. If the religious tradition saw childhood as the decisive phase for the inculcation of Christian doctrine, the later guidebooks to child care, addressed to a secular audience and more influenced by the medical sources, provided practical advice about the child's diet, preparation for a future career, and the methods of discipline.

While the etymological approach of Isidore of Seville remained the starting point for any definition of infancy and childhood, a host of classical and Arabic sources were now adduced to provide a broader scheme of developmental psychology, drawing on examples taken from natural history. The needs of the cloister no longer governed the rearing of children. After about 1260, a time coinciding with the height of the demographic rise, when presumably larger numbers of children required attention, the emphasis was more on the physical needs of the child. Conrad of Megenberg cautioned parents to confine the child's play to home or courtyard, because there is some danger he may inadvertently fall into a pit, be snared by a trap laid for animals, or be attacked by wild beasts.[74] The tale of Guinefort, the greyhound who became a patron saint of children, was largely a product of the thirteenth century.[75]

Such advice takes on particular significance in the light of the considerable number of childhood accidents which are found in contemporary miracle collections, which graphicallly portray the fears of infertility, infant mortality, childhood disease and accidents, which afflicted all levels of society. The argument that caring parents were a rarity in the middle ages is somewhat belied by the scores of cases of parental solicitude found in hagiographical sources. Instances of children falling victim to insufficient or tainted milk, fire, disease, plague, collapsing walls, ditches, wild beasts, or mill machinery, are found among rich and poor, rural and urban folk throughout Europe. The more complete documentation now available, which required the attestation by several witnesses of every alleged miracle permit us to discover the measures undertaken to secure the child's recovery and the concern expressed not only by grieving parents, but also by friends and neighbors over the loss of a child or his undue suffering. The vagaries of childhood played a significant role in the miracles attributed to St. Yves among the rural sea-going folk of Brittany in the early fourteenth century; in the miracles of Thomas Cantilupo throughout England; of Raymund of Penyaforte, reported at Barcelona or 1278; and of the Franciscan Gerard Cagnoli in Pisa and Sicily on the eve of the Plague.[76] The argument advanced by Philippe Ariès in his now classic *Centuries of Childhood* that the middle ages possessed no clear notion of childhood as a separate developmental phase can thus certainly be laid to rest.

IV. *Notes*

1. Isidore of Seville, *Etymologiae*, 2 vols., ed. W.M. Lindsay (Oxford, 1911), XI.1; Vincent of Beauvais, *Speculum maius*, 4 vols. (Douai, 1624), *Speculum naturale*, XXXI. cc. 76-79; *Speculum doctrinale*, XII. c. 25 ff. on infancy; Bartholomaeus Anglicus, *De rerum proprietatibus*, ed. Georg Barthold (Frankfurt, 1601), I. cc. 71-75. 78; Pierre Bersuire, *Dictionarium*, II, 360, and *Reductorium*, III. 2, in *Opera omnia*, 6 vols. (Cologne, 1731); Thomas of Cantimpré, *Liber de natura rerum. Text*, ed. H. Boese (Berlin, 1973), I. 71-75, 78.

2. On infant care, see Luke Demaitre, "Child Care in the Middle Ages," *Journal of Psychohistory*, 4 (1976/7), 461-490; Albrecht Peiper, *Chronik der Kinderheilkunde* (Leipzig, 1955); Karl Sudhoff, *Erstlinge der pädiatrische Literatur* (Munich, 1925) for treatises on the treatment of childhood diseases; Jean-Noel Biraben, "La médicine et l'enfant au moyen âge," *ADH*, 8 (1973), 73-5; Ephraim Kanarfogel, "Attitudes toward Childhood and Children in Medieval Jewish Society" in David R. Blumenthal, ed., *Approaches to Judaism in Medieval Times*, II (Chico, Ca., 1985), 1-34.

3. Isidore of Seville, *op. cit.*; Jerome, *Liber interpretationis hebraicorum*, ed. Paul de Lagarde, in *Corpus christianorum. Series latina*, 72 (Turnhout, 1959), 57-161.

4. "Vita S. Albertis confessoris ordinis Carmelitarum," *AB*, 17 (1899), 318: "sic merito nomen sequatur rei proprietatem, ut dicit philosophus sepe hoc accidere."

5. Raymund of Capua, *Legenda Agnetis de Montepolitano*, in *ASS*, 20 April II: 790.

6. Ralph Bocking, *Vita Ricardi episcopi Cicestrensis*, in *ASS*, 3 April I: 285.

7. Caesarius of Heisterbach, *Vita, Passio et Miracula S. Engelberti*, in *ASS*, 7 November II: 146.

8. James of Voragine, *Legenda aurea*, ed. Th. Graesse (Leipzig, 1890), 752; Caesarius of Heisterbach, *Vita Elisabethae*, in *Die Schriften des Caesarius von Heisterbach über die heilige Elisabeth von Thüringen*, ed. Albert Huyskens, *Publikationen der Gesellschaft für rheinische Geschichtskunde*, 43, pt. 3 (1937), 348.

9. James of Voragine, *op. cit.*, 662.

10. In general, see Francesco Lanzoni, "Il sogno presago della madre incinta nella letteratura medievale e antica," *AB*, 45 (1927), 225-261; Peter of Monte Rubiano, *Vita et miracula Nicolai de Tolentino*, in

ASS, 10 September III: 644; *Vita anonymi Angeli*, in *ASS*, 6 February I: 936.

11. Peter Calo, *Vita S. Thomae Aquinatis*, ed. Dominic Prümmer, *Fontes Vitae S. Thomae Aquinatis* (Toulouse, 1911), Fasc. 1, 17; "Vita S. Alberti confessoris ordinis Carmelitarum," *AB*, 17 (1899), 318; William of Tocco, *Vita S. Thomae Aquinatis* in *ASS*, 7 March I: 659.

12. Israel Abrahams, ed., *Hebrew Ethical Wills*, 2 vols. (Philadelphia, 1926), II, 165-96.

13. Peter Calo, *op. cit.*; Raymund of Capua, *op. cit.*; Arsenio Frugoni, ed. "L'Autobiografia di Pietro Celestino," in *Celestiniana* (Rome, 1954), 46; *AB*, 13 (1894), 417.

14. The chief contemporary text is Giles of Rome, *De formatione corporis humani in utero* (ca. 1276/90). Much of this is discussed in Danielle Jacquart and Claude Thomasset, *Sexualité et savoir médical au moyen âge* (Paris, 1985).

15. Bartholomaeus, *op. cit.*, VI.4; Bersuire, *Dictionarium*, IV, 359-60; *Reductorium*, III.2 (pp. 62-4). See Constantinus Africanus, *Locus medicus [Liber pantechni]*. III. 33 and I.2, in *Opera omnia*, 2 vols. (Basel, 1636-9), which is a major source for both Bersuire and Bartholomaeus; on Constantine, see Heinrich Schipperges, *Die Assimilation der arabische Medizin durch das lateinische Mittelalter* (Wiesbaden, 1964), 45-54 and *passim*.

16. *Biblia sacra cum glossis interlineari et ordinaria*, 7 vols. (Venice, 1588), *Liber Sapientie*, VII.2 makes extensive use of Aristotle's *De generatione animalium* for the discussion of the biology of infancy.

17. Bersuire cites Galen, *Commentaria in Hippocratis Aphorismos*, ed. C.G. Kühn in *Opera omnia*, 20 vols. (Leipzig, 1821-1833), XVII; Augustine, *Super Joannem*, X. 12-13 (*MPL*, 35: 1461); Constantinus Africanus, III. 34.

18. Augustine, *De trinitate*, XV, iv.6 (*MPL*, 42: 894-5); idem, *Homilia super Joannem*, X. 10-12 (*MPL*, 35: 1471-2).

19. Although the *De anatomia* is cited, this appears to come from Hippocrates' work on dentition, Hippocrates, *Oeuvres complètes*, ed. E. Littré, 10 vols. (Paris, 1839-1861), VIII, 545-9.

20. Vincent of Beauvais, *Speculum naturale*, XXXI, cc. 76 ff.; Augustine, *De Civitate Dei*, XXI. 14-15 in *Corpus christianorum. Series latina*, 48 (Turnholt, 1955); idem, *Confessiones*, I, 7, ed. W. Watts (Cambridge, 1950); Solinus, *Collectanea rerum memorabilium*, I. 72, ed. Th. Mommsen (Berlin, 1895), 18; Bernard of Clairvaux, *De consideratione libri quinque*, II. 17-8 (*MPL*, 182: 753); Pliny, *Historia naturalis*, ed. L. Ian and C. Mayhoff, 6 vols. (Stuttgart, 1967), VII.1: Peter Comestor, *Historia ecclesiastica, Genesis* 18, (*MPL*, 198: 1071) cites

Isidore and Josephus on the naming of Adam and Eve, and how wailing led to the naming; William of Conches, *De philosophia mundi*, IV. 17 (*MPL*, 172: 91); William of St. Thierry, *De natura corporis et animae libri duo*, in *MPL*, 180: 715.

21. Nicholas of Lyra, *op. cit.*, *Genesis*, II says that the "Ah" is for the A in Adam, and "Eh" for the E in Eva.

22. M. Anthony Hewson, *Giles of Rome and the Medieval Theory of Conception* (London, 1975), 58 cites Michael Scot, *Physiognomia* (Paris, 1505), XI. 26.

23. William of Conches, *De philosophia mundi*, IV. 14-18 (*MPL*, 172: 89-91): Augustine, *De trinitate*, CIV.7 (*MPL*, 42: 1041); Gregory of Nyssa, *De opificio hominis*, I.7 (*MPG*, 44: 139-42).

24. Aristotle, *De generatione animalium*, ed. A.L. Peck (London, 1963), II. 6 on infants. For Latin edition, trans. William of Moerbeke, ed. H.J. Drossaert Lulofs, *Aristoteles latinus*, 17, 2.v. (Leiden, 1966).

25. Innocent III, *De contemptu mundi*, in *MPL*, 217: 704-6; cf. also William of Conches, *Dragmaticon*, Stanford University Ms. M412, 69v; Charles Trinkaus, *In Our Image and Likeness. Humanity and Dignity in Italian Humanist Thought*, 2 vols. (Chicago, 1970), I, 173-99 points out that Petrarch's (1354/7) *De remediis utriusque fortunae*, II.93 constitutes an early refutation of Innocent's view of the wretchedness of the human condition.

26. Augustine, *De civitate Dei*, xxi. 14-15, in suggests that death is preferable to a return to infancy because of the sufferings which attend life. On such vices as jealousy, which beset infants, see idem, *Confessiones*, I. 7; William of Conches, *De philosophia mundi*, iv. 17, in *MPL*, 172: 91. Recent studies of the trauma of childbirth indicate that at the neonate is strengthened through the production of hormones, cf. Hugo Lagencrantz and Theodore A. Slotkin, "The 'Stress' of Being Born," *Scientific American*, 254, no. 4 (April, 1986), 100-107.

27. Bersuire, *Dictionarium*, vol. IV, p. 360. His treatment is interspersed with verses summarizing his views, e.g. : "Infans faciliter, cadit, & vix revelatur; plorat, & vix pacificatur; se maculat, & vix emundatur; infirmatur, nec cito sanatur; decipitur, nec fraudem rimatur; se denudat, nec verecundatur; ridet, atque jocundatur; petit, & morte gravatur"; or "Criminalem culpae pravitatem, Virtualem vitae sanctitatem, Naturalem carnis vanitatem."

28. Shulamith Shahar, "Infants, Infant Care and Attitudes towards Infancy in the Medieval Lives of Saints," *Journal of Psychohistory*, 10 (1983), 281-309; Christiane Klapisch-Zuber and David Herlihy, *Les toscanes et leurs familles* (Paris, 1978), *passim*; James Bruce Ross, "The Middle Class Child in Urban Italy - Fourteenth and Early Fifteenth Century,"

in Lloyd De Mause, ed., *History of Childhood* (New York, 1974), 182-222.

29. Giles of Rome, *De regimine principum* (Rome, 1607), I. IV. 1-3; III. 1, 16; II, II.1-17, III. III.3; Vincent Licitra, ed. "Il *Liber legum moralium* e il *De regimine vite et sanitatis* di Bellino Bissolo," *Studi medievali*, Ser. 3, 6 (1965), 432.

30. Isidore of Seville, xi. i. 77; Avicenna, *Liber canonis*, trans. Gerard of Cremona (Venice, 1507), I. iii. 1, 2. "Jacobus", in his entry under *Lac* (*B.M. Royal* 6 E. VII, pt. 2, f. 404r-406r) discusses the problem of milk production at great length.

31. Vincent of Beauvais, XXXI. 79; al-Razi [Muhammed ibn Zakariya Abu Bakr], *Liber Rasis ad Almansorem* (Venice, 1497); Avicenna, *Liber canonis*, I. fen. iii. doctr. I, c. 1-2 on infant care. Among the lines cited are *Sententiae Varronis*, 58a, ed. Peter Germann, *Die sogenannten Sententiae Varronis* (Paderborn, 1967); Quintillian, *Institutio oratoria*, I.ii.6, ed. H.E. Butler, 2 vols. (Cambridge, 1921-2); Horace, *Epistulae*, I. ii. 69-70, ed. H. Rushton Fairclough (Cambridge, 1955).

32. Constantinus, *op. cit.*, III.33; John of San Gemignano, *Summa de exemplis et rerum similitudinibus* (Venice, 1584), VI.17.

33. *Hebrews* 5.12: "Anyone who lives on milk, being an infant, does not know what is right. But grown men can take solid food; their perceptions are trained by long use to discriminate between good and evil."; Razi, *op. cit.*, IV.31; Avicenna, *op. cit.*, I.III.iii.4; Haly Abbas ['Ali ibn al-Abbas], *Liber regalis*, trans. Stephen of Antioch, in *Liber totius medicine...* (Lyons, 1523).

34. *Philippians*, 3.17: "You have us for a model; watch those whose way of life conforms to it."

35. Adam of Perseigne, *Lettres*, ed. J. Bouvet (Paris, 1960), 69, 1-5; *MPL*, 211: 612-4.

36. Isidore, *op. cit.*, XI.2. 10 ff.; Vincent of Beauvais, XXXI.80; Bartholomaeus Anglicus, VI.5. I am unable to locate the source of Isidore's line "Iam puerile iugum tenera cervice gerebat."

37. Thomas of Cantimpré, I.79.

38. William of St. Thierry, *Physica corporis et animae libri duo*, in *MPL*, 180:715.

39. On this theme see Ernst R. Curtius, *European Literature and the Latin Middle Ages*, trans. R.W. Trask (New York, 1968), 98-101; among the commonly used phrases are *puer senilis, cor gerens senile, puer senex, corpore iuvencula sed animo cana*; some examples include *Vita B. Alpaidis*, in *ASS*, 3 November II.1: 175; Eva of St. Martin (?), *Vita Iulianae*, in *ASS*, 5 April I: 443; Bernard of Clairvaux, *Life of St. Malachy of Armagh*, trans. H.J. Lawlor (London, 1920), I.i; Simon

of Trebnitz, *Vita maior S. Hedwigis*, in *ASS*, 17 October VIII: 225. Thomas of Cantimpré, *Bonum universale de apibus* (Douai, 1627), II. 28 arguing that no age should be exempt from service to God, provides examples of virtuous and saintly children who preached like the aged, such as Albertus Magnus and the child Achas.

40. *Vita Iulianae*, *op. cit.*, 443; see the testimony of Elizabeth's four maidservants in Albert Huyskens, ed., "Zum 700 Geburtstage der hl. Elisabeth von Thüringen," *Historische Zeitschrift*, 28 (1907), 811.

41. Vincent of Beauvais, XXXI.80; Augustine, *Confessiones*, I.viii.13; I.ix.14-15; I.xx.31; idem, *De civitate Dei*, XXI.xiv. 5-12; XXII.xxii.22-48; *Ecclesiasticus* 40.1; 30.12; *John* 7.1; *Psalms* 76.10.

42. Vincent of Beauvais, XXXI.81; Avicenna, I.III.iii.4; Razi, IV.31; Haly Abbas, II.i.22.

43. Bartholomaeus Anglicus, VI.5; Aristotle, *De generatione naturalium*, IV.8.

44. Horace, *De arte poetica*, 158-60, ed. F. Vollmer, *Q. Horatii Flacii Carmina* (Leipzig, 1912); Ovid, *Epistulae*, IV. 10-3, ed. R. Ehwald (Leipzig, 1897); idem, *Ars amatoria*, I. 185, ed. J.H. Mozley (Cambridge, Mass., 1962); Varro, *Sententiae*, 73-4; Virgil, *Bucolica*, III. 92-3 in *Opera*, ed. O.E. Ribbeck (Leipzig, 1894).

45. Aristotle, *De generatione animalium*, IV.8; Bartholomaeus Anglicus, VI.5; Bersuire, *Reductorium*, III.3; *Dictionarium*, V, 342-4.

46. Bernard Gordon, *De conservatione vitae* (Leipzig, 1570).

47. Bersuire, *Reductorium*, III.3; *Dictionarium*, V, 342-4; on the virtues of children, with examples, see Johannes Gobi, *Scala coeli* (Lübeck, 1476), cccxxvii, *puer*.

48. John de Orta, *Vita S. Ludovici episcopi Tolosani*, in *AF*, VII (Quaracchi, 1951), 337; Eustace of Faversham, *Vita sancti Edmundi*, ed. C.H. Lawrence, *St. Edmund of Canterbury* (Oxford, 1960), 291; Guibert of Tournai, *Sermo tercius ad conjugatas*, in Carla Casagrande, ed., *Prediche alle donne del secolo XIII* (Milan, 1978) 92: "in puericia non didicerunt vix in senectute addiscere poterunt." Guibert is here commenting on *Ecclesiasticus* 7.23: "Have you sons? Discipline them and break them in from the earliest years." He notes that an old horse can't learn to walk, and repeats the tale found in Pseudo-Boethius' *De disciplina scolarium* of a man about to be executed for theft who chastized his father for not having disciplined him in childhood for his thieving ways.

49. Thomas of Celano, *Vita prima S. Francisci*, in *AF*, 10 (Quaracchi, 1926-41), fasc. 1, 1 ff.; Chiara Frugoni, "La giovinezza di Francesco nelle fonti (testi e immagini)," *Studi medievali*, Ser. 3, 25.1 (1984),

115-144 brings together all the contemporary material on Francis' early life.

50. Conrad of Megenberg, *Ökonomik*, 2 vols., ed. Sabine Kruger, *MGH. Staatsschriften des späten Mittelalters*, 3 (Stuttgart, 1973), 80, 92. This work was dedicated to Bishop Leopold of Bamberg. Conrad was also the author of a *Speculum felicitatis humanae* (ca. 1348) intended for the education of Duke Rudolph II of Austria; a partial translation of Thomas of Cantimpré's *De natura rerum*, entitled *Das Buch der Natur*; a translation of John Holywood's *Sphera*; and *vitae* of Sts. Erhard and Dominic; along with works supporting the papal position against Louis the Bavarian, and an anti-heretical tract. See August Pelzer and Thomas Kaeppeli, "Conrad de Mégenberg," *Revue d'histoire ecclésiastique*, 45 (1950), 559-616.

51. See also Pseudo-Boethius, *Disciplina scolarium*, c.5, in *MPL*, 64: 1253 "Sunt autem quidam vehementer obtusi, alii mediocres, tertii excellenter acuti." This was probably written in the early thirteenth century.

52. See e.g., Wicbert, *Vita Sancti Leonis*, in *MPL*, 143: 468; Anon. of Molesmes, *Vita Roberti*, in *MPL*, 157: 1271.

53. Christopher of Parma, "Legenda beati Francisci de Senis," *AB*, 14 (1895), 176; A charismatic figure to whom the conversion of many Dominicans was attributed was Jordan of Saxony, see Marguerite Aron, *Un animateur de la jeunesse au xiiie siècle. Vie, voyages du Bx. Jourdain de Saxe* (Paris, 1930).

54. Caesarius of Heisterbach, *Vita, passio et miracula S. Engelberti*, in *ASS*, 7 November III: 146. The virtues of the ideal child according to Johannes Gobi, *Scala coeli*, *Puer*, are "mitis, sobrius, docilis, solaciosus."

55. James of Voragine, *Legenda aurea*, ed. Th. Graesse, 3rd ed. (Leipzig, 1890), 753: "auctor naturae supra naturam quodammodo extulet."

56. Decima L. Douie and Hugh Farmer, eds., *Magna vita sancti Hugonis*, 2 vols. (London, 1961), I, 6-7.

57. Gisbertus et al., *Vita Ambrosii*, in *ASS*, 20 March III: 180-3; Conrad of Castellario, *Vita Benvenutae...*, in *ASS*, 29 October XII: 153; cf. A. Poncelet, ed., "Vita Beatae Margaretae virginis de Civitate Castelli," *AB*, 19 (1900), 24.

58. Honorius of Autun, *De vita claustrali*, in *MPL*, 172: 1247-1248.

59. For a survey of monastic didactic literature see Philibert Schmitz, *Histoire de l'ordre de Saint Benôit*, 7 vols. (Maredsous, 1948-1956), II, 375-383.

60. *Constitutiones Hirsaugiensis*, in *MPL*, 150: 939 ff.; Edmond Martène, *De antiquis monachorum ritibus* (Bassano, 1758), 230.

61. *Vita S. Stephani*, in *ASS*, 8 March 1: 799-808; *MPL*, 152: 667-720.

62. Adam of Perseigne, *Lettres*, 110-129.

63. For the canonical legislation see *Decretales Gregorii noni*, III. 31, in E. Friedberg and E. Richter, eds., *Corpus iuris canonici* 2 vols. (Leipzig, 1879-1881). Livario Oliger, "De pueris oblatis in ordine minorum," *Archivum franciscanum historicum*, 8 (1915), 389-447; 10 (1917), 271-288.

64. Bonaventura, *Regula novitiorum*, 7.1, in *Opera omnia*, 10 vols., ed. PP. Collegii S. Bonaventurae (Quaracchi, 1948), VIII, 483.

65. Eadmer, *Vita sancti Anselmi*, ed. R.W. Southern (London, 1962), 20; Anselm, *De similitudinibus*, c. 176, in *MPL*, 159: 695.

66. Hugh of St. Victor, *De institutione novitiorum*, 7-8, in *MPL*, 176: 931-2. On the wax image see Giles Constable, "Renewal and Reform in Religious Life," in Giles Constable and Robert Benson, *Renaissance and Renewal in the Twelfth Century* (Cambridge, Mass., 1982), 46; see also Stephen Gersh, *From Iamblichus to Eriugena: An Investigation of the Prehistory and Evolution of the Pseudo-Dionysian Tradition* (Leiden, 1978), 236; and Robert Javelet, *Image et ressemblance au douzieme siècle: De Saint Anselme à Alain de Lille*, 2 vols. (Strassbourg, 1967), I, 83, 365; II, 56, n. 126.

67. Eva of St. Martin (?), *Vita Iulianae*, in *ASS*, 5 April II: 442: "Inter omnia visibilia quibus humana natura de facili ad bonum flectitur vel ad malum, exemplum videtur praecipuum esse. Non sicut impressionem cera recipit sigillo, sic vitae formatur moralitas ab exemplo."

68. Eadmer, *op. cit.*, 37-9, 90-1, 149.

69. Walter Daniel, *Vita Ailredi Abbatis Rievall*, ed. F.M. Powicke (London, 1963), 16-17.

70. Douie and Farmer, *op. cit.*, 130, 6-7: "iocos numquam didici."

71. Conrad of Megenberg, *op. cit.*, I. ii. 13.

72. Conrad of Megenberg, I, 89; Giles of Rome, II.ii. 10: "Circa locutionem quidem iuvenes tripliciter peccare videntur. Primo quia de facili loquuntur lascivia. Secundo, quia de levi locuuntur falsa. Tertio, quia ut plurimum loquuntur fatua et impraemeditata."; cf. Aristotle, *Politica*, VII. 17; *Rhetorica*, II. 12.

73. Conrad of Megenberg, 91 ff; Giles of Rome, II.ii.16; Julius Blintz, *Die Leibesubungen des Mittelalters* (Gutersloh, 1880), 8 ff.

74. Conrad of Megenberg, 90ff.

75. Jean-Claude Schmitt, *Le saint Lévrier, Guinefort guérison d'enfants depuis le XIIIe siècle* (Paris, 1979).

76. *Miracula ex processu canonizationis Thomae episcopi Herefordensis*, in *ASS*, 2 October I: 585-696; Jose Rius-Serra, ed., *Sancti Raymundi di Penyaforte Opera omnia* (Barcelona, 1949-1954), III, 182ff; A. de La Borderie, et al., eds., *Monuments originaux de l'histoire de S. Yves* (Saint Brieuc, 1887), 1-199; Bartholomew Albizi, "La Leggenda del B. Gerardo, O. Min (1267-1342) di Bartolomeo Albizi O. Min (d. 1351)," ed. Filippo Rotolo, *Miscellanea francescana*, 57 (1955), 367-446; *idem*, "Il trattato dei miracoli del B. Gerardo Cagnoli, O. Min. (1267-1342) di Frà Bartolomeo Albizi O. Min (d. 1351)," ed. Filippo Rotolo, *Miscellanea francescana*, 66 (1966), 128-192.

V. *Adolescence*

Vincent of Beauvais' discussion of adolescence, the most thorough of the earlier encyclopedists, commenced with the Isidorean placement between fourteen and twenty-eight, and noted that reason, intelligence and the ability to act are greatest at this age.[1] Like other contemporaries, his treatment of *adolescentia* concentrated on the male, rather than the female youth. In Giles of Rome, the term youth (*pueritia*) was employed somewhat imprecisely,[2] at times melding together the three discreet periods of infancy, childhood and adolescence. To Giles, the period of adolescence, which ends sometime between twenty-one and twenty-seven, is to be highlighted by training in the arts of war and the encouragement of the bellicose instincts of youth; the son of the citizen will be trained for the defense of the republic.[3] Nevertheless, because the youth is still subject to conceit and venery, he must remain under the control of his guardians or elders. Physical beauty is a sign of this period because this attribute allows the adolescent to fulfill necessary tasks through the agency of an agile and well-ordered body, which is the best vessel for the performance of such deeds.

A similar chronological imprecision marked Bersuire's treatment of adolescence. Despite the traditional definition of *iuventus* as lasting from twenty-one to forty-eight[4] which Bersuire cited in his *Reductorium moralis*, in the *Dictionarium* he preferred the more modern meaning of the term in the sense of adolescence or youth, a time of graciousness, joy, strength, subtlety, agility, and beauty.[5] Those who do not turn such natural virtues to good advantage, are characterized by foul conversation, slowness to act, ignorance, weak resistance to evil; in a word, they are "juvenile". Those who (*Psalms* 103.5: "and my youth is ever new like an eagle's") allegedly rejuvenate themselves in old age are akin to the eagle, the phoenix and the palm tree.

Virtues and Vices of Youth

To Vincent of Beauvais and Dante, perhaps the chief characteristic of the adolescent was his physical beauty and health, a necessary concomitant of the dangers of youth. The maintenance of good health was demanded through a proper regime of diet, rest, good air and exercise, as a means of guaranteeing the conformity of one's physical and spiritual well-being. Modesty as an antidote to lust should be cultivated in order to enhance one's beauty, which will in any case fade with age.[6] For, as Petronius had said, "beauty and wisdom make a rare conjunction."[7] Otherwise, the moral weakness of adolescence may be paralleled by the physical weakness of which Razi, Halys and other physicians warned.[8] When the youth's body reaches the height of its natural growth, it may be filled with superfluities, causing diseases, which develop rapidly. As an antidote, warm baths, phlebotomy, laxatives, moderate exercise and diet should be applied. Spicy and hot food should be avoided, although wine may be introduced, provided it is mixed with cold water.

The virtues to be inculcated among the young (*iuvenes*) include liberality, hope, magnanimity, kindheartedness, compassion and modesty.[9] Youths are naturally giving because the goods they possess are not acquired by their own labor, but by others. They are hopeful and spirited because of the natural warmth which burns in them. Possessing few enemies, they live in the future and delight in considering future achievements. Their magnanimity is caused by heated passions and the desire to excel. For just as in the universe the warmer elements -- fire and air -- always overcome the colder (i.e. earth and water), so their warm natures lead the young to desire glory and honor. Their inexperience, however, leads them to be trusting and good-hearted, judging others according to what they see in themselves; this breeds a compassionate belief that others may be suffering unworthily. Their modesty, like that of women, derives from a fear of ingloriousness. At the same time, in accordance with contemporary moral teaching, the virtues of youth were balanced by vices such as changeability, excessive trustworthiness, stubbornness, mendacity and intemperance. The concupiscence and intemperance of youth are a consequence of their heated passions, whereby they are subject imprudently to instinct unmitigated by reason. The constant movement of the humors in the body creates a changeability which can lead easily to error and reduce one's willpower. Their trusting natures may lead to gullibility, entering for example into business transactions without carefully checking the consequences. While the desire of the young to excel may be praiseworthy, this can encourage uncalled-for stubbornness, and even mendacity out of a desire to display wisdom, despite a lack of experience. The virtues of temperance, bravery, loving-kindness, courtesy and loyalty required by the adolescent were to Dante exemplified by Aeneas, and by Adrastus, King of the Argives, who displayed modesty and awe, which taught them to respect their elders.[10]

Images of Youth

Berengar of Landorre employed a number of sometimes contradictory natural images in his treatment of adolescence. It is comparable to mid-day, when the sun is highest in the heavens, the air is calm, the tempests have temporarily ceased and blood has been drawn up to the brain by the sun's warmth.[11] It is the contrary of midnight, which is comparable to death; when the sun is down, the storm may be at its height, blood has concentrated in the heart and the body is cold. Adolescence is also likened to springtime, which is the optimal season for growth, but is also a time which requires special solicitude lest such adverse conditions as melancholia develop which will permanently hamper one's life; the best antidote is concentration on matters spiritual, in order to develop the habits which will last throughout a lifetime.[12] Air is a particularly suitable metaphor in adolescence, because it is the most porous of elements, readily penetrated by the aqueous vapors and warm fires which generate storms, making it the most "tempestuous" time of life.[13] These outside influences may of course prove to be temporary, since when air comes into contact with water it is only barely affected, and cannot be consumed by fire. Like the air which is constantly seeking purification and purgation by lightning and hail, so adolescence may also be cleansed of sin through chastity. If however, one is suffused with the waters of earthly pleasure like the sky filled with clouds, it is difficult to be moistened by the dew of grace or inflamed by the ardor of divine charity.[14]

The tempestuous character of adolescence merited comparison to the genesis and development of storms and winter floods.[15] Such floods are generally preceded by three signs: falling stars, heavy, dark clouds, and an overwhelmingly threatening calmness. The falling stars represent the saints or guardian angels who have abandoned the youth: the approaching porous clouds filled with rain represent the perils which threaten the adolescent; and the calm before the storm stands for the false phase of security which deludes him.

In an extended metaphor adolescence was likened by Berengar to running water in a stream. A staff or twig thrust into such flowing water appears upon observation to be broken in the middle. This branch represents the hope which may defend us in life against the beasts of prey sent by Satan, but which in adolescence may appear vain and broken. Just as the stick appears distorted in running water, so also on a bright day the visibility of the stars is impeded by the sun, and one may see them clearly only in certain northern regions where the sky is darkened; if one stands in the bottom of a well and peers skyward; or with the aid of a lens. Likewise, in the heat of the day the sun stands over our hearts and we may be blinded by earthly light, but will be aided by chastity to perceive the celestial beauty and grace. But the flowing water of adolescence may nevertheless be therapeutic, for just as water restores stones and pebbles which had been unsuitable for building, but become spherical and usable through collision with the running water, so one's evil deeds may be corrected in youth. This life-giving water lifts ships on high with its waves; just as in adolescence we are lifted up and our souls are made more amenable to Heaven. Elsewhere, Berengar compared adolescence to the morning,[16] when the young warrior is at the height of his strength, girded and ready for battle, able to suffer every peril. Although just a short time ago he was asleep, perhaps blinded by sin, he can make a quick recovery.

Finally, the youth recalled to Berengar a new home,[17] in which voices loudly resound and which is easily battered by stormy weather. The adolescent, untainted by sin, will hear God's word, but can at the same time be destroyed by tempests sent by the Devil. Bersuire in his *Dictionarium*, noted that the natural malleability of adolescence makes the youth impressionable, like a new plant whose crooked branches, if not straightened in time, cannot be rectified later on.[18] This same image was also employed by Giles of Rome and Bellino Bissolo.

The optimal time for the correction of faults by one's companions or tutors is adolescence, because the body is strong, the time is appropriate, the rewards acquired will be more valuable, and the tasks of correction which are imposed will be less arduous and easier to bear. Impressionability enhances the possibility of conversion in adolescence because of the long endurance of any changes wrought in youth and the ready acceptability of good morals. The receptivity of youth is paralleled in young animals, whose flesh is soft, more malleable and easily handled. Bersuire likened man to a brass vase which becomes discolored and corroded with age, poisoning the liquid contained therein. In youth one may shine with good works, but beauty disappears with age, as one becomes rusted with sin. As a consequence God shows greater pleasure for the untarnished deeds performed by such youths as David and St. John. Like new brass, pearls conceived in the morning are brighter and more beautiful than those conceived at night.

Several creatures were likened to the adolescent. Just as the young bees carry the pollen from flower to flower, while the older bees remain in the hive protecting the honey and cells, likewise in the Church the young are fit to labor outside in the world, while the aged remain sequestered, given over to contemplation, devotion and prayer.[19] Although honey is generated in both spring and autumn, the highest quality is produced in the spring, just as the man in the spring of his youth produces finer deeds than in the autumn of old age (cf. *Proverbs* 24.13). Bersuire also likened the adolescent to the obstinate, untameable, undomesticated wild ox, who refuses to be yoked or chained and, it is said, can only be captured with the aid of a virgin. The beast is comparable to the indomitable, evil man, who can only be harnessed by the Blessed Virgin (cf. *Job* 39.9-12). Nevertheless, in adolescence, despite the difficulties, we must labor hard and learn to bear the burden, like the vanquished beast.

The principle of *assimilatio* permitted the appropriation of other symbols to represent the adolescent. Both Bersuire and Berengar likened the youth to a warrior (like Goliath in his youth) who is far better equipped to do battle with the world, the flesh and the Devil than the child or the aged; he is girded with fortitude, armed with the shield of patience, the breastplate of penance, the sword-belt of friendship, the lance of truth and justice, and the sword of persuasive speech. Also, just as the vine bears its finest fruit when ripe, so an adolescent will flourish through penance and correction, bursting forth with the fruits of virtue. Its wine may be naturally warm and wet; but outside influence may dissipate this warmth and transform it into dry, cold vinegar. A good man, warmed by charity and dampened by piety, may be poisoned by the corruption of avarice and lust. In another metaphor, the youth who sustains tribulations was likened to a new building strengthened with new columns, which may weaken with age.

The disorder of youth requires control and repression, lest lust and ambition become overweaning, in accordance with the injuction of *Ecclesiasticus* 30. 11-12: "Do not give him freedom while he is young or overlook his errors. Break him in while he is young, beat him soundly while he is still a child, or he may grow stubborn and disobey you and cause you vexation." Employing the cliche of the impressionable wax, Bersuire suggested effective education in youth, since in old age learning becomes more difficult (*Ecclesiasticus* 6.18: "My son, seek wisdom's discipline while you are young, and when your hair is white, you will find her still.") Like the bee who carried the honey first with his front feet, then his middle, and then his hind legs, wisdom acquired in youth will remain in old age (*Proverbs* 22.3 "Start a boy on the right road and even in old age he will not leave it.") Also, one might note the example of the dog found as a puppy who will remain forever faithful (also *Ecclesiasticus* 25.3: "If you have not gathered wisdom in your youth, how will you find it when you are old?") The young person should likewise be occupied with useful labor and the performance of good deeds with his friends. As Pliny pointed out, the young bee leaves the hive to work while the aged remain behind, just as one should undertake good deeds and acts of repentance in youth so that in old age one may retire to a life of prayer and contemplation. Also, the young knight who possesses a strong horse should go out to do battle. Our bodies are akin to the young horse, ready for battle, as the young bees gather honey.

To Dante, in adolescence reason and the soul are still developing, and one is still governed by natural passions, so that one may therefore still be subject to a guardian in certain matters.[20] The ancient sources in particular stress that adolescents should be subjected to the wise counsels of the aged, who can provide the discipline necessary to rein in the energy of youth. One of the sobering lessons which the old teach the young is the transience of youth. For regardless of one's condition, the length of life is not fixed and death may lurk at every turn. The brevity of life ("the young man must store up, the old man use") had been a common theme in classical literature.[21]

Monastic Education

The chief means of controlling adolescent passion and preparing the youth for the responsibilities of adulthood was education. The genesis of late medieval pedagogical theory must largely be sought in the Gregorian period, which had witnessed an efflorescence of interest in monastic circles concerning the training of novices. Thus, many of the educational commonplaces which one encounters in late thirteenth century lay manuals echo their Gregorian predecessors. Pedagogical theory received considerable attention in monastic circles due to the large number of novices and oblates entrusted to the care of the church. The demographic 'revolution' of the eleventh century may well have contributed to the publication of educational manuals as a consequence of the large number of younger sons who, either through choice or force of circumstance, found themselves within the cloister. The consequent establishment of cathedral and monastic schools engendered an interest in problems of curriculum, discipline, vocation and child development. In the thirteenth century, this was succeeded by the foundation of lay, usually urban schools, and the integration of classical, largely Aristotelian theories of education into a moralizing tradition of Christian pedagogy.

The early monastic educational treatises had noted the dangers to the adolescent in the crowded environment of the cloister. A characteristic such work was Abbot John of Fruttuaria's (1028-1074) *Tractatus de origine vitae et morum instructione*, which owed much to Ambrose's *De officiis ministrorum*.[22] In it, John focused on the vices common to youth and the disciplinary techniques necessary to ward them off. In old men, he argued, religious observance is weakened by foolishness and depravity. In adolescence, rashness and shamelessness or the love of carnal pleasures are the most common causes of laxness. The primary virtue which must be encouraged in adolescence is therefore shame, accomplished through the avoidance of indecent speech and visual temptations, such as the sight of women. The best remedy for lustfulness is fasting. "It is better for one's stomach to suffer than one's mind", he said, in order to stanch the flames of hot-blooded adolescence. Among the problems of monastic youth cataloged by John were autoeroticism, narcissism, homosexuality and voyeurism.

John further described effete mannerisms, histrionics and the imitation of a broken feminine voice as widespread among novices, and worthy of condemnation. Perhaps the best cure for this is taciturnity and silence, he said. Following a catalogue of sins common in the monastery, John argued that the best antidote is fatigue of the body through fasts, prayers, vigils and manual labor, and the encouragement of such virtues as humility, obedience, prudence, fortitude, justice and temperance. All of these virtues are weapons in a kind of military campaign waged in youth against the temptations of the world. He praised the value of conversations between the old and the young, citing the examples of Mark and Barnabas (*Acts* 15.37), Paul and Silas (*Acts* 40), Timothy (*Acts* 16.3) and Titus (*Galatians* 2.1); for the youth who embarks on life's journey without a guide faces grave dangers.

Example thus remained the most effective tool of the clerical pedagogue. The saint's life, tailored to the disciplinary needs of each religious order, was the educational tool par excellence for teaching the child and adolescent the required virtues. It is therefore suitable that the canonization bulls issued by Rome beginning in the late twelfth century invariably emphasized the exemplary role of the saint, and that popular preaching made increasing use of such exemplary cases in order to instruct the laity.[23]

As Eva of St.Martin had said "among all visible things which human nature undertakes with ease, one may note either examples of good or evil".[24] As a consequence, the saint's exemplary conformity to a long tradition of virtuous behavior was a cornerstone of Christian hagiography. Raymund of Capua in his life of Catherine of Siena suggested consulting the *Vitae patrum* for comparable examples of piety, and cited a string of Biblical and patristic examples to which her life conformed.[25] Similarly, nearly every saint was explicitly compared to some distinguished predecessor. In Caesarius of Heisterbach's *Vita* of Engelbert of Cologne, comparisons to King Solomon, Judah the Maccabee, Abel, Thomas Becket, and the martyrs of Cologne (Evergislus and Agillolfus) became the structural framework around which the martyred archbishop's life was constructed.[26]

The same search for the outer symptoms of disease undertaken by the physician was used by the clerical pedagogue and physician of souls in the diagnosis of the spiritual disorders of adolescence. In his treatise on the raising of novices, Hugh of St. Victor (1096-1141) had laid stress on uncontrollable gestures as the surest signs of inner disorder, which can be expunged in adolescence; fatness reveals lasciviousness, loose movements negligence, lateness indolence, excessive speed inconsistancy, insolent mannerisms pride, and wild behavior indicates anger. The surest antidote was discipline, which will train the mind to control the movements of the body and will suffocate illicit appetites such as cupidity, lasciviousness, elation, anger and intemperance.[27]

Stephen of Salley (d. 1252) in his *Tractatus de informatione novitii*,[28] provided suitable spiritual medicine for each sin which the novice encounters, providing particular details concerning the means of dealing with nocturnal emission. He counseled the novice not to be saddened, but rather to attend mass the next morning and indicate with a sign to his minister what had transpired. Odilo of Cluny had even composed a prayer especially designed to free the sinful monk from the fires of concupiscence through the intercession of the martyrs and saints.[29] This fear which contemplation of the body might unleash may be illustrated in the life of Anselm, which tells the story of a young man who had decided never to lay a hand on his genitals. The Devil, however, had other ideas,[30] and made him feel unbearable pain in his member. He felt as though a pendulous weight was pulling down his whole body. When Anselm, in the presence of an aged monk, examined the affected area, the pain disappeared.

Lay Education

Until the mid-thirteenth century, such dour educational manuals were intended to meet the needs of clerical, monastic consumers, still wed to the institutional requirements of the monastery, which called for the use of the rod, regimentation and the suppression of natural impulses. It had been a rare preacher such as Hildebert of Lavardin (1069-1133) who had been concerned with Christian values among the laity; he produced a kind of catechism which parents and priests could teach their charges, including proper belief and conduct, both moral and physical.[31]

Although referred to in conciliar legislation, the regular instruction of children outside the monastery was spotty.[32] Such mendicant orders as the Dominicans, however, undertook to raise the educational level of the laity, perhaps with the aim of shoring up wavering Christian belief in the face of the heretic threat. Mendicant educational theory thus placed stress on the responsibility of the parent to provide a suitable education for his progeny. After about 1260, treatises directed at the laity stressed parental responsibility and the bond of love binding parent and offspring. In this, the influence of Aristotelianism, along with the secularization of culture and the demographic revolution, are evident. Many historians of education have specifically identified the educational system of the Italian friars as the presumed progenitor of humanistic education.[33]

Much attention was now devoted by the Augustinian friar Giles of Rome to the solicitous attention which parents owe their children, based on the undeniable fact that their progeny are an extension of themselves; they are superior and therefore responsible for their offspring, and a natural love cements them together. The affection felt by parents for their children is greater because: 1) parents display their love immediately, while children learn to love over a longer period of time; 2) parents are sure of their offspring, particularly mothers, who naturally identify them; and, 3) the children are a part of their parents and tied to them by a natural unity. The love of parents proceeds from cause to effect, from the upper to the lower; while the love of children proceeds from effect to cause, from lower to upper, just as it is natural for the superior to flow toward the inferior, and not vice versa. The genesis of parental love according to Giles may be compared to the view of the non-Christian "Bryson" that parents love their progeny because they are born of their own seed, which is the cause of pleasure in coition.[34] Parents were enjoined by Giles to instruct their progeny in the precepts of their faith, to perfect their habits and virtues, and to provide for their physical comfort. From the moment we suckle at our mother's breasts, we feel carnal pleasure and concupiscence, and are subject to animal passions, which parents should correct.

A work such as the Dominican William of Tournai's *De instructione puerorum* (ca. 1249/64) retained the monastic preference for "word, example and the rod" as the primary pedagogical tools.[35] It is divided into five parts dealing with: 1) love as the foundation of all education; 2) the importance of pedagogical work; 3) the educator and his special skills; 4) the ends of education, namely faith, good behavior and knowledge; and, 5) examples of sermons to be directed at children. But William lay the prime responsibility to provide a proper education whose fruits remain in adulthood upon the shoulders of the child's spiritual and/or carnal parents. For sin was inevitably considered the consequence of poor grounding in childhood, and parents were responsible for their offspring's moral transgressions. Unlike his pre-mendicant predecessors, William did not exclude the need to educate women, serfs and servants. The standard virtues of justice and temperance to which the adolescent is amenable were to be inculcated, although the continuing stress on the dire effects of lust remained.

Raymund Lull's *Doctrina pueril*, composed at Palma de Majorca or Montpellier (ca. 1275/83), was a kind of pocket catechism of essential knowledge for the young, addressed to a son named Dominic.[36] Raymund here remarked that nature knows how to raise children better than one's mother does, and that an education which ignores human nature is doomed to failure, a view which seems to contrast markedly with the largely monastic treatises which preceded Raymund's work. He took note of the intellectual and physical superiority of poor over rich children, who have been excessively spoiled by an overabundance of food and clothing. The mutual responsibility of the parent and child to nurture and sustain each other was stressed, motivated by feelings of mutual love. Many of Lull's remarks on the four humors, diet, disease prevention, the amusements of children and the virtues to be inculcated, appear derived from the standard contemporary encyclopedias of medical literature. Philip of Novara's *Les quatre âges de l'homme* (1259/65) undertook to provide advice not simply to the young, but to all four ages of man -- childhood, adolescence, youth and old age.[37] He argued that the education provided should be suitable to the class to which the child belongs. As a member of a class which had often witnessed the aggressive behavior of the young, Philip warned against the irascibility and quarrelsomeness of youth, and the naive acceptance of false counsel, which may lead to the loss of honor and inheritance. Youth ought therefore to be subject to the restraints of their elders, prelates, counsellors and espoused wives.

While practical advice concerning the choice of an occupation only appeared in Christian admonitory guides in the late thirteenth century, the Jewish tradition of autobiographical testaments addressed by learned scholars to their sons, included more practical remarks on such subjects as conjugal relations and the search for employment. Many such works, including Nahmanides' (1197-1270) letter to his son Solomon, who held a position at the Castilian court, and the *Gates of Instruction* attributed to Maimonides, were largely collections of moral injunctions. Others, such as the testament (ca. 1190) by the physician and translator ibn Tibbon, contained considerable biographical material, particularly about family life, a subject often lacking in their Christian counterparts, which until the late thirteenth century had emphasized spiritual development and were written by celibate clerics.[38] Ibn Tibbon began with a lament that he had been left a lonely exile by his children, and recounted the great sacrifices he suffered in order to secure food, clothing and education for his son. His accusatory epistle was replete with citations from Scripture and particularly from *Ben Mishle*, Samuel Hanagid's commentary on *Proverbs*. He lamented the fact that while other scholars were willing to learn from him, his own sons had turned away. Much of the advice he gave was practical: perfect your Arabic; develop good penmanship; learn medicine and Torah; cultivate good habits; keep away from evil company. Much attention was devoted to the financial and physical dangers he had undergone for the sake of his children, berating his son for profligacy and for not soliciting his literary criticism. Ibn Tibbon also advised treating one's wife and hired nurse with respect. He concluded with fatherly advice to his son to rear his own children as he had, and to care for their health.

The *Guide to Knowledge* (1332) addressed by Joseph Bonafos ibn Kaspi (1279-1340) to his son Solomon, while mostly a spirited defense of philosophy by a partisan of Maimonides, provided a detailed graded plan of intellectual development, which outlines a kind of periodization of life. Until age fourteen one studies Scripture and Talmud; between fourteen and eighteen one studies mathematics and moral texts; at eighteen one reviews former studies and adds the natural sciences. At twenty, the time has come to build a family and to add theology to one's pursuits. The focal point is at twenty, when one no longer needs to rely on faith to achieve the truth, but may be aided by the intellect; although for some, true knowledge may not be achieved until forty or fifty. Joseph thus provided the kind of graded system of education which has been a hallmark of modern pedagogy.[39]

The only such work which combines the tradition of practical advice with the characteristically Christian hagiographical admixture of prophecy and miracle is the testament of Judah ben Asher ben Yehiel (1290-1349) of Toledo.[40] Written in a rather patriarchal, preachy tone, he admitted to having borne children purely out of duty (hardly a comfort to his children); he voiced complaints about his financial situation, and recalled the adolescent difficulties he faced after the age of thirteen, when he was taken from Germany to France, and then to Spain, and had to acclimatize himself to a different educational tradition; Judah also spoke much of the near-blindness which inflicted him in infancy.

The qualities of the ideal teacher and student in the lay environment received ample attention from Bernard Gordon, William Peraldus and Giles of Rome, among others. To Bernard Gordon,[41] the pedagogue should be learned, knowledgeable enough to base his teachings on facts rather than hearsay and rumor; he should be wellspoken and honest, humble and eloquent, for language is the chief instrument by which learning is imparted. His knowledge should be all-inclusive, the sign of a truly educated man, taking care to suit the instruction to his audience. Such flexibility requires him to observe his students carefully in order to determine their proper disposition. William Peraldus[42] summarized the qualities of the good teacher as "mens ingeniosa, vita honesta, humilis scientie, eloquentia, docendi peritia." The tutor should first and foremost concern himself with the outer signs of his charge's character, namely his gestures, bearing, speech, eating and drinking habits, and marital continence, inculcating those virtues which will last into adulthood. Each of the senses must be harnessed through its own peculiar disciplinary technique, whereby the soul and body learn to function in unison. "Bryson" stressed love of God, the prophets, angels, religious institutions, rulers and elders as a major goal of education.[43]

To Bernard,[44] the student should love and fear God, which is the beginning of wisdom, and be of blessed life and pious behavior. He should ban pride, sloth, gluttony and intemperate drinking, and be open and frank in his speech, humble, willing to confess what he knows and methodical. One should not waste time studying *curiositates* which require great labor but offer little of value. The student ought to be modest in dress and control his tongue, which is the guardian of the soul, the means whereby one praises God, confesses one's sins and expresses virtue. When others speak, one should always listen, regardless of whether a youth or an old man, a sage or a fool, a foreigner or a local is speaking. In addressing God, especially in a holy place, one should display reverence and fear. Concerning diet, shelter and dress, Bernard preached the Aristotelian doctrine of moderation and avoidance of excess, providing what life requires for sustenance and protection.

V. *Notes*

1. Vincent of Beauvais, *Speculum maius*, 4 vols. (Douai, 1624), *Speculum naturale*, XXX.82; Isidore of Seville, *Etymologiae*, ed. V.M. Lindsay, 2 vols. (Oxford, 1910), XI.2.15-16; "Jacobus", *Omnebonum*, *B.M. Royal* 6. E. VI, f. 59r suggests that adolescence may extend to twenty-four. Elsewhere (*B.M. Royal* 6 E. VII, pt. 2, f. 247r) he extends it to twenty-five.

2. Giles of Rome, *De regimine principum* (Rome, 1607), *passim*.

3. *Ibid.*, II.ii.17 speaks of the concerns of adolescence: "circa bonam dispositionem corporis, cira ordinationem appetitus, et circa illuminationem intellectus."

4. Pierre Bersuire, *Dictionarium*, I, 80, *Opera omnia*, 6 vols. (Cologne, 1731); Berengar of Landorre, *Lumen animae*, ed. Matthias Farinato (Augsburg, 1477), Tit. XVI, "Jacobus", *Omnebonum*, *B.M. Royal* 6.E. VI. f. 59S, placed *iuventus* between 21 and 31 or 35.

5. Bersuire, *Dictionarium*, IV, 427-8 (*iuventus*).

6. On beauty in youth, see Vincent of Beauvais, XXXI,85; Isidore of Seville, IV.2.2 on defenses against degeneration in youth. The classification of the sources of danger to health in this period is found in Hugh of St. Victor, *Liber exceptionum*, I.i.20, ed. Jean Châtillon (Paris, 1958), cited by Vincent; see also Hugh of St. Victor, *Didascalicon*, ed. and trans. Jerome Taylor and Henry Buttimer (New York, 1961), II.26; Haly Abbas, ['Ali ibn al-Abbas], *Liber regalis*, trans. Stephen of Antioch, in *Liber totius medicine...* (Lyons, 1523), II.I.24; Seneca, *Epistulae*, 78 in R.M. Gummere, ed., *Senecae Epistulae*, 3 vols. (Cambridge, 1953); Jerome, *Contra Iovinianum*, 2 (*MPL*, 23); on the health required of athletes, or soldiers for Christ, see A. Hilka, ed., *Das Leben und Sentenzen des Philosophen Secundus* (Breslau, 1910), 17 on the transitory character of beauty.

7. Vincent of Beauvais, XXXI, 86; Petronius, *Satyricon*, 94, ed. Michael Heseltine (London, 1919); Ovid, *Ars Amatoria*, I. 509, 6-3-4, in Ovid, *Ars Amatoria*, ed. J.H. Mozley (Cambridge, Mass., 1962); II. 113-5; Valerius Maximus, IV.6. Ext. 1, in *Factorum et dictorum memorabilium libri novem*, ed. C. Kempf (Leipzig, 1888); Calpurnius, IV. 24, 32, in C. Giarratano, ed., *Calpurnii et Nemesiani Bucolica*, 3rd ed. (Turin, 1951); Ovid, *Tristia*, III.vii.33-8, ed. A.L. Wheeler (Cambridge, 1953); idem, *Fasti*, I.419, ed. J.G. Frazer (Cambridge, 1931); Ambrose, *De Josepho* V. 22, in *CSEL*, 32.2 (Leipzig, 1897) tells of how Joseph in the house of Potiphar (*Genesis* 39.6-7) did not take unfair advantage of his comeliness, but rather cultivated modesty, thereby enhancing his beauty.

8. On the moral weakness of youth, Ambrose, *In Psalmum cxviii Expositio*, 18.31 (*MPL*, 15: 1463c); Annaeus Seneca, *Tragoediae*, ed. R. Peiper and G. Richter (Leipzig, 1902); Sallust, *Catalina*, ed. A. Ahlberg (Leipzig, 1919), 14; Ovid, *Fasti*, V. 273; Ovid, *Amores*, I.ix.1-3, in *Heroides and Amores*, ed. G. Showerman (Cambridge, 1971).

9. Giles of Rome, *op. cit.*

10. Dante Alighieri, *Il Convivio*, ed. G. Busnelli and G. Vandelli, 2nd ed. (Florence, 1964), IV. Statius, *Thebais*, I.462 ff., ed. Alfred Klotz (Leipzig, 1973); see also *ibid*, IV. 551 and his *Achilleade*, I. 43 on Aeacus.

11. Berengar of Landorre, Tit. XVI. *De adolescentia*, CXXVII. *De juventute*. On the predominance of blood in adolescence, and the distribution of the humors, see Galen, *De sanitate tuenda*, VI.2, ed. C.G. Kühn, *Opera omnia*, 20 vols. (Leipzig, 1821-1873), VI.382; *Quod animi mores...*, IV.10, in *Kühn*, IV, 810. On humoral balance, see *Definitiones medicae*, CIV, in Kühn, XIX, 374; on changes from age to age, *Hippocratis Aphorismi et Galeni in eos Commentarii*, V.9, in Kühn, XVII, pt. 2, 781 ff.

12. A somewhat more comprehensive adaptation of the same imagery is found in P. Boffito, ed., "Il 'De principiis astrologiae, di Cecco d'Ascoli," *Giornale storico della letteratura italiana*. *Supplemento* 6 (1903), 10-11, who paralleled the four parts of the Zodiac, the four ages of man and history, and the four seasons. For example, the period from Aries to Gemini, springtime, is comparable to *pueritia*, characterized by heavy humidity and the dominance of blood. In the sixteenth century, Pedro Mexia, *Silva de varia leccion* (Madrid, 1673), I.43, noted that the seven ages of man are governed by seven heavenly bodies.

13. On the porousness of air, Berengar cites Avicebron [Ibn Gebirol], *Fons vitae*, trans. John of Spain and Dominicus Gundissalinus, ed. C. Baeumker, *Beiträge*, 1 (1895).

14. The character of tempests is discussed in Aristotle, *Problemata* XXV, 4, in *Aristotelis Opera*, ed. Academia regia Borussica, 5 vols. (Berlin, 1831), II, 458. This pseudo-Aristotelian tract had been translated by Bartholomew of Messina in 1254/65, and retranslated at Padua in 1310. See also Yuhanna ibn Masawaih [John Mesue], *De consolatione medicinarum antidotorum*, VI, ed. Daniele Jacquart and Gerard Troppeau (Paris, 1980).

15. Albertus Magnus, *De impressionibus*, in *Liber IV Meteorum* IV, in *Opera omnia*, ed. August Borgnet, 38 vols. (Paris, 1890), V, 477-508. He also cites Avicenna's commentary on Aristotle's *Meteora* III.3, and a tract by Alcabitius. These citations are probably paraphrased, and rather difficult to locate. On Alcabitius, see Francis J. Carmody,

Arabic Astronomical and Astrological Sciences in Translation (Berkeley, 1956).

16. Aristotle, *Problemata*, XXVII.5; see also John of San Gemignano, *Summa de exemplis et rerum similitudinibus* (Venice, 1584), IX. 85.

17. Among the other sources cited by Berengar are the *Secretum secretorum*, Avicenna's *De diluviis*, Alfarabi's *De mixtibilibus et mixtis*, Plato's *Timaeus*, Claudius Ptolemy's *Almagest* and John Mesue's *Aphorisms*.

18. Bersuire, *Dictionarium*, I, 79 ff. (*adolescentia*); Vincenzo Licitra, ed., "Il *Liber legum moralium* e il *De regimine vite et sanitatis* di Bellino Bissolo," *Studi medievali*, Ser. 3, 6 (1965), 421. The *Liber* contains moral advice to his young sons, with considerable material on the selection and upkeep of one's wife, child-rearing, relations with neighbors, and old age. The *De regimine* is largely dietary.

19. Bersuire relies on Ambrose, Pliny, Aristotle; see also John of San Gemignano, VI. 29.

20. Dante, *Il Convivio*, IV.

21. Vincent of Beauvais, *op. cit.*, c. 82 ff. On the transience of youth, cf. Seneca, *Epistulae* xxxvi. 4; Cicero, *De senectute*, XI.38; IX,29; XIX, 68, in I. Huxley, *Cato maior*, new ed., 2 vols. (Oxford, 1957); Ambrose, *Sermones in Psalmum cxviii*, 19.19 (*MPL*, 15: 1474c); Ovid, *Amores*, I.viii.49-50; Seneca, *Epistulae*, xxv.8.

22. *MPL*, 184: 559-584; André Wilmart, "Exorde et conclusion du traité de Jean l'Homme de Dieu," *Revue bénédictine*, 38 (1926), 310-320; Caroline Bynum, *Docere Verbo et Exempla. An Aspect of Twelfth Century Spirituality* (Cambridge, Mass., 1979), *passim* deals with the didactic sources of the twelfth century.

23. Stephan of Bourbon, *Anecdotes historiques, légendes et apologues*, ed. A. Lecoy de la Marche (Paris, 1877), 4 notes the impressive value of tales drawn from the saints' lives. See e.g., the canonization bulls of Anthony of Padua (1232) and of Edmund of Canterbury (1246), in *Bullarium romanum*, ed. C. Coquelines, 14 vols. (Rome 1739-1744), III, 271-2, 307.

24. Eva of St. Martin, *Vita Iulianae*, in *ASS*, 5 April II: 442.

25. Raymund of Capua, *Vita Catherinae*, in *ASS*, 30 April III: 877-8, 866.

26. Caesarius of Heisterbach, *Vita, Passio et Miracula S. Engelberti*, in *ASS*, 7 November III: 662.

27. Hugh of St. Victor, *De institutione novitiorum*, cc. 10-21, in *MPL*, 176: 934-52; Peter of Porto, *Regula clericorum*, in *MPL*, 163: 703-48 shows special solicitude for the disabilities of the aged and those under

sixteen. Both are limited by their weak constitutions from taking full part in the common life (*ibid.*, II. cc. 25-6).

28. Edmond Mikkers, ed. "Un 'Speculum novitii' inédit d'Étienne de Salley," *Collectanea ordinis Cisterciensium reformatorum*, 8 (1946), 17-68.

29. "Un opuscule inédit de saint Odilon de Cluny," *Revue bénédictine*, 16 (1899), 477-488.

30. Eadmer, *Vita sancti Anselmi*, ed. R.W. Southern (London, 1962), 23-24.

31. Hildebert of Lavardin, *Sermones*, in *MPL*, 171: 921.

32. *Decretales Gregorii noni*, III. T.1. c.3, in E. Friedberg and E. Richter, eds., *Corpus iuris canonici*, 2 vols. (Leipzig, 1879-1881).

33. James Bowen, *A History of Western Education*, 3 vols. (London, 1975), II, 180 notes that Dante's Christian Aristotelianism was presumably acquired at the Dominican school of Santa Maria Novella. See also Gaston Mialaret and Jean Vial, eds., *Histoire mondiale de l'education*, 4 vols. (Paris, 1981), II, 304; William Harrison Woodward, *Vittorino da Feltre and Other Humanist Educators* (New York, 1963), 182 ff.

34. Martin Plessner, ed. "Der OIKONOMIKOC der Neupythagorers 'Bryson' und sein Einfluss auf die islamische Wissenschaft," *Orient und Antike*, 5 (Heidelberg, 1928).

35. James A. Corbett, ed., *The De instructione puerorum of William of Tournai O.P.* (Notre Dame, Ind., 1955) for text; R. Fluck, "Guillaume de Tournai et son traité 'De modo docendi pueri'," *Revue des sciences religieuses*, 27 (1953), 333-356.

36. Raymond Lull, *Doctrine de l'enfant, version médiévale*, ed. Armand Llinares (Paris, 1969) for a French version; for a Catalan edition, see Ramon Llull, *Doctrina pueril*, ed. Gret Schib (Barcelona, 1972).

37. Philippe de Navarre, *Les quatres âges de l'homme*, ed. Marcel de Fréville (Paris, 1887).

38. Israel Abrahams, ed., *Hebrew Ethical Wills*, 2 vols. (Philadelphia, 1926), I, 51-92 for ibn Tibbon's will.

39. *Ibid.*, 130-161. Speaking of medieval education, Philippe Ariès, *Centuries of Childhood*, trans. Robert Baldick (New York, 1962), 145, said: "Nobody thought of having a graduated system of education, in which the subjects for study would be distributed according to difficulty, beginning with the easiest."

40. Abrahams, II, 165-196.

41. Bernard Gordon, *De conservatione vitae* (Leipzig, 1570), 31ff.
42. William Peraldus, *De eruditione principum*, in Thomas Aquinas, *Opera omnia*, 34 vols., ed. S.E. Fretté (Paris, 1871-1880), XXVII, 609.
43. Plessner, *op. cit.*
44. Bernard Gordon, 34.

VI. The Sexual Strains of Late Adolescence and Early Adulthood

The sexual tension of adolescence and early adulthood became the focal point whose resolution would determine the model of adult development, both male and female. The chief task of late adolescence and early adulthood was to overcome the dangers of unbridled lust, armed with a moral education. Some would choose the monastic or clerical vocation; others found a suitable haven within the confines of sacramental marriage.

Control of Male and Female Passion

Vincent of Beauvais' extended treatment of the moral dangers of adolescence relied on selections from the early fathers and the Latin classics, such as this remark from Seneca the Elder's *Controversiae*, which stressed the sexual confusion of youth: "Look at our young men: they are lazy, their intellects asleep... Libidinous delight in song and dance transfixes these effeminates, braiding the hair, refining the voice till it is as caressing as a woman's, competing in bodily softness with women, beautifying themselves with filthy fineries-- this is the pattern our youths set themselves... Born feeble and spineless, they stay like that throughout their lives, taking others' chastity by storm, careless of their own."[1] As Augustine had noted, in adolescence he had sought both chastity and lust, had yearned to both love and be loved; Jerome adduced a series of Biblical citations in his *De interpellatione Job et David* concerning the havoc wrought by the bodily passions in youth.[2]

In *Omnebonum*, the adolescent was portrayed poised between sin and virtue, between the "via avis vel sagitte", as Hostiensis said; he is thus comparable to the Jewish people who wavered between God and Satan. Following Isidore, Bersuire argued that adolescence derives from *adolere*, which implies burning, because of the fires of lust which threaten to consume the youth and influence his appetites, due to an overabundance of viscosity and humidity. The adolescent lacks stable foundations, is rather vain and inconsistent, akin to the chameleon whose skin has no permanent hue.[3] Nevertheless, despite its recklessness and unprovoked violence, the natural humility and malleability of youth allow correction.

Reflecting its non-Christian origin, "Bryson" suggested that after fourteen the young should become accustomed to sexual relations, although excessive coition can be debilitating. In the Hebrew version it was suggested that one ought not to learn about sexuality until after marriage. Thomas of Cantimpré noted that the adolescent possesses seminal virtue and is capable of generation, although the precise age of puberty may vary.[4] At the very moment when the body ought to possess its greatest strength, the passions are aroused and draw away the natural virtues so that the body and soul are weakened and one becomes effeminate. He therefore advised marriage. The flux of the libido tends to diminish after about twenty-two, when growth ceases.

Giles of Rome, on the other hand, argued that, ideally, males should marry at thirty-six, females at eighteen, the ages of perfection. But since by that time the generative power has become somewhat corrupted, marriage should occur sometime after twenty-one. He opposed marriage in youth for the following reasons: young parents are not yet themselves in a state of perfection so their progeny will be less than perfect; women at an early age are intemperate and lascivious and will thus harm their offspring; an early pregnancy may be dangerous; too much venery in young men leads to corpulence.[5] Conrad of Megenberg noted that in fact child-bearing and marriage vary with circumstance, and under certain conditions, the age of matrimony may be accelerated.[6] The selection of an honest wife was regarded by Bissolo as the surest means of avoiding illicit vices; although virginity may be praiseworthy, he said, marriage is also a good according to the law.[7] The selection and maintenance of a wife were given considerable attention in Bissolo's work, which is essentially a treatise on household management.

At the same time, a growing number of educational and medical manuals devoted attention to the needs of women, including many in the vernacular, which made them more accessible to their intended audience. Such a work as the novel *Flamenca* (ca. 1240/50), and *Le ménagier de Paris* (1392/4), a guide to household management, were to make learned doctrine more widely known.[8] King Louis IX of France, for example, composed two letters, one to his daughter Isabella, queen of Navarre (1255), and another to an unknown daughter, in which he provided largely moral advice on good conduct, stressing the love of God, frequent confession, patience, love of the Church, alms-giving, modesty, humility, truthfulness and obedience to one's husband and parents. The same kind of advice urging temperate behavior, proper deportment, appearance and manners was to be found in such works as the *Chastoiement des dames* (1250-1275) by Robert of Blois; the *Reggimento e costumi di donna* (1307-1315) by Franceso Barberino, which offered advice to women at different stages of their lives (young women ready for marriage, those unlikely to marry, wives, widows, widows who will remarry); the anonymous *Die Winsbekin* (13th century), apparently composed by a Bavarian noblewoman; and the *Dodici avvertimenti che deve dare la madre alla figliuola quando la manda a marito* (ca. 1300), containing twelve precepts of advice from an Italian mother to a daughter about to marry. In addition to these vernacular sources, many of the mirrors for princes and the regimens for health contained advice concerning the upbringing and health of women.[9]

Giles of Rome, an Aristotelian, in his *De regimine principum* (1277/9), viewed woman as an incomplete man, "quasi masculus occasionatus", somewhat like a boy whose use of reason is incomplete and puerile; some women are even akin to wild animals, although capable of domestication.[10] On the other hand he did praise some "womanly" virtues, although the causes may be unfortunate. They may be modest, because of a desire to be praised and commended, and because of a natural timidity. Their piety and mercy are a consequence of the same softheartedness found in children and the aged. William Peraldus, on the other hand, whose sources were largely Scriptural, stood for greater equality between the sexes.[11] Eve was not created out of Adam's head, and should thus not govern man. Nor was she created out of his foot, and ought therefore not to be trodden upon. She was rather born of Adam's rib, his waist, the mid-portion of his body, and is thus meant to serve as a companion. One's wife should properly belong to the same social class and be of comparable age and beauty. As a helpmate, the noblewoman should assist her warring spouse through acts of charity; and cultivate gentleness in order to restrain his cruelty. Her prayers will bring God closer; her patience will help her to ameliorate her husband's errors.

To Giles, whatever attributes a woman possesses are characterized by intensity; when pious, she is deeply so; when cruel, she is downright ferocious; when modest, she is very modest.[12] At the same time women are by nature intemperate, garrulous, quarrelsome, and unstable as a result of their weak constitutions. In order to ward off laziness they should be occupied with suitable employment, such as knitting, reading and perhaps some arithmetic, rather than frivolity and adornment, a view shared by Bernard Gordon and William Peraldus.[13] Conrad of Megenberg, like others, attributed the puerility of women to their softer physical constitutions, which requires greater guidance and direction. They ought therefore to be confined to the home, protected physically and emotionally from the snares of the world.[14] Their lesser moisture implies that they require less food, can fast more, but can be lured into bed easily by drink. When their breasts are two digits in length they are already heated up by sexual desire, and should therefore be restrained from reading books which stir the appetite; they may also be ready for marriage earlier than men.

According to Gilbert of Limerick (d. 1140), the ideal role of the Christian woman was to "serve those who pray, plough and fight". She is "a servant, mild, obedient, humble, patient, sweet, charming, innocent, devoted, faithful in her deeds, easy to those complaining, amicable to those giving birth, pious to the suffering... and gracious to all and sundry on every occasion."[15] In a sermon directed at women Humbert of Romans (1194-1272) suggested that women remain humble, chaste, pious, taciturn and charitable stay-at-homes, following the examples of Agnes, Catherine, Caecilia, Lucia and Esther.[16] Although such sermons were largely antifeminist, and woman was depicted as the temptress, an element of partnership in marriage is found. Guibert of Tournai (d. 1284) went beyond the rather passive image of womanhood by suggesting that married women are charged with: 1) learning to deal severely with wayward servants, whose good morals are their responsibility; 2) undertaking the proper management of the household; and, 3) caring for and educating their children, whose faults in later life can be traced to poor training in childhood.[17]

These discussions of the differences between the sexes, the nature of adolescent sexuality, and the suitable age of marriage, were not merely academic exercises, but must be understood in the light of the many changes which the late middle ages witnessed in domestic mores, marriage legislation and family structure, and which in recent years have received considerable attention. Within the Church, a determined effort was made to impose celibacy not only on the monks, but also on the clergy.[18] Beginning in the eleventh century the European family had begun to undergo drastic change as the first signs of urbanization and the agricultural revolution became evident, leading in some areas to a replacement of the large, extended partriarchal clan by the nuclear, urban family.[19] While, for example, all sons formerly shared the inheritance equally, now only the eldest son often inherited, and the younger sons might be forced to seek their fortunes elsewhere, leaving a residue of resentment which was difficult to heal. Traditional family obligations -- vengeance, group fines, family honor -- were being redefined, and the dislocation inevitably caused many a crisis, sometimes leading to bloodshed and intrafamilial warfare. This was aggravated by a crisis of over-population, during which many presumably unwanted children had entered the world robbed of the security which the feudal estate had formerly provided, and were forced to pursue the monastic life against their wills.[20]

At the same time, the new heretical sects suggested a sexual ethic opposed to the Catholic program. The more radical, such as the Brethren of the Free Spirit, were accused of sexual libertinism, including polygamy and the holding of orgies in which acts against nature were performed.[21] Cathar theology, on the other hand, implied the prohibition of sexual intercourse leading to generation for all, not simply the clergy, thereby destroying the Church's traditional boundary between the total celibacy of the clergy and the monogomous marriage of the laity. Raymund of Toulouse, for example, complained in 1177 that the Cathars have thrown "discord into all families, dividing husband and wife, son and father, daughter-in-law and mother-in-law." These Cathars denied that salvation can be achieved through sexual generation in marriage, although they might be amenable to contraception and other restrictions on procreation. Nor was marriage seen as a sacrament, a view which coincided with the secular predisposition to regard marriage as a contractual relationship between two families, not necessarily requiring the couple's consent, and which was dissoluble in pursuit of material interest.[22] Women had proven particularly amenable to the 'snares' of heresy, since many of the sects accorded them a higher status than Catholic Christianity.[23]

The Church's attempt to severely restrict marriage through a severe definition of consangunity, caused the greatest political conflict by limiting the opportunities for an advantageous match. By 1215, Rome was forced to relent and reduce the prohibited grades of consangunity from seven to four.[24] But the struggle continued. A majority of marriages apparently continued to be performed outside the physical confines of the Church, and might be termed "clandestine", in order to circumvent the Church's demand that matrimony be sacramental, consensual and based on ties of affection. For Christian ideology was working to weaken the authority of the family over its offspring.

As a consequence of this weakening of parental authority, the expansion of career opportunities and opposition to the Catholic notions of sexuality and sainthood, most vocally expressed by the heretics, a new series of options faced the budding adolescent and young adult. The tripartite scheme of the ages of man prevalent in hagiography now recognized new idealized forms of adulthood. Contemporary hagiographers undertook to classify the saints in accordance with their status in adulthood. Caesarius of Heisterbach spoke of four categories of saint, each personified by its own figure: martyrs (Demetrius), confessors (Nicholas of Myra), virgins (Catherine of Alexandria), and widows (Elizabeth of Thuringia). He emphasized that married persons may be included.[25] Sicco Polentino spoke of four *ordines*: preachers, martyrs, hermits and mendicants, noting how rare it is to find someone who voluntarily abandons family and fortune for a life of poverty and pilgrimage.[26]

The traditional notion of sexual chastity confined to the clergy and monks thus became only one of several strategies of post-adolescent development. Among women, a new ideal of Christian matrimony permitted the expression of female piety within the framework of marriage. Among men, the tertiary orders provided for the realization of lay spirituality within a modified penitential framework. The three developmental options - celibacy, mental chastity for men and for women - warrant attention.

The Resoltuion of Male Sexuality

The critical choices of adolescence were graphically illustrated in the saints' lives, which served as living *exempla* of the crises which faced every believer. Since the "temptations of the flesh are violent during youth, whereas after the age of fifty concupiscence dies down",[27] the snares of sexuality the Devil lays in adolescence were a feature of the earliest saints' lives. Jerome's life of Paul the Hermit noted the first bloom of manhood and the overcoming of the temptations of a lustful harlot as the prerequisites of sainthood and adulthood.[28] A crisis occurred when Paul feared the betrayal of his newly-won Christianity by his brother-in-law, which led him to flee the world and become a hermit. Structurally, this high point was followed by an undifferentiated life of piety until old age. Athanasius' life of Anthony likewise dwelt on the lascivious tricks of the Devil which began to beset the saint in adolescence.[29] The temptations of lustful women nearly caused Benedict to abandon his hermitage, until he "conquered pleasure through suffering" by throwing himself naked on a bed of brambles and nettles. In Martin of Tours' life the trauma of adolescent sexuality was replaced by the difficulties of service for a Christian in the Roman army, which interrupted his earlier inclinations to religion.[30]

The stress on the sexual struggle of the adolescent which was likewise found in later hagiography must thus be seen as essentially a continuation of such themes found in early Christian biography, adopted with little change by later authors. In the thirteenth century, the dangers of adolescent sexuality were now supported by arguments drawn not only from Scripture and the fathers, but also from classical and Arabic sources. But although the fires of lust which burn in youth must be stanched, marriage rather than total abstinence was increasingly viewed as another option to the control of passion.

The ideal of sexual 'purity', which regarded all emissions as a kind of ritual impurity, was even more severe than the prohibited abominations of Leviticus. This program of sexual purification necessitated the creation of new forms of monastic life which would ensure the pursuit of chastity as a prerequisite to Christian sanctity. All bodily discharges were regarded as defiling, and disqualified the monk (whose physical separateness signified his holiness) from the pursuit of his goal of unity with the Godhead. The new religious ideal, which demanded solitude, self-flagellation, penitential discipline and poverty, was achieved through a reform of the statutes governing the rearing of oblates and child-monks. In contemporary hagiography, which had both a reflective and didactic role to play, childhood and adolescence were therefore often described in detail, as was the crucial transitional stage from late adolescence to adulthood, when lustful longings are stanched in favor of spiritual perfection.

The decisive character of the adolescent crisis of sexuality as a touchstone to religious *conversio* (i.e., either admission to the monastic life, or simply a religious *crise de conscience*) was to become commonplace in hagiography after the Gregorian age. Adolescence thus took its place beside infancy and childhood as a distinctly recognizable phase of human development, despite an occasional frustrating imprecision in the use of such terms as *adolescentia, pueritia* and *iuventus*, which may be used interchangeably. The late tenth and early eleventh centuries began to supply graphic examples of the struggles of adolescent sexuality, perhaps because of the increasing use made of saints' lives in order to encourage the young to abandon the world for a life of monastic celibacy and to strengthen the faith of those already cloistered. Such stress on celibacy and the control of sexual desire may be seen as a logical response to the nascent crisis of overpopulation which had begun to afflict Europe in the tenth century, and whose contours have not been fully mapped out, but which by the late eleventh century had spawned new social and familial problems.[31]

The stress on adolescence, which often possessed a sexual dimension, and led to a break with one's family, had been graphically illustrated in Cluniac hagiography. Gerald of Aurillac (d. 909) became physically active upon reaching adolescence.[32] In his case, however, "while he was growing up his bodily strength consumed the harmful humor of his body" and despite his noble, military training, he was "not puffed up, as youths often are". Nevertheless, tests of his chaste nature abound during this critical turning point of his life; he provided a dowry to a poor girl to whom he was attracted in order to hasten her marriage to another, rather than ignite his own ardor. He often shrank from suggestions of marriage and, suffering nocturnal emissions, had a change of clothes and water available at night to remove any telltale signs of involuntary sin. Odo of Cluny (d. 942) likewise suffered an adolescent crisis of divided loyalty in which his dedication to God and his natural inclination to devote himself to noble pursuits were in conflict.[33]

The life of Peter Damian (ca. 1007-1072)[34] contained many of the elements which were to become the stock-in-trade of later medieval biography: parental cruelty, sexual conflict, the cult of the Virgin. As Mary McLaughlin has noted, Peter presented a classic case of the abandoned battered child, born into a large, fatherless, impoverished family.[35] Peter's mother was so struck with depression -- perhaps *post partum* -- that she refused to nurse him. Close to death, he was saved by a priest's concubine. His mother briefly fulfilled her maternal duties, but Peter, soon orphaned, was raised by an older brother and his cruel, merciless wife. At about twelve, he was transferred to the care of a more kindly sibling. Nevertheless, Peter began to devote himself to a regimen of self-denial and degradation. Sexuality was especially described in his writings in the most pejorative terms, the product of lust rather than love. The pangs of birth are the just punishment of the pleasures of conception; while the desire to bear children is a sign of the unwillingness to abandon the sensual world, even after one's death. We are all born in "hideous putrefaction and filth". Animals, he says, are merely concerned with conception; mankind seeks the satisfaction of lust. The human body is described as dirt, filth, or ordure, consumed by the fires of lust, particularly in youth. In a suggestive cry of despair, Damian once addressed the Virgin Mary in this way: "O my glorious mother, mirror of virginal purity and standard of virtue. How have I, a wretched and unhappy creature, offended you by the filthy putridness of my flesh, and have violated the chastity of my body, of which you are mother and author!" When he was attacked by the pangs of desire in the middle of the night, and a nocturnal emission threatened, Peter customarily jumped out of bed and threw himself naked into ice cold water. When these diabolical urges had subsided, he recited a series of Psalms, and went back to sleep. Thus, his purity was restored after defilement.[36]

Following the Gregorian ideal of sexual chastity enunciated by such as Peter, sexual abstinence and abandonment of worldly concerns were more severely enforced as elements of the monastic ideal. While in an earlier period family ties had been maintained, total separation from family was now a *sine qua non* of monastic conversion. This ideal was represented by the newly formed Camaldolensian and Vallumbrosian orders, which sought to return to the eremitical ideal of each monk isolated in his own cell, reliving the temptations and physical self-denial of the Christian hermits in the Sinai and the Judean deserts. Both orders were established by men who found life in the older monasteries too free and affluent, and who had withdrawn for a period of preparation and solitude before pioneering a new way of life. Withdrawal and suffering now became a permanent feature of both monastic and eremitical biography, played out in adolescence and early adulthood. The founders of both orders experienced the kind of conflict with their families which was to become characteristic of many of the saints who spurned the martial ideals of feudal society and the mercantile values of the city.[37]

Romuald of Salerno (ca. 952-1027), founder of the Camaldolensian order, was born into a ducal family of Ravenna and was allegedly given over to vice in his youth.[38] When he failed to take part in a family feud over land claims, his father threatened to disinherit him. In the course of the fight which ensued between two branches of the clan, Romuald's father killed a relative; feeling responsible for his father's crime, although there is no evidence that he was involved, he fled to the monastery of Saint Apollinaire in Classe to do penance for forty days. Because of his rigidity in application of the monastic rule, he was forced by his fellow monks to leave the monastery and become a wandering hermit. John Gualberti (d. 1073), founder of the Vallumbrosian order, was born into a wealthy Florentine family.[39] His father was an aggressive soldier who vigorously opposed to his son's entry into the Benedictine monastery of San Miniato in 1013. After his brother's murder, John returned home, and was expected to avenge his brother's death. He refused, however, and returned to the monastic life, where he was appalled by the easy living of his fellow monks and quarrelled violently with the abbot. He was thus forced to leave Florence in order to establish his own house at Vallombrosa (ca. 1036).

The Cistercian Bernard of Clairvaux (1090-1153) also faced attempts by a knightly brother to dissuade him from joining the Cistercians at twenty-two (in 1112 A.D.). The paradigmatic sexual temptation of adolescence confronted Bernard thrice in the form of lustful women according to James of Voragine's widely distributed thirteenth century biography; and as a youth he stanched the fires of lust by jumping into cold water until he was nearly bloodless.[40]

William of Oliva (1174-1240), for example, was likewise buffeted about by sexual temptation, trying to outdo his fellow youths in debauchery.[41] Plagued by lust, he left home and wandered about at sea, until several visions induced him to become a hermit. Even after the fateful decision, he was visited by "demons who took the form of beautiful women", who danced about and sang in order to seduce the nascent saint. In order to stanch the fires of lust, he prostrated himself in prayer, thrust himself into cold running water, in winter ran about naked in the snow, and flagellated himself. In the autobiography ascribed to Pope Celestine V, the inner sexual turmoil resulting from a nocturnal emission just before he performed the mass, led to a vision which reaffirmed the saint's sense of mission.[42]

The conversion crisis, (which appeared in much contemporary biography as an ilustrative example of the schematic approach to the life cycle) which may have sexual overtones, served as a dramatic denouement dividing the life into two parts, before and after the religious transformation. Indeed, Rufus Jones has pointed out the rather remarkable similarity between the conversion experiences of such diverse figures as Peter Waldo, Francis of Assisi and Raymund Lull.[43] Peter's conversion -- which resulted in the establishment of the Waldensian sect -- began after he had seen a dear friend at the height of his powers fall dead before his eyes. It was hastened along by the singing of a wandering minstrel who bemoaned the debased condition of the Church and recited the popular tale of St. Alexis, who had deserted his wife in pursuit of religion. Peter then sought out a spiritual guide who told him that "If thou wilt be perfect, sell all thou hast and give to the poor and come and follow me." The autobiography attributed to the Catalan philosopher Raymund Lull, the *Vita coetanea* (1311), was intended to report his "conversion to the penitential life and his other deeds".[44] He reported that while writing a love poem addressed to a woman, presumably not his wife, a series of visions of the crucified Christ appeared to him, leading to his abandonment of his family and the Majorcan court in favor of the Christian mission.

Elsewhere, a 'crisis of conversion' in adulthood may be the result of political conflict, which forced a reassessment of one's life. Facio of Cremona (d. 1272), for example, was forced to leave Verona as a result of unspecified 'persecution'.[45] He then undertook a life of penance and pilgrimage, establishing the *Confraternità di Santo Spirito*, although the contemporary biographer noted that Facio had always engaged in charitable activities. A similar path was followed by Lucchesio of Poggibonsi (d. 1226), who was forced to leave home with his wife and children for apparently political reasons (although signs of piety had already appeared in his youth).[46]

Female Chastity

By the thirteenth century, following the establishment of penitential orders, the dangers of sexuality increasingly found their solution within the framework of a chaste form of Christian marriage. The growing involvement of women in the affairs of the Church, represented by a concomitant increase in the number of female saints, demanded new images of female piety. For the cloistered woman, the danger of adolescent sexuality remained a centerpiece of the transition from childhood to adult saintliness. A celibate figure such as the Dominican tertiary of Forlì Benvenuta Bojani (1235-1295), was visited by a malign spirit who asked, "Why do you behave this way? You can do it at another time. For I have come and let us experience the pleasures of the world."[47] How much greater, however, was the temptation of the marriage bed experienced by the lay saint, who might find an ideal in a figure such as St. Alexis, who had renounced marriage.[48]

The increasing involvement of the laity in pioneering new forms of Christian piety, along with the larger numbers of women drawn to the monastery, demanded adaptation of earlier ideals to changing circumstances. The ideal of monastic celibacy was not always a viable option, and required a suitable response in the face of heretical attack. Perhaps the most representative innovation of late thirteenth century piety was the encouragement of female piety as personified by the married female saint.[49] The encouragement of images of female marital piety may be understood in light of the reassertion of antimatrimonial views in vernacular French literature composed between 1260 and 1300, perhaps under the influence of Ovid's *Ars amatoria*. Women were portrayed as capricious, scheming, frivolous, jealous -- in short, the ruin of men, both spiritually and economically.[50]

Up until the twelfth century a pessimistic view of marriage had dominated hagiography, which idealized the virgin martyr of antiquity who had preferred torture at the hand of her pagan suitor to marriage; or the nascent Christian saint who had either fled her proposed groom or invented subterfuges in order to avoid sexual relations. The Church had often seemed dominated by the views of Tertullian, Clement of Alexandria, Jerome or Gregory, who expressed a general distaste for matrimony. By the thirteenth century, however, marriage had become a sacrament, and a spiritual justification for its existence was sought in both Scripture and the fathers. The life of the married female could become a vehicle to explore the ideal of sacramental marriage and conjugal love. Increasingly, such figures as Margaret of Hungary, who bore three children, and Bridget of Sweden, who bore eight, were to become popular.[51] The sacramentalization of marriage in the late thirteenth century paralleled the inundation of medical knowledge concerning sexuality and female anatomy, leading to a more 'scientific' approach to human generation.[52]

But just as the monastic saint passed through a crisis wherein the sexual awakening of adolescence gave way to a celibate resolution, so also the married female, despite the obedience to spouse and family which she was expected to display, necessarily experienced an adolescent crisis which balanced the demands of the marital debt and the strivings of sanctity. St.

Paul had said (I *Corinthians* 7.3-6): "A wife has no authority over her body, but her husband; likewise the husband has no authority over his body, but his wife. You must not refuse each other except perhaps by consent, for a time, that you may give yourself to prayer and return together again lest Satan tempt you, because you lack self-control." Paul thereby enunciated the doctrine of marital debt and the requirement of spousal consent for the cessation of sexual relations.

As Augustine had argued, sex in marriage may be blameless when concupiscence has been tempered through fulfillment of the marital good, namely when one's desires have been mitigated by procreative intent. Marital intercourse, on the other hand, which has been motivated by lust is a venial sin. In *The Good of Marriage* (401) Augustine even praised marriage as the first natural tie of society on which all other institutions are based, for the patriarchal order of the family properly reflects the natural social and heavenly order.[53] Marriage permits the achievement of five praiseworthy goals: 1) the procreation of offspring to people the City of God; 2) personal companionship; 3) the channeling of lust into honorable directions; 4) individual purification through the overcoming of lust and temptation; and, 5) the suppression of more unlawful forms of concupiscence. Marriage was regarded as indissoluble and sacramental, and its only worthy fruit was children. In the *City of God*, Augustine argued that in the ideal marriage the sexual organs obediently serve only their procreative function; the genitalia are subject to one's will and offspring are produced without lust or shame. Only the saints, however, achieve complete self-control and can go beyond the limits of nature to rein in their bodies.[54] One ought not to marry out of ignoble lust, but rather to bear children and avoid fornication. The fact that only married persons -- Noah and his family -- survived the Deluge, indicated to Peraldus the blessedness of the marital state; concubines and prostitutes perished. Further, the Virgin Mary was married.[55]

Sensual pleasure in marriage was therefore sinful and intercourse could rarely occur without sin; sin was only absent if pleasure was absent, as Gratian had said.[56] Connubial rights might of course be suspended in extraordinary cases, when an impediment to marriage had existed or in cases of adultery; on holy days, in sacred precincts, during a woman's purification period or *menses*, abstinence was likewise called for. Conjugal duty was nevertheless obligatory, and could only be evaded by mutual consent, which once given, could not be taken away. Even after the death of one's spouse, if one were to remarry, the children of the second marriage were illegitimate if the first couple had vowed mutual continence. These dicta would lay the groundwork for the sexual conflict found in the married saint of the thirteenth century. But because women were instructed to obey their husbands -- "the wife ought to suffer and let the husband have the words, and to be master, for it is a shame to hear strife between them" -- the onus of responsibility for initiating a virginal marriage usually rested on the woman, who was to counsel her husband sweetly in the marriage bed.[57] For even canon law permitted a man to chastise and beat his wife to correct her faults, just as a schoolmaster may moderately beat his charges with rods.[58]

At the same time, consent had become the foundation of the Christian conception of marriage. And while the mutual marital debt should be honored, chastity should be voluntary. Among those whom circumstances brought to the marriage bed, the three-part division of life into childhood, adolescence and adulthood still applied; but the crisis of adolescent sexuality was played out in the struggle with one's spouse. The late thirteenth century represented a turning point in the documentation of hagiography by providing verbatim connubial conversations concerning the marital debt among the blessed, based upon either accounts by the saint's confessor, or by other reliable eyewitnesses. These are among the earliest examples of immediate personal testimony concerning the solution of the sexual crisis of adolescence.

The vagaries of married life were recorded in the 1363 canonization record of Dauphine of Languedoc (d. 1361) in which her confessor Guillaume de Saint Martial, her personal physician Durandus Andree and her lifelong companion Garsenda Alphanta gave testimony; this is corroborated by the canonization trial (1330) of Elzéar (1283-1323) himself, in which other eyewitnesses had spoken.[59] The primary weakness of such testimony lies in its selectiveness, for the witnesses were requested to respond to particular questions posed by their inquisitors in accordance with a specific papal injunction to seek out evidence of Dauphine's "exemplary life and perfect chastity, the rejection of fleshly desire and the relegation of earthly longings."[60] Her adamant refusal to marry and subsequent vow of chastity were the cornerstones of their testimony; they report her willingness to suffer poverty and the physical abuse she underwent because of the refusal to consider suitors who sought her valuable dowry. She consented to marry Elzéar rather than incur the wrath of King Charles II of Sicily to whose court at Marseilles she had been sent in 1297, on condition that she could abandon her husband when she so desired. The marriage was contracted in February 1300, when Dauphine was twelve and Elzéar was fifteen. Dauphine immediately tried to induce her husband to maintain celibacy by citing the examples of such saints as Caecilia, Valerianus and Alexis, who had sworn vows of chastity with their spouses.[61] Dauphine supposedly said to her husband after the celebration of their marriage: "I was forced into the married state by my parents; I came unwillingly..."[62]

Still callow, Elzéar was grasped by divine fear, and the bridal night was spent in tearful sleeplessness. Elzéar nevertheless persisted, and she consequently simulated illness; the ruse turned into a serious inflamed throat, and the doctors feared for her life. Lying in bed, Dauphine reportedly said: "You know, Elzéar, that unless you consent not to bother me any more about carnal intercourse, I will never get out of this bed alive, since you know I'd rather die than consent to carnal relations."[63] As a result, Elzéar agreed to mutual chastity. They shared the same bed except when he was abroad; she slept fully clothed, and did not touch her husband except to kiss his brow when he was ill. Their marriage lasted twenty-seven years. It was widely believed that Dauphine's *conversacio* with her husband was the principle cause of his virginity and sanctity. The veracity of the witnesses' testimony could be corroborated by those ladies-in-waiting and servants who slept in the couple's bedchamber at the behest of Elzéar's parents, who feared they would not bear children. The two saints played a kind of cat and mouse game with such spies, making believe they were asleep; when the women left the room, they would jump out of bed and pray.[64] Eventually, after spending five chaste years in Italy, Elzéar returned to Provence and the holy couple publicized their secret arrangement on the feast of Mary Magdalene.

The dilemma of marriage as a turning point parallel to the sexual cravings of the cloistered saint was likewise illustrated in the life of Cunegunda of Cracow (d. 1292), who in the course of the licentious banquets preceding her marriage tried to convince her husband Boleslas to maintain his virginity.[65] They agreed to remain chaste for a year; Cunegunda customarily spent the night secretly in a convent. She managed to elicit a promise to extend the arrangement one more year. But by the third year, the duke bridled at the restriction and became involved with other women. He approached Cunegunda's confessor to convince his wife to relent. But she refused to do so; the duke forced himself upon a noblewoman and, consumed with anger, refused to talk to his wife. The couple was eventually reconciled; two women nevertheless slept with them in their bedroom, and when the duke had fallen asleep, Cunegunda arose to pray. After Boleslas' death in 1279 she became a nun. In giving in to her husband's needs reluctantly, the duchess had fulfilled another marital good praised by Augustine, namely the avoidance of a greater sin -- adultery -- caused by the duke's frustrated lust. Cunegunda's case recalled that of Elizabeth of Thuringia (1207-1231), who had not accepted a forced marriage in order to satisfy her own lust, but rather in order to raise children to the service of God, and had found no pleasure in the marriage bed.

Another saint whose life was based on her confessor's testimony is Dorothy of Montau (d. 1394) whom, it was said, consented to marry "out of fear of God, not out of lust". Her marriage was characterized by the three Augustinian goods of wedlock, namely "faith, fertility and sacrament", which fulfilled the marital debt exacted by her sometimes brutal husband.[66] Such obedient fulfillment of God's will to bear children rather than the satisfaction of lust as a motive for the sex act was noted by Hedwig of Silesia's (1174-1243) learned biographer: "Like another Sarah, in fear of the Lord rather than because of her lust, she consented to marry the nobleman".[67] Nevertheless, she fulfilled Paul's injunction to maintain an "unstained marriage-bed". Her salvation was to be achieved through the generation of children. Hedwig of Silesia pointedly kept away from her husband til the very end of each pregnancy in order to avoid the sin of barren sexuality.

Jewish Late Adolescence

In contradistinction to the sexual crises revealed in Christian hagiography, the Jewish sources were bound by the Biblical requirement to "increase and multiply" as the first commandment of God to man, which is repeated four times in Scripture, indicating its centrality to both Jewish ritual and belief.[68] Some went so far as to argue that the failure to multiply is akin to the shedding of blood in its iniquity. Marriage increasingly bore a sacramental character and was further required as: 1) the means of preventing the release of uncontrollable passions which cause transgressions; and, 2) in order to allow man to reach his complete spiritual fulfillment, since an unwed person was regarded as an incomplete human being. As in Christianity, consent was required to marry, although the desireable age remained flexible.[69] Talmudic commentators suggested that one may in fact be forced to marry by age twenty, and everyone must be wed by twenty-four. Further, Jewish hortatory literature contained much frank advice concerning sexual relations and the responsibilities of both parents and children. Jewish pietism, perhaps under the influence of Christian penitential movements, on the other hand, did require chastity of the potential *chasid* (or holy man) and cautioned the avoidance of female companionship. At the same time, the overpowering influence of wives on their husbands was recognized; a good woman could reform an evil man; while an evil woman could lead a virtuous man astray.[70]

As a consequence of such emphasis on the continuation of the species as a divine commandment, although the marriage ceremony may be a chronological turning point initiating its participants into the responsibilities of family and community, in Judaism it was not fraught with the same traumatic and spiritually creative consequences found in Christianity. Only among those who discarded the Jewish faith, did the burden of marriage entail a frustratingly long delay in the appearance of a 'conversion crisis' until middle age. Two earlier examples will suffice. Born Judah son of David and Zipporah of Cologne, the Praemonstratensian Hermann of Scheda (ca. 1107-1170) dated his earliest memory of Christian yearnings to an allegedly prophetic vision at the age of thirteen, which had been interpreted to him in a superficial, materialistic (i.e. Judaical) manner by a respected relative.[71] Sent to Mainz on business at the age of twenty, he became acquainted with the Christian faith under the tutelage of Bishop Ekbert of Münster (1127-1132), learning to penetrate the deeper meaning of Scripture; as a result of conversations with Christian theologians his doubts grew. When they heard of the dangers which Hermann's continued stay in Mainz might entail, his parents had the youth married to a coreligionist, thus delaying his final decision to convert. Samua'al al' Maghribi (ca. 1167) also long nourished religious doubts, but a sense of duty kept him bound to his ancestral faith.[72] This period of uncertainty came to an end in 1163 with a vision of his namesake the prophet Samuel explaining the words of *Deuteronomy* 18.18, "I will raise up for them a prophet like you, one of their own race, and I will put my words into his mouth", as a herald of Mohammed's coming. In a second vision he was accompanied by two Sufis to meet the Prophet, who told him to prepare for a journey to China. He then saw three Sufi ascetics in the marketplace dressed as warriors in the humble dress of Holy War. When he awoke, Samau'al reported his conversion, although for three years he preferred to attribute this pious change of heart solely to rational arguments rather than the prophetic dreams he had experienced; in the end he affirms that the dreams "served merely to alert and to prod me out of my procrastination and inertia..."

Thus, the picture of adolescence was one of both danger and opportunity. The budding youth stands at a crossroads in which his lustfulness blocks the path to moral development. The fires of sexuality must be stanched otherwise the vices of youth will remain his permanent companions, and endanger his everlasting soul. The earlier educational manuals, which largely served a clerical, monastic public, had stressed the repression of such urges through celibacy. By the late thirteenth century, the stress was on marriage as the best means of controlling the youth's sexuality, an antidote long recognized in Judaism. The lives of the saints and the handbooks of advice presented a laudable model of conjugal Christian bliss. The bearing of children, in the framework of a form of wedded harmony in which the sexual urge was kept under firm control, was thus legitimized.

VI. *Notes*

1. Vincent of Beauvais, *Speculum maius*, 4 vols. (Douai, 1624), *Speculum naturale*, XXX.82. Annaeus Seneca, *Controversiae, Praef.* 8-9, ed. A. Kiessling, *Annaei Senecae Oratorum et Rhetorium Sententiae, Divisiones, Colores* (Leipzig, 1872); for English translation, see *Declamationes*, ed. M. Winterbottom, 2 vols. (Cambridge, 1974).

2. Augustine, *Confessiones*, II.i.2; ed. W. Watts (Cambridge, 1959); Ambrose, *De interpellatione Iob et David*, I.vii.21, ed. C. Schenkl, *CSEL*, 32.2 (Leipzig, 1897). "Jacobus", *Omnebonum, B.M. Royal* 6. E. VI, f. 58r.

3. Pierre Bersuire, *Dictionarium*, I, 70 ff; IV, 427-8, in *Opera omnia*, 6 vols. (Cologne, 1731).

4. Thomas of Cantimpré, *De natura rerum. Text*, ed. H. Boese (Berlin, 1973), I.80; Martin Plessner, ed., "Der OIKONOMIKOC der Neupythagorers 'Bryson' und sein Einfluss auf die islamische Wissenschaft," *Orient und Antike*, 5 (Heidelberg, 1928).

5. Giles of Rome, *De regimine principum libri III* (Rome, 1607) II.i.16; this is based on Aristotle's *Politica*, VII.16.

6. Conrad of Megenberg, *Ökonomik*, 2 vols., ed. Sabine Kruger, *MGH. Staatsschriften des späten Mittelalters*, 3 (Stuttgart, 1973), I, 116 ff.

7. Vincenzo Licitra, ed., "Il *Liber legum moralium* e il *De regimine vite et sanitate* di Bellino Bissolo," *Studi medievali*, Ser. 3, 6 (1965), 427-9.

8. Eileen Power, *Medieval Women*, ed. M.M. Postan (Cambridge, 1975), 76-88; "Enseignements à sa fille Isabelle," ed. P.C.F. Daunou and J. Naudet, in *La vie de saint Louis par le confesseur de la Reine Marguerite*, in M. Bouquet et al., eds., *Recueils des historiens des Gaules et de la France*, 24 vols. (Paris, 1869-1904), XX, 82-3; "Conseils de Saint Louis à une de ses filles," ed. J.N. de Wailly, et al., in *Recueils des historiens des Gaules et de la France*, 23 (Paris, 1894), 132.

9. Robert of Blois, *Robert von Blois sämtliche Werke*, ed. Jacob Ulrich, 3 vols. (Berlin, 1889-1895), III, 57-78; Francesco Barberino, *Reggimento e costumi di donna*, ed. E. Sansone (Turin, 1957); Albert Leitzmann, ed., *Winsbekische Gedichte nebst Tirol und Fridebrant*, ed. I. Reiffenstein, new ed. (Göttingen, 1962), 46-66; Pietro Gori, ed., *Dodici avvertimento...* (Florence, 1885); on "courtesy" books, see Diane Bornstein, *The Lady in the Tower. Medieval Courtesy Literature for Women* (Hamden, Ct., 1983), 46-75, 133-4; Alice A. Hentsch, *De la littérature didactique du moyen âge s'adressant specialement aux dames* (Halle, 1903).

10. Giles of Rome, *op. cit*, III.1.18; II.2.3; cf. Claude Thomasset, "La représentation de la génération dans la pensée scientifique médiévale," in *Love and Marriage in the Twelfth Century*, ed. Willy van Haecke and Andries Welkenhuysen (Louvain, 1981), 7, who cites Giles of Rome's *De humani corporis formatione*.

11. William Peraldus, *De eruditione principum*, in Thomas Aquinas, *Opera omnia*, 34 vols., ed. S.E. Fretté (Paris, 1871-1880), XXVII, 628.

12. Giles of Rome, *De regimine*, I. i. 18ff.

13. Bernard Gordon, *De conservatione vitae* (Leipzig, 1570), 39-40; William Peraldus, *op. cit*, 647 ff. An old view held that women were colder and more moist than men, more desirous of coitus in order to expel the excess dampness, wanting to associate themselves with the warmth of the male. See Adelard of Bath, *Quaestiones naturales*, ed. Martin Müller, *Beiträge*, 31.2 (Munich, 1934), c. xlii.

14. Conrad of Megenberg, *Ökonomik*, 109 ff. Philippe de Navarre (1259/60), *Les quatres âges de l'homme*, ed. Marcel de Fréville (Paris, 1888), I.21 suggests that chastizement is the best means of insuring woman's moral virtue.

15. Gilbert of Limerick, *Liber de statu ecclesiae*, in *MPL*, 159: 997: "Nec dico feminarum esse officium orare, arare, aut certe bellare; sed tamen subserviunt, qui orant, et arant, et pugnant." Hugh of Floreffe, *Vita Idae*, in *ASS*, 29 October XIII: 109.

16. Humbert of Romans, *Ad juvenculas sive adolescentulas seculares*, in Carla Casagrande, ed., *Prediche alle donne del secolo XIII* (Milan, 1978), 49 ff.

17. Guibert of Tournai, *Sermo ad conjugatas*, in Casagrande, *op. cit.*, 92 ff. For five sermons on marriage and widowhood (nos. xvii-xxii), see L. Bianchi, ed. *Le prediche di San Bernardino da Siena*, 3 vols. (Siena, 1880).

18. The classic account remains Henry Charles Lea, *The History of Sacerdotal Celibacy in the Christian Church*, 2 vols., 3rd ed. (New York, 1970); E. Jombart, "Célibat des clercs. - en droit occidental," *DDC*, II: 132-146; E. Vacandard, "Célibat ecclésiastique," *DTC*, II.2: 2068-88; P. Delhaye, "Le Dossier anti-matrimonial de l'*Adversus Jovinianum* et son influence sur quelques écrits latins du xiie siècle," *Mediaeval Studies*, 13 (1951), 65-86; A. Fliche, *La Réforme grégorienne*, 3 vols. (Louvain, 1924-37), *passim*.

19. Cinzio Violante, "Quelque characteristiques des structures familles en Lombardie, Émilie et Toscane aux XIe et XIIe siècles," in Georges Duby and Jacques Le Goff, eds., *Famille et parenté dans l'Occident médiéval* (Rome, 1972), 116 speaks of the creation of the conjugal family.

20. Georges Duby, "In Northwestern France: the Youth in Twelfth Century Aristocratic Society," in *Lordship and Community in Medieval Europe*, ed. F. Cheyette (New York, 1968), 198-209; Jane K. Breitscher, "'As a twig is bent': Children and their Parents in an Aristocratic Society," *Journal of Medieval History*, 2 (1976), 181-191.

21. Robert E. Lerner, *The Heresy of the Free Spirit in the Later Middle Ages* (Berkeley, 1972), 20-34 argues that the accusations of unrestrained fornication are without foundation. He takes note of the widespread sermon literature attacking heretics as lecherous. For the marriage doctrines of the early heretics, see Malcolm Lambert, *Medieval Heresy. Popular Movements from Bogomil to Hus* (New York, 1976), 61-2, 109-113, 26-31; cf. also R.I. Moore, *The Birth of Popular Heresy* (London, 1975), *passim*.

22. E. Le Roy Ladurie, *Montaillou, village occitan, de 1294 à 1324* (Paris, 1976), based on the inquisitorial investigation of a small village in Southern France in which heresy and sexual non-conformity were rife, indicates the wide gap between the Church's declarations and the peasants' behavior; on the institutional and theological ramifications of heresy, see Christine Thouzellier, *Catharisme et Valdéisme en Languedoc* (Paris, 1969); Walter Wakefield, *Heresy, Crusade and Inquisition in Southern France 1100-1150* (Berkeley, 1974); J. Guiraud, *Histoire de l'Inquisition au moyen âge* (Paris, 1935-1938).

23. William Harold May, "The Confession of Prous Boneta Heretic and Heresiarch," in *Essays in Medieval Life and Thought Presented in Honor of Austin Patterson Evans*, ed. John H. Mundy, et al. (New York, 1955), 3-30, for the testimony of a female heretic. On women and heresy see Gottfried Koch, *Frauenfrage und Ketzertum im Mittelalter* (Berlin, 1962); idem, "Die Frau im mittelalterlichen Katholismus und Waldensertum," *Studi medievali*, Ser. 3, 5 (1984), 741-774.

24. J. Alberigo et al., eds., *Conciliorum oecumenicorum decreta*, 3rd ed. (Bologna, 1973), 257-8 (c. 50). The extent to which natural philosophy had penetrated theology is indicated by the justification for reducing the prohibited degrees from seven to four: "quia quattuor sunt humores in corpore, quod constat ex quattuor elementis".

25. Caesarius of Heisterbach, *Sermo de Translatione beate Elyzabeth*, in A. Huyskens, ed., *Die Schriften des Cäsarius von Heisterbach über heilige Elisabeth von Thüringen*, in *Publikationen des Gesellschaft für Geschichtskunde*, 43.3 (1937), 388.

26. Sicco Polentino, "Vita beati Antonii Peregrini," *AB*, 13 (1894), 417.

27. Gregory the Great, *Dialogi*, ed. Adalbert de Vogüé and Paul Antin, 2 vols. (Paris, 1978-1980), I.3

28. Jerome, *Vita Pauli Thebaei*, in *MPL*, 20: 159-76.

29. Athanasius, *Vita S. Antonii*, in *MPG*, 26: 835-976.

30. Sulpicius Severus, *Vita S. Martini*, ed. Jacques Fontaine, 3 vols. (Paris, 1967-1969), II.2.

31. Leopold Génicot, "La population en Occident du XIème au XIIIème siècle," *Cahiers d'histoire mondiale*, 1 (1953), 446-462; Georges Duby, "Au XIIème siècle: les 'jeunes' dans la société aristocratique," *Annales (Économies, Sociétés, Civilisations)*, 19 (1964), 835-846; B.H. Slicher von Bath, *The Agrarian History of Western Europe*, trans. Olive Ordish (London, 1963), 78. Many of the religious consequences are dealt with in Lester Little, *Religious Poverty and the Profit Economy in Medieval Europe* (Ithaca, 1978), 79 ff.

32. Odo II of Cluny, *Vita Geraldi Aurilacensis*, in *MPL*, 133: 644: "incitamentis coruptae maturae, solent parvuli irasci, et invidere, et velle ulcisci vel alia huujusmodi attentare."

33. John of Cluny, *Vita Odonis*, in *MPL*, 133: 43-86. This life is based on a conversation held at Rome ca. 939/43 between the author and his subject, and thus comes closer to autobiography than most contemporary sources.

34. John of Lodi, *Vita Petri Damiani*, in *ASS*, 23 February III: 412-433.

35. Mary McLaughlin, "Survivors and Surrogates: Children and Parents from the Ninth to Thirteenth Centuries," in *The History of Childhood*, ed. Lloyd de Mause (New York, 1974), 101-181.

36. John of Lodi, *op. cit.*, 424.

37. For a typology of religious orders, see Raymond Hostie, *Vie et mort des ordres religieux* (Paris, 1972); on the adolescent conversion crisis see Michael Goodich, "Childhood and Adolescence among the Thirteenth Century Saints," *History of Childhood Quarterly*, 1 (1973), 283-309. On monasticism and society, Barbara Rosenwein and Lester Little, "Social Meaning in Monastic and Mendicant Spiritualities," *Past and Present*, 63 (1974), 4-32; Heribert Roggen, "Die Lebensform der hl. Franziskus von Assisi in ihrem Verhältnis zur feudalen und bürgerlichen Gesellschaft Italiens", *Franziskanische Studien*, 46 (1964), 1-54, 287-321.

38. Peter Damian, *Vita Sancti Romualdi*, in *MPL*, 144: 953-1008.

39. *Vitae* by Andrew of Strumi and Atto of Pistoia in *MPL*, 146: 667-703, 765-790.

40. James of Voragine, *Legenda aurea*, ed. Th. Graesse (Leipzig, 1890), 527-38. For the various lives of St. Bernard see M.-M. Canivez, "Bernard de Clairvaux," *DHGE*, VIII, 610-644.

41. Anon., *Vita Gullelmi*, in *ASS*, 11 February I: 496 ff.

42. A. Frugoni, ed., "L'Autobiografia di Pietro Celestino," in *Celestiniana* (Rome, 1954), 67.

43. Rufus Jones, *Studies in Mystical Religion* (London, 1909), 132. Raymund says, "Raymundus tunc sancti Francisci provocatus exemplo venditis mox possessionibus suis." (B. de Gaiffier, ed., "Vita beati Raimundi Lulli," *AB*, 48 [1930], 150).

44. De Gaiffier, *op. cit.*, 130-178 for autobiography. The study of Lull and Lullism has reached mammoth proportions. One may profitably consult J.V. Hillgarth, *Ramon Lull and Lullism in Fourteenth Century France* (Oxford, 1971), 46; E.W. Platzeck, *Raymond Lull*, 2 vols. (Dusseldorf, 1962), I, 10-41; Miquel Batllori, "Sur l'édition de l'Autobiographie de Raymond Lulle par le père de Gaiffier", *AB*, 10 (1982), 683-689.

45. André Vauchez, ed., "Sainteté laïque au XIIIe siècle: la Vie du bienheureux Façio de Crémone, c.v. 1196-1272," *Mélanges de l'Ecole Française de Rome. Moyen âge. Temps modernes*, 84 (1972), 13-53.

46. Martio Bertagna, "Note e documenti intorno a S. Lucchese," *Archivum franciscanum historicum*, 62 (1969), 452-457 for the *Legenda*.

47. Conrad of Castellario, *Vita Benvenutae de Foro-Julii*, in *ASS*, 29 October XIII: 154.

48. On Alexis, see Enrico Josi, "Alessio," *BS*, I, 814-823; Bandouin de Gaiffier, "Intactam sponsam reliquens. À propos de la vie de S. Alexis," *AB*, 65 (1947), 157-195; James of Voragine, *Legenda aurea*, ed. Th. Graesse (Leipzig, 1890), 403-406 for his life. He convinced his wife in their marriage bed to live a life of chastity, divided their wealth, and sailed to Edessa. According to James, Alexis composed an autobiography.

49. On married saints see Selden P. Delany, *Married Saints* (New York, 1935); Marc Glasser, "Marriage in Medieval Hagiography," *Studies in Medieval and Renaissance History*, ser. 2, 4 (1981), 3-34; Richard Kieckhefer, *Unquiet Souls. Fourteenth Century Saints and their Religious Milieu* (Chicago, 1984). For a list of twenty-one *vitae* in which the renunciation of marriage occurs, see de Gaiffier, "Intactam"; Caroline W. Bynum, *Holy Feast and Holy Fast. The Religious Significance of Food to Medieval Women* (Berkeley, 1987); 21, 314 on the considerable rise in female saints in the thirteenth century.

50. Jean-Claude Payen, "La crise de mariage à la fin du XIIIe siècle d'après la littérature française de temps," in Duby and Le Goff, *op. cit.*, 413-430; cf. also D. D'Auvray and M. Tausche, "Marriage Sermons in *Ad Status* Collections of the Central Middle Ages," *AHDLMA*, 47 (1981), 71-119.

51. Glasser, *op. cit.*; Elizabeth Makowski, "The conjugal debt and medieval canon law," *Journal of Medieval History*, 3 (1977), 99-114;

Georges Duby, *Medieval Marriage*, trans. E. Forster (Baltimore, 1978) on changes in matrimony in the later middle ages.

52. Danielle Jacquart and Claude Thomasset, *Sexualité et savoir médical au moyen âge* (Paris, 1985); cf. also M. Anthony Hewson, *Giles of Rome and the Medieval Theory of Conception* (London, 1975).

53. Augustine of Hippo, *The Good of Marriage* (*De bono conjugali*), trans. Charles Wilcox, in *Treatises on Marriage and Other Subjects* (New York, 1955), 3-51.

54. Augustine, *De civitate Dei*, IV. xiii.15-26, in *Corpus christianorum. Series latina*, 48 (Turnholt, 1955).

55. William Peraldus, *op. cit.*, 626-7.

56. Gratian, *Decretum*, C. 32, q. 2, c.1, in *Corpus iuris canonici*, ed. E. Friedberg and E. Richter, 2 vols. (Leipzig, 1879-1880), citing Ambrose, *Super Lucam*, I. c. 1, and Jerome, *Epistolae ad Ephesios* 5, c. 2 cites Augustine, *De bono conjugali*, 6 on the moderate use of marriage to satisfy immodest desire as a venial sin; cf. also c. 6 on the dissolution of marriage. James Brundage, *Law, Sex and Christian Society in Medieval Society*, (Chicago, 1987), 23 ff. on late medieval marriage.

57. Geoffrey de la Tour Landry [1371], *The Book of the Knight and of the Tower*, ed. T. Wright, *EETS*, 33 (1906), 23.

58. "Jacobus," *Omnebonum*, in *B.M. Royal* 6 E.VI., 214r makes the comparison, citing Gratian, *Decretum*, 2. c. vii.q.1.; I. Dist. xxv.c.3. One reason for the establishment of matrimony was to subject women to the domination of men as punishment for the first sin. See Nicholas of Lyra, *Biblia sacra cum glossis interlineari et ordinaria*, 7 vols. (Venice, 1588), *Genesis* III.

59. Jacques Cambell, ed., *Enquête pour le procès de canonisation de Dauphine de Puimichel comtesse d'Ariano* (Turin, 1978); *Processus canonizationis S. Elzeari*, in *ASS*, 27 September VI: 539 ff.

60. Cambell, *Enquête*, 9, 17-18.

61. *Ibid.*, 36. For the *passio* of St. Caecilia, see H. Delahaye, *Études sur le légendier romain des saints de novembre et décembre* (Paris, 1936), 73-76, 194-200. The precedents of the saints were likewise employed by Jane Mary of Maillé (d. 1414), who elicited a vow of chastity from her husband on their marriage couch. See the life by her confessor, a Franciscan of Tours, in *ASS*, 28 March III: 738: "Domino cooperante ipsamque dirigente ut ambo relictis nuptiarum copulationibus, spretaque liberorum propagine, Sponso, qui in caelis est, perpetim se disposuerint applicare"; 745 on her invocation of the saints. Margery Kempe read the vernacular life of Dorothy of Montau and was acquainted with James of Vitry's life of Mary of Oigniès. See W.

Butler-Bowden, trans., *The Book of Margery Kempe* (New York, 1944), I.17, 58, 62. The spiritual lives of many of these figures are discussed in Kieckhefer, *op. cit., passim*.

62. *Processus, op. cit.*, 548.

63. *Enquête, op. cit.*, 36-37.

64. *Enquête*, 40: "ipsius domine conversacio, cum divino adiutorio fuit principium et causa virginitatis [ac] honestatis eiusdem mariti sui."

65. *Vita et miracula Sanctae Cunegundae ducissae Cracoviensis*, ed. W. Ketrzynski, in *MPH*, IV, 690-4.

66. John of Marienwerder, *Vita Dorotheae*, in *ASS*, 30 October XIII: 512: "In quem tamen timore Domini, non attracta libidine consensit."

67. Simon of Trebnitz, *Vita maior S. Hedwigis*, ed. A. Semkowicz, in *MPH*, IV: 514: "Hunc utique nobilem virum ut altera Sara in timore domini non cum libidine consensit suscipere. Non in contrahendo matrimonium illud suorum pocius progenitorum quam voluntatem propriam creditur implevisse, ut ex post facto constare sufficientissime potuit, dum tam notabili se continencie loro strinxit. Coniugali enim vinculo alligata studebat secundum doctrinam apostoli honorabile connubium et thorum immaculatum in omnibus custodire, leges et iura matrimonii peroptime conservare." Another similar case is that of Salome of Poland (1211-1268), see *Vita sanctae Salomae*, in *MPH*, IV: 776 ff.

68. The following is based largely on Elyakim Ellinson, ed., *Ish ve-Ishto, Mekorot halachtiim mevooarim* (Jerusalem, 1979), 37 ff. which contains a selection of primary sources; Ze'ev Falk, *Jewish Matrimonial Law in the Middle Ages* (Oxford, 1966), 41 ff. The didactic Aharon Halevi of Barcelona (?) (13th century), *Sefer ha-Hinukh* (Jerusalem, 1966) which lists the traditional 613 *mitzvot* (commandments) of the Jewish faith, ranks "increase and multiply" as number one, although the obligation clearly rests on the man rather than the woman.

69. Abraham ha-Kohen of Lunel, *Orhot Haim*, ed. Elyakim Schlesinger (Berlin, 1902), pt. 2, 42.

70. *Sefer ha-Hasid* [ca. 1140-1217], ed. R. Margalith (Jerusalem, 1957), cc. 9. 13, 139. Although attributed to Yehudah ha-Hasid, this is probably an early thirteenth century collection of religious and ethical precepts produced in the Rhineland.

71. Hermannus Iudaeus, *De conversione sua*, ed. Gerlinde Niemeyer, *MGH. Quellen zur Geistesgeschichte des Mittelalters*, 2 (Weimar, 1963).

72. Samau'al al Maghribi Ifham al-Yahud, *Silencing the Jews*, ed. and trans. Moshe Perlman (New York, 1962).

VII. *Adulthood and Old Age*

Despite the distinct periods listed in the encyclopedist's introduction, which may reach seven, following adolescence the pattern tended to break down. The classic fourth age, *iuventus*, was often absorbed by adolescence. Thomas of Cantimpré defined the fourth age as *robur*, which begins at thirty-five, when one has reached the height of one's power; but as a result of growing weakness one becomes angry and resentful. This age ends at fifty.[1]

Adulthood

Both Bartholomaeus and Bersuire included chapters under the rubric *vir* which, according to Isidore, derives from *virium*, or strength, since a man is stronger than a woman and ought to control her as the head controls the body.[2] The marital condition was described in a commentary on Fulgentius' interpretation of the marriage at Cana, regarded as a metaphor for the relations between the Church (the bride) and Christ (the bridegroom), who carries his wife away to the marriage bed of Paradise.[3] Just as a man ought to abandon family, friends and country for his wife's sake, exposing himself to death if necessary, so Christ left the family of the angels for the sake of the Church. Somewhat in contrast to the Pauline assertion of male superiority in marriage, Bersuire suggested that man and woman are equal, since Eve was not created out of Adam's feet, but rather his rib, and they are thus more like sister and brother; and just as Christ is productive, a man ought to perform useful labor and good deeds. The defense of a woman by her husband was comparable in Bersuire to the prelate's role in the Church: defending her against tyrants, driving the Devil away by prayer, preaching against the heretics, and eliminating sin through correction.

A citation from *Daniel* 10.5-7 was interpreted by Bersuire to describe the virtues which a man ought to possess: "I looked up and saw a man clothed in linen with a belt from Ophir round his waist. His body gleamed like topaz, his face shone like lightning, his eyes flamed like torches, his arms and feet sparkled like a disc of bronze, and when he spoke his voice sounded like the voice of a multitude." Here, the decorous dress, chaste body, strong soul, handsome countenance, shining intellect, honest labor, charitable heart and truthful speech of man are summarized. A man is especially warned to avoid any hint of effeminacy, citing an ancient philosopher who constantly stroked his beard in order to remind himself of his manhood. An interpretation *in malo* speaks of the leprosy, verbosity, quarrelsomeness, pomposity, mendaciousness, hatefulness, foolishness, greed, lust and cruelty to which a man may be prey.

Bersuire's moralized account of adulthood contained Scriptural citations in which man appears as the personification of Christ, the prelate, a friend, the Devil, and an evil man. Ideally, he is noble, glorious, strong, vigorous, pernicious, impetuous and lazy. In married life, a man ought to love his wife, defending her against evil. At the same time, as the preacher emphasized, in mid-life one should be well on the path to the salvation laid down in adolescence, and take care to scrutinize one's life, assisted by the physician, who cares for one's body, and the priest, who ministers to one's soul.

To Dante, the virtues of manhood, the prime of life, which lasts from twenty-five to forty-five, are that same temperance, fortitude, loyalty, courtesy, justice and love which one at first possesses for oneself in mid-life, and in old age are displayed toward others.[4] The irascibility and lust derived from the uncontrolled appetite of youth are constrained by the bridle of temperance and the spur of courage, like an unbridled horse. The example cited by Dante is again Aeneas, who followed a praiseworthy path after being received by Dido, and even faced the dangers of Hell, armed with courage and temperance, accompanied by the Sybil in search of his father Anchises. Having reached the pinnacle of the arc, in manhood one ought to display love of one's elders who have guided us, and of the young whom we are to guide, in imitation of Aeneas, who commended the Trojan elders to Acestes and instructed his son Ascanius. Courtesy was exemplified when he cut wood for the fire to burn the dead; and loyalty when he established games to honor his dead father, judging the competitors with justice.

"Middle age" generally was given rather short shrift, being vaguely defined by Giles of Rome as the period between youth and old age, possessing the virtues of both; for example, timidity and audaciousness may appear, depending on circumstances.[5] "Virility" is here tempered by a life of reason, suitable to middle age, the most judicious period of all. Many of the prescriptions for health which Giles provided, conforming to the contemporary *Regimen sanitatis*, appear to have been directed at middle age, requiring temperance in food and drink, especially wine. The control of the five senses, the avenues through which temptation enters, is achieved through the moderation preached by Aristotle. Healthy games to Giles are a way of avoiding illicit pleasures; clothes should be selected for pleasure, utility and honor, diversified according to age, class, country, time and complexion.

Many of the regimes for health, along with the *Oecumenicus* of "Bryson" and the mirrors for princes (which often included guides to health) were in fact directed at adult men.[6] While varying little and often quite derivative, they may differ in emphasis depending on the audience to which they were directed. The pseudo - Aristotelian *Secretum secretorum*, probably composed in the tenth century, may properly be regarded as the ancestor of many of the *regimina* directed at adults.[7] Couched as a response to Alexander the Great's request for advice on how to administer his newly-won empire, 'Aristotle' warned against the traditional vices which may weaken his rule, vices which may bedevil every man. Arrogance, bloodthirstiness, and a failure to follow the example of one's ancestors are duly condemned; the basis of one's power is loyalty and the honoring of treaty obligations, otherwise men are in danger of returning to the condition of savage beasts. Learning, especially among one's own progeny, should be encouraged. One should beware of women, whose poisonous (literally) deeds may fell an empire. The author suggested consulting the stars at all times, since God does nothing without cause or reason, which can be revealed through the advice of the learned. Health is to be maintained through an equilibrium of the humors, revealed to the natural philosophers. Evacuation, sleep, rest, motion, diet, etc. should be regulated according to medical guidance, which will determine each person's condition and circumstance. The special diets noted in the *Secretum* were intended to undo the changes of bodily equilibrium which are caused by the seasonal predominance of one human over the others. These prescriptions were found in the encyclopedic and medical sources, and became the common heritage of the educated classes. To judge by their wide dissemination, 'adults' were much concerned to maintain a proper regime of health. Man's microcosmic character, his similarity to other creatures, minerals and plants, was emphasized.

A typical regime of health, for example was Maimonides' *Regimen sanitatis*, which became available in a translation of about 1290 by either Armengaud Blasius of Montpellier (d. 1313) (physician to both James II of Aragon and Pope Celestine V), or John of Capua, from the Hebrew version.[8] While clearly intended to assist adults in the maintenance of good health, Maimonides also commented on childhood, adolescence and old age. Proper washing, diet and moderate exercise were suggested, beginning at the age of three, though no regime which dries out the body is recommended. Children should be fed softened food in order to aid digestion; chicken is especially salubrious, while certain fruits and vegetables should be avoided. Sleep should not be forced on the child, but only when he is tired. Concerning youths, Maimonides allowed the introduction of wine to the diet as an antidote to the feared black bile, which is eliminated through urination. Wine dries out certain organs which ought to be dry, and raises the body temperature, which is good for youths.

Like all the physicians, as opposed to the Christian moralists, Maimonides praised the natural and necessary character of sexual relations. He further provided prescriptions for the treatment of the aged. He laid stress on the psychosomatic treatment of disease. A strong man, possessing a powerful voice and a shining countenance, for example, will appear completely transformed when he hears bad news; his voice will weaken, his face grow pale. A weak-looking man appears revived by the advent of good news, as natural warmth rises to the surface. The physician should therefore observe his patients in order to determine their disposition, especially melancholics, and should learn ethics and philosophy in order to cope with the emotional dilemmas they face. The expulsion of black bile was regarded as particularly important in order to prevent melancholia, which is more common among those inflicted with chest, stomach and foot problems, leading to delirium, confusion and an irrational fear of the dark and of death. An anonymous Hebrew treatise on melancholy, probably based on Constantine the African, suggested that melancholia is more common among the aged because of bad blood and the reduction of warmth in the body, leading to a tearful, sad mien. It may be accompanied also by such disorders as melanoma, epilepsy, tremors and weakened reason.[9]

Maimonides' *Regimen* may be contrasted with the widely read *Book of Beliefs and Opinions* (933) by Saadia Gaon, which had been translated into Hebrew from the Arabic by Judah ibn Tibbon of Lunel in 1186.[10] The first systematic presentation of Judaism as a rational set of beliefs, it contained a chapter on longevity in which Saadia spoke of certain people who believe that one should seek to extend the span of one's life in order to truly realize one's spiritual and physical needs. Such persons recommend regular eating and drinking habits, moderate sexual intercourse, cheerfulness and the avoidance of fearful situations. These suggestions, Saadia argued, conflict with reality, since those who follow such prescriptions do not necessarily extend their lives; one who lives longer in fact suffers more cares, sins more and is more corrupt. Such a pessimistic message strongly contrasted with the guarded optimism of the thirteenth century texts.

This optimism found expression in the work of ibn Falaquera, who argued that, were it not for the conflict and disorder to which man is heir, he would be immortal. Man's body was likened by him to a boat at sea, and his soul to a ship's captain, who steers his craft safely into harbor.[11] Ibn Falaquera's Aristotelian prescription of moderation as a means of sustaining life was a product of the reappearance of such works as *Politics* and the pseudo-Aristotelian *Oecumencius*, which encouraged the publication of manuals of household and family management, such as Bissolo's *Liber legum moralium*. Bissolo strongly praised marriage and suggested how best to maintain a wife's allegiance: refrain from public quarrels; rear one's children well; keep a well-ordered home; and speak in moderate tones. Advice was provided on child-rearing and diet, along with relations with one's guests and neighbors.[12] Bissolo's brief *De regimine vitae et sanitatis* detailed the means of insuring a good life: proper sleep, diet, daily ablutions, piety, avoidance of the cold, moderation in drug-taking and the pursuit of pleasure. The many other *regimina* for health followed a similar formulary pattern, dealing successively with exercise, massages, baths, food, drink, rest, sexual intercourse, evacuation, and the symptoms of disease. Some, like Bernard Gordon's manual, dealt with the control of the emotions, following the Aristotelian principle of moderation: "The body follows the soul in its actions, just as the soul follows the body in its passions."[13]

Old Age

What we have termed middle age was followed by *senectus*, a period which we have seen bore a variety of names. It commences at about fifty and is a consequence, according to Avicenna, of the diminution of the blood supply; those more lacking in blood are more likely to die sooner.[14] All the vices likewise diminish, with the exception of cupidity and tenacity, which dominate, even if one is buffeted by reverses. Thomas of Cantimpré noted that the ancients placed the end of this period at eighty, the moderns at seventy, followed by *decrepita*, which he described as a time when a man's stature is reduced and his intellectual and physical strength are sapped.[15] Those who survive beyond the proverbial seventy rarely recover from illness. Such survival merely increases grief and sorrow. The other encyclopedists, while recognizing the existence of periods after *senectus*, did not elaborate on their character.

According to Isidore, the term *senectus* was derived from *sensus*, because the senses are diminished, when the blood runs cold and men become foolish.[16] As Ambrose noted in his commentary on the *Hexameron*, old age is sweetened by wise counsels and one becomes better equipped to face death, made heroic by the reduction of fleshly lusts.[17] Infirmity of the body likewise produces sobriety of the mind. An oft-repeated tale concerned Sophocles, who was asked in old age whether he still suffered from the pangs of lust.[18] He replied that he was happy to be free, and no longer tyrannized by lasciviousness. Old age could thus be regarded as a time of moral behavior, like the palm tree which only bears fruit as it ages, not in its youth (*Wisdom* 4.9: "an unspotted life is the true ripeness of age.") There are many who may still be saved in old age, which affords an opportunity to exercise prudence and discretion in matters pertaining to salvation, and permits one to contemplate the errors of youth.

A commentary *in malo* of old age took note of the lethal sin and corruption which the physical disfigurement of aging may signify.[19] For the aged possess their own peculiar vices. They are easily angered, rapacious and tenacious, but weak in sustaining what they already have. Their irascibility is a product of coldness, of the lack of vital spirits and heat, which are the sources of pleasure and enthusiasm. Because of their dry constitution, Halys cautioned the aged to reside in more tropical regions; they should avoid excessive exertion, although a brisk, accompanied walk may be salubrious.[20] They ought to bathe in sweet, warm water, refreshing themselves during the day; eat easily digestible food thrice daily, avoiding foods which could cause melancholia or make them phlegmatic, avoiding excessive coition. Avicenna agreed that the expulsion of phlegm from the body is necessary, and may be accomplished through massages and exposure to redolent fragrances.

As Innocent III (d. 1216) had said in his oft-cited *De contemptu mundi*: "The aged are easily challenged, but not easily revived; quick to believe, they are slow to disbelieve; quick to speak, but slow to listen and not slow to quarrel."[21] In Horace's words, "Many ills encompass an old man, whether because he seeks gain, and then miserably holds aloof from his store and fears to use it, or because, in all that he does, he lacks fire and courage, is dilatory and slow to form hopes, is sluggish and greedy of a long life, peevish, surly, given to praising the days he spent as a boy and to reproving and condemning the young."[22] The aged ought to possess the virtue of clear sense and prudence, even if youthful in appearance. All of their physical characteristics possess a moral equivalent. They are bent over from contemplating death and from humility; white-haired out of innocence and purity; dry through the sobriety of abstinence; sad out of the anxiety of divine wrath; slow due to the maturity of deliberation.[23] The ideal of aging was considered to be Abraham (*Genesis* 24.1), of whom it was said: "By that time Abraham had become a very old man, and the Lord had blessed him in all that he did."

John of San Gemignano made use of a passage from *De abusionibus saeculi* attributed to Cyprian[24] describing the physical decrepitude of old age as a means of elaborating on the wretched condition of the sinner in his dotage: "While the eyes grow blind, the ears hear with difficulty, the hair falls out, the face acquires a pallor, the teeth are reduced in number, the skin dries up, breathing becomes labored, the chest feels clogged, a cough roars, the knees tremble, swelling overcomes the ankles and feet."

The loss of natural color in old age, for example, implies the extinction of the warmth of charity found in the sinner. The dissolution of the humors of lust and the flux of concupiscence in the sinner are likened to the loss of humor among the aged.

The attributes of the aged -- incredulity, suspicion, pusillanimity, illiberality, hopelessness, and immodesty -- are the opposite of those found among the young.[25] As a result of long experience the old believe that everyone is trying to deceive them, suspecting most people of evil intentions. Their lack of humor and cold constitution lead to timidity and fear. Because the aged do not expect to earn or accumulate in the future, they are often uncharitable and tight-fisted. They live in the past because there is no hope for the future; nor are they easily embarrassed. On the positive side, they often possess the virtues of temperance, compassion, moderation and a healthy scepticism. The libido at this age is less active, although rather desirous of retaining what it already possesses. The compassion of the aged derives from a desire for friendship and a foolish hope of being treated compassionately by others. Unlike the young, they will not cling pertinaciously to doubtful opinions.

To Dante[26] old age -- *senettute* -- demands the prudence, justice, bountifulness and affability exemplified by Cato and King Aeacus, in order to instruct the young by one's example. At this age, one ought to dispense wisdom freely; this includes physicians and lawyers, although they may charge for the advice directly related to their skills which they have themselves purchased; they ought to take care to pay the tithe and give charity to the poor. One's wisdom should serve as a beacon to others, which is why the Roman senate was made up of the aged. The fourth age of decrepitude in Dante -- *senio* -- is the time when the noble soul has returned to its home port after a long sea journey or its native city after a temporary stay at an inn. Just as the good sailor lets down sails after a long voyage and is met at the gates by the city's citizens, in death one ought to be prepared to encounter the residents of heaven. Two examples of noble souls who disregarded their worldly occupations, even marriage, and retired to religion at the end of their lives, were Lancelot and Guido da Montefeltro (1223-1298).[27] Like the merchant who returns to port thankful for the profits he has made and able to reap their benefits, the noble soul ought to look back at the past without regret. Bernard Gordon[28] suggested that in old age men ought to indulge in contemplation and speculation, concerned with matters divine and angelic (like the Trojan elders) in accordance with their own abilities and needs, governed by prudence and wisdom.

Many observers have noted the increasing interest in approaching death and the tormenting fires of the next world which almost obsessively pervaded European culture after the Black Death. As Chiffoleau has shown, after 1380 the use of the testamentary will became nearly universal, affecting all classes.[29] But this concern with the disposition of one's property in this world and one's soul in the next had already been well established in the late thirteenth century. Between about 1290 and 1330 deathbed testaments included commendation of the soul to God; and the fear of dying intestate and without confession (particularly encouraged by the mendicant orders) became endemic. The loss of attachment to one's traditional roots and family which we have already observed in contemporary autobiography found expression in: 1) the adolescent crisis of sexuality and conversion; and, 2) the theme of spiritual and physical wandering found in such figures as Celestine V, Lull, Abulafia and others. This loss of roots presumably contributed to the sense of melancholia which so many contemporary treatises addressed. The aged were thus warned to come to terms with the next world, where they would stand in judgement, unprotected by the honors of this world and the protective ties of family. In order to avoid the terrors of Hell, the moralists, in an oft-quoted verse, thus demanded a confession before death which would be "simple, humble, pure, faithful, utterly truthful, spare, discreet, free, modest, completely secret, tearful, quick, accusatory and compliant."[30] This interest in complete confession before death parallels the fear expressed by parents that a new-born would die before baptism, and thus fail to achieve salvation.

The effectiveness of the Church's campaign in the late middle ages to inculcate the importance of confession before death is well illustrated by an episode drawn from the canonization records of Charles of Blois (d. 1364), Duke of Brittany, held at Angers, and reported by several eyewitnesses, including the parish priest of Ploegeznou in the diocese of Tréguier. It had occurred on the tenth night after the feast of Epiphany, 1369; a certain Evenus Floci in the village of Pabu had lain near death for several days and was attended by family and neighbors.[31] Suddenly, although all signs of his coming death had appeared, he excitedly arose as if from a deep sleep and said, "have you all seen what I saw?" The assembled bystanders asked what he had seen, and he recounted the following vision: "It seems to me that my soul had exited from my body, and that immediately two horned, black, terrible demons came to snatch away my soul to Hell, because I had been condemned, as it seemed to me, as a result of a horrible sin I had committed seven years ago [1362], which, because of shame, I had not wanted to confess to anyone, and which I had remembered, although I had confessed other sins. I then recalled the Lord Charles, and invoked him in my heart that he should give me succor. Said Charles then appeared to me garbed in white clothes, holding a lance in his hand, with which he drove away the demons, and then left, and thereby saved my soul from them. He told me to confess that sin quickly, if I would like to be saved; that I had only a brief time more to live, that I would shortly die, and he disappeared with them." After these words, the priest Jacobus Dren was called. Evenus showed due contrition, confessed his horrible sin, was absolved, and died. Thus, if such a strong sense of penitential guilt had reached the peasantry of Brittany, it may be supposed that the Church had done an effective job inculcating its ideology to a very wide circle.

A similar tale intended to illustrate the grave danger which threatened those who failed to confess, especially if they offended a particular saint by their omission, comes from the protocol of miracles attributed to the shepherdess Giovanna da Signa (d. 1307).[32] During the plague year of 1348, twenty-four men joined together to found the *Compagnia della Spirito Santo:* under the patronage of the Carmelites of Tuscany, with the aim of providing material and spiritual aid to plague victims. Having taken counsel with the provincial prior, the men confessed and held communion before undertaking their task, with the exception of one Morozzo Tendi da Signa, who promised to confess at a later date. Dressed in white, swearing mutual aid, they began a procession through the territory of Gangalandi, which took them to the parish church at Signa, which housed relics belonging to Giovanna. In the course of a solemn mass when her relics were displayed, the aforesaid Morozzo, who hadn't confessed for twenty years, tried three times unsuccessfully to kiss the relics and was driven back as if by a demon, falling to the ground with a loud crash. Gripped by fear, his confession was heard by all the onlookers, and three days later he died. While the narrator intended to demonstrate the great power of the saint and her revenge against those who ill-treated her relics, this story further indicates the kind of fear which the Church sought to engender among those who had failed to confess.

Extension of Life

The description of old age thus stressed the physical and moral corruption to which the aged are heir, and the terrors which awaited the unconfessed sinner. At the same time the translation of Aristotle's *Parva naturalia* containing treatises dealing directly with the vicissitudes of aging and the conditions necessary for the prolongation of life, led after about 1240 to a lively commentary on the Aristotelian texts at Paris and a heightened interest (albeit apparently largely academic) in the care and treatment of the aged and the possibilities of extending the human life span.[33]

In his treatise on the length and shortness of life Aristotle had noted the vast differences between *genera* and species and even within the same genus (for example, two men) with respect to the duration of life, and inquired whether there are single or multiple causes to these differences.[34] All things are in a permanent state of transition and are acted upon by the environment in either a favorable or unfavorable way, which permits their natures to be more or less enduring. The Aristotelian position argued that if contrary qualities are contained within the same object, it cannot endure, or remain eternal, especially if it contains matter, which is changeable and destructible. Since man is composed of four constituent elements -- earth, air, fire and water -- their relationships may have some bearing on the duration of life. Averroes (d. 1202) (whose commentary was read in conjunction with Aristotle) added that the preponderance of active elements (fire and water) over passive (air and earth) is a further condition.[35] Among the animals, blood-bearing creatures such as elephants and men are longest-lived. As a rule, the larger outlast the smaller. Corporeal beings consist of hot, dry, cold and moist materials, and old age represents a predominance of the dry and cold; while animals are naturally moist and warm. A long life demands a sufficiently high concentration of warmth and moisture to retard congealing.

To Aristotle, the coursing of the blood through the body originating in the heart is the giver of life; when the heart grows cold, death ensues. Furthermore, in order to avoid degeneration the production of waste should be minimized, as should excessive copulation of seed, which is a form of waste which causes dryness, as does physical labor. Those who dwell in warm, humid climates are likely to outlive others; nourishment and fat further increase life expectancy. Johannes Magistri disputed the life-giving properties of humidity and moisture on the grounds that during the summer meat putrified more rapidly; one might even argue that coldness and dryness by their nature possess qualities which repel outside poisons. In the end, he concurred, however, with Aristotle, since dead animals are demonstrably cold and dry.[36]

Plants tend to outlive animals because their viscosity allows them to retain moisture and to continually renew themselves. And since every part of the plant potentially includes a root and stem, longevity is enhanced. Aristotle believed that the male tends to outlive the female because the upper half of the male body is larger and possesses warmth, since the cold resides in the lower half. Averroes listed those who are likely to live longer, differing somewhat with his mentor: *castrati* outlive those who copulate; mules outlive horses; women outlive men; those who dwell in warm, moist climates outlast denizens of other regions; warm, wet serpents outlive others; those who dwell in sea isles outlast continental inhabitants.

Peter of Spain's (d. 1277) commentary on Aristotle argued that the warmth which supports life is supplied by sperm, which is sustained by the daily intake of nourishment in moderate and temperate doses, a view to which Giles of Rome also subscribed.[37] Thus, those creatures which preserve their sperm are more likely to live longer. Of the four elements, air is the least destructible, and thus its retention is a further spur to the prolongation of life. To Peter of Spain, during the first four ages of life (*iuventus, pueritia, adolescentia* and *perfecta iuventus*) til age forty-eight, one retains the necessary warmth and humidity. In old age, coldness and dryness set in, although excessive warmth may indeed also dissipate the body's natural humidity. There are, he said, six principle ingredients which affect the body's longevity: 1) the combination of the four elements; 2) the diversity of the complexions; 3) the disposition of the humors; 4) the integrity of the body's members; 5) the perfection of the virtues; and, 6) the strength of the operations and the condition of the spirit. Other factors include age, coloring, sex, weight, etc. Peter agreed with Aristotle that the male outlives the female, although the excessive emission of sperm induces dessication and death, as do labor and continuous movement. The controversy over which climate is most salubrious was resolved by Peter with a citation from Constantine the African, who noted that animals in temperate climates live longest.

In his commentaries on the Aristotelian corpus, Albertus Magnus (ca. 1200-1280) generally followed Avicenna in providing a four-part division of life into *pueritia* (til age 30), *status protensus* (til 35/40), *aetas diminuendi* or *aetas virilis* (til 50) and *senectus*.[38] In the *De aetate* he noted Ptolemy's parallel between the waning of the moon and the aging of man; the *Meteora* related the ages to the seasons, elements and parts of the day; a scheme which, we have seen, was adopted by Dante.

Perhaps the most interesting treatment of the Aristotelian corpus is found in the works of Roger Bacon (ca. 1219 - ca. 1292), although as George Sarton has said: "The bibliography of Bacon's work is made especially difficult because of his habit of rewriting some of them many times or of using the same material over and over again in different ways."³⁹ Thus, Bacon's treatment of aging and the ages of man appeared in several treatises, although the same themes tended to be repeated. The earliest work, his *De retardatione accidentum senectutis* (which appeared in both a long and short version) was begun in about 1236 at the request of an unidentified Jean de Châtillon and Philip de Grève, chancellor of Paris (1218-1236). It was dedicated to a secular prince, possibly Alphonse de Poitiers, brother of Louis IX (who suffered from an incurable disease in 1252, but recovered and died in 1271) and was sent to Pope Innocent IV (1244-1252).⁴⁰ The work may have been occasioned by a study of Aristotle's *Parva naturalia* and relied heavily on the chapters in Haly Abbas' *Liber regalis* concerned with aging (translated by Stephen of Antwerp in 1127).

With Aristotle, Bacon argued that the decline of natural heat, caused by infection, negligence or ignorance, is the primary cause of senescence -- which parallels the aging of the world -- causing the decay of natural moisture and an increase in extraneous moisture, a process which accelerates after forty-five or fifty. This aging process can be retarded by a proper regime of health, or by the application of occult medicines. Among the causes of such reduced heat are the motions of the body and mind, poor digestion, the consumption of meat, evil thoughts and cares, and an increase of phlegm. The natural moisture which strengthens life is situated in the heart, veins and arteries. Among the accidents of old age enumerated by Bacon are gray hair, paleness, wrinkled skin, bleary-eyedness, weakness of one's faculties and strength, an overabundance of phlegm or mucous, foul excreta, shortness or weakness of breath, an angry or disquieted disposition, and a loss of sensory power.

In his *Liber de conservatione iuventutis*, agreeing with Aristotle, Bacon argued that the dryness and coldness which weaken the natural body heat, may be caused either by the course of nature or by improper care.⁴¹ In order to correct this imbalance, warmth and moisture can be retained through attention to a proper diet, digestion, sleep or rest, bowel functions, good air, exercise, control of the passions, and pleasurable activity. People will age even before the high point of beauty and strength between forty-five and fifty because of insufficient concern for good health. Man is by nature potentially immortal, and even after having sinned could live a thousand years, as Joseph did. Since this abbreviation is accidental it can in part be repaired, for the corruption does not derive from Heaven, but is a result of ill health. In the *Opus maius* (1266/7), he argued that the corruption of the fathers (especially immoral activity, which weakens the body) may be inherited by the sons.⁴² Because of the hereditary character of corruption, this degeneration continues from generation to generation, and the reduction of life multiplies. If this process were to continue, the human race would eventually come to an end. The suitable remedy for this state of affairs is a proper regimen of health beginning in youth, in order to guarantee that one lives at least as long as one's parents. Education, which is aided by the natural innocence of youth, is one of the means recommended to suppress natural vice.

Old age occurs as a result of the weakening character of nature, the loss of the humors, excessive coition, bloodletting or phlegm, and can be restored through proper food and drink, long sleep, rest and quietude, pleasant odors, sights and sounds, use of a soft bed, and the avoidance of unpleasantness. In the *De conservatione iuventutis* Bacon devoted much attention to the potions and medical aids which can be applied against aging, and such rejuvenating pleasures as good music, reading, conversation and gazing at handsome persons.

On several occasions Bacon argued that art can improve upon nature, and that through a knowledge of astrology, alchemy, mathematics (perspective) and scientific experiment the duration of life may be extended, since the shortening of life is a consequence of human error, which can be ameliorated.[43] The role of the sun's rays in particular was stressed as a catalyst in the preparation of therapies for the prolongation of life. The final aim is the restoration of the balance of complexions in the body, as had been the case before the Fall. For after corporeal death, God is able to reconstitute human remains at the Resurrection in such a way as to guarantee an immortal equilibrium of the elements; and through 'artificial' means man can likewise invigorate himself through the application of reason. Several examples of wonder drugs were cited by Bacon from unspecified papal letters, Aristotle, Pliny, Avicenna and others.

In his version of the *Secretum secretorum* Bacon had spoken of a special medicine which had cured Alphonse of Poitiers of a disease which had made him greedy, pusillanimous, sad, melancholy, weak, weighed down in body and soul.[44] The *De retardatione* likewise contained a list of *occulta* or secret remedies which allegedly helped to retard old age, among them gold, rosemary, ambergris, viper's flesh, human blood, the bone of a stag's heart and pearls.[45] Bacon often returned to the theme of the occult medicines, noting that there are some remedies which have not as yet been discovered, but which will be found through experiment and through observing the habits of animals, some of which have been described by Aristotle, Pliny, Artephius and others.[46] On several occasions Bacon reported a rustic ploughman in the time of King William of Sicily (1151-1189) who had discovered the elixir of life buried in a golden vessel; after drinking the beverage and washing himself in it, his youth was restored and he was made a porter to the king. Bacon reported that Augustus Caesar lengthened his life through goodness and a certain potion. He also told of a man held captive by the Saracens who acquired a medicine which allowed him to live five hundred years; of the Briton Nemus who lived three hundred years by smearing an unguent over all of his body, except the soles of his feet; and of Artephius, who lived 1025 years by studying the life-giving properties of herbs, stones and animals. Bacon noted that in his own day in rural areas there were men who lived 160 years without the aid of physicians.

Engelbert of Admont in his *Liber de causis longaevitatis hominum ante diluvium*,[47] drew many of the same conclusions as Bacon concerning the possibility of prolonging life through an intelligent reading of the stars, proper regimen of health and artificial means. He attempted to wed natural science to Scripture by beginning with a long discussion of life span prior to the Deluge, arguing that life expectancy has been progressively growing shorter. Before the Flood there had been those who lived up to one thousand years, while afterwards the patriarch Abraham only reached one hundred and seventy-five. In Abraham's time, the third age of the world, men could still father children in their eighties, and women in their sixties. In David's time, the fourth period of history, life expectancy had been reduced to the seventies or eighties, with rare exceptions.

Engelbert argued that the long life span of our ancestors had been caused by the will of God, since the natural conditions which obtained prior to the Flood might in fact shorten one's life. Herbivorous animals, for example, live shorter lives, he said, while many creatures only became carnivorous after the Flood. Nevertheless, the pure air and water along with the restorative power of plants assisted the extension of life, even after the expulsion from Eden. The lives of all men have been shortened to a large extent because of the corrupting character of lust, and the further we get chronologically from Paradise, the shorter our lives become. Following the Deluge, the turbulence, infection, and putrefaction of the Flood further hastened death. Still, he added (in agreement with the other scholastics) that life may be prolonged through such extrinsic causes as place, time, food, drink, rest, sleep, movement, exercise, leisure, the passions, climate, etc. Following Aristotle, he also stressed the retention of warmth and moisture as the means of extending life. But because humans are more dissimilar to their parents than are other creatures, the likelihood of breaking the precedent of an ever-shortening life span is greater. Engelbert placed the maximum life span in his day at eighty-five years old: thirty-five years of youth; fifteen years of *status*; and thirty-five years of old age.

VII. Notes

1. Thomas of Cantimpré, *De natura rerum, Text*, ed. H. Boese (Berlin, 1973), I, 81.

2. Isidore of Seville, *Etymologiae*, ed. W.M. Lindsay, 2 vols. (Oxford, 1911), XI.1; Pierre Bersuire, *Dictionarium*, IV, 210-222, in *Opera omnia*, 6 vols. (Cologne, 1731); Bartholomaeus Anglicus, *De rerum proprietatibus*, ed. Georg Barthold (Frankfurt, 1601), VI. 13.

3. Fulgentius, *Liber ad Scarilam de incarnatione filii...*, 41, in *Opera Fulgentii*, ed. J. Fraipont, *Corpus christianorum. Series latina*, 91 (Turnholt, 1968), 346.

4. Dante Alighieri, *Il Convivio*, ed. G. Busnelli and G. Vandelli, 2nd ed. (Florence, 1964), IV.

5. Giles of Rome, *De regimine principum* (Rome, 1607), II. IV. V. 4.

6. Martin Plessner, ed., "Der OIKONOMIKOC des Neuphythagorers 'Bryson' und sein Einfluss auf die islamische Wissenschaft," *Orient und Antike*, 5 (Heidelberg, 1928).

7. For editions, see Reinhold Möller, ed., *Mittelhochdeutsche Prosaübersetzung des 'Secretum secretum'* (Berlin, 1963); see also M. Grignaschi, "L'origine et les metamorphoses du 'Sirr-al asrâ,'" *AHDLMA*, 43 (1976), 7-112.

8. I have used the Hebrew edition, R. Moshe ben Maimon, *Hanhagat ha-Briut be Tirgumo shel Moshe ibn-Tibbon*, ed. S. Muntner (Jerusalem, 1957). Another thirteenth century regimen (in poetic form) is by the encyclopedist Shemtov ben Joseph Falaquera, *Iggeret Battei Hanhagat ha-Guf ve-ha-Nefesh, oh Battei Hanhagat ha-Guf ha-Bari*, ed. S. Muntner (Jerusalem 1950). A treatise which draws heavily on both Maimonides and Aristotle is Henry Malter, ed., "Shem tov ben Joseph Palquera II. His 'Treatise of the Dream'," *Jewish Quarterly Review*, N.S. 1 (1910-11) 451-501 [Hebrew], which advises holding one's tongue, i.e. not criticizing either religion or the head of state, as a means of prolonging life, for conflict is the cause of a shortened life. The rather 'puritanical' tone of this work, somewhat unusual in Jewish sources, suggests that Falaquera was celibate.

9. S. Muntner, "Al-ha-Melancholia, le Regel Yovel ha-Elef le-Moto shel Yizhak ben-Shlomo Yisrael," *Ha-Rofeh ha-Ivri*, 25 (1952), 85-94 also notes other texts devoted to melancholia.

10. Saadia Gaon, *The Book of Beliefs and Opinions*, trans. Samuel Rosenblatt (New Haven, 1967), Treatise X. c. 11.

11. Falaquera, *Iggeret, op. cit.*

12. V. Licitra, ed., "Il *Liber legum moralium* e il *De regimine vite et sanitatis* di Bellino Bissolo," *Studi medievali*, Ser. 3, 6 (1965), 405-454.

13. Bernard Gordon, *De conservatione vitae* (Leipzig, 1570), 79.

14. Avicenna, *Liber canonis*, trans. Gerard of Cremona (Venice, 1507), I. III.iii.1; Bersuire, *Dictionarium*, VI, 86-7 (*senectus*). Some of the following material is dealt with in Georges Minois, *Histoire de la viellesse* (Paris, 1987).

15. Thomas of Cantimpré, I. 82-3.

16. Isidore of Seville, XI. 2. 27-30; Vincent of Beauvais, *Speculum maius*, 4 vols. (Douai, 1624), *Speculum naturale*, XXXI. 87.

17. Ambrose, *Hexameron*, in *Opera omnia de Sant'Ambrogio. I sei giorni della creazione*, ed. Gabriele Banterle (Milan, 1979), I.viii.31.

18. Valerius Maximus, IV.iii.2 in *Factorum et dictorum memorabilium libri novem*, ed. C. Kempf (Leipzig, 1888); Vincent of Beauvais, XXXI. 87 also cites Cicero, *De senectute*, ed. W.A. Falconer (Cambridge, Mass, 1964), XI. 39, 49, 24-5; Jerome, *Super Joannem*, 13 (*MPL*, 35: 1472-3); Fulgentius, *Mitilogiarum libri tres*, III.iv. 711, ed. R. Helm, *Opera* (Leipzig, 1898).

19. Bersuire, *Dictionarium*, VI. 86-7.

20. Avicenna, *Liber canonis*, I. Gen. II, doct. III, c.I.; Haly Abbas ['Ali ibn-Abbas], *Liber regalis*, trans. Stephen of Antioch, in *Liber totius medicine*... (Lyons, 1523), II. I.2; al-Razi [Muhammed ibn Zakariya Abu Bakr], *Liber Rasis ad Almansorem* (Venice, 1497), IV. 31.

21. Innocent III, *De contemptu mundi*, I. 10-11 (*MPL*, 217: 706).

22. Horace, *De arte poetica*, 169-74, in *Carmina*, ed. F. Vollmer (Leipzig, 1912); on the discomforts of old age see A. Hilka, ed., *Das Leben und die Sentenzen des Philosophen Secundus* (Breslau, 1910), 19; Cicero, *De senectute*, XI,34, 36, ed. E. Behrens (Leipzig, 1883); Virgil, *Georgics*, III. 66-8, 97-100 in *Opera*, ed. O.E. Ribbeck (Leipzig, 1894); Quntillian, *Institutio oratoria*, I, ed. H.E. Butler, 2 vols. (Cambridge, 1921-2); Publilius Syrus, *Sententiae*, 212, ed. E. Woefflin (Leipzig, 1869), 80.

23. Bersuire, *Dictionarium*, IV. 86-7. These characteristics of aging come from the standard medical sources.

24. John of San Gemignano, VI.52; *Summa de exemplis et rerum similitudinibus* (Venice, 1584), VI. 52; Cyprian(?), *De duodecim abusionibus saeculi tractatus*, in *MPL*, 4:949. P. Godet, "Cyprien (Saint)," *DHGE*, III.2: 2465 notes that this work remains of unknown authorship and provenance.

25. Giles of Rome, *De regimine principum* (Rome, 1607), II. IV. c. 3.

26. Dante Alighieri, *op. cit.*

27. Guido da Montefeltro, a Ghibelline *capitano*, became a Franciscan in 1296, and appears in Dante's *Inferno*, XXVII. 61 ff.; see Robert Davidsohn, *Geschichte von Florenz*, 8 vols. (Berlin, 1908), II, *passim.*

28. Bernard Gordon, *op. cit.*, 10.

29. Jacques Chiffoleau, *La comptabilité de l'au dela. Les hommes, la mort et la religion dans la region d' Avignon à la fin du moyen âge (vers 1320-vers 1489)* (Rome, 1980), *passim.*

30. Thomas of Argentina, *Compendium theologice veritatis* (Strassbourg, 1489), IV.24.

31. François Plaine, et al., *Monuments du procès de canonisation du B. Charles de Blois duc de Bretagne 1320-1364* (Saint-Brieuc, 1921), 313-318.

32. *Vita et miracula B. Ioannae de Signa*, in *ASS*, 9 November IV: 287. Another tale of the vengeance wreaked on a woman who hadn't confessed for forty years is found in the *Miracula* of Bridget of Sweden (d. 1373), in *ASS*, 8 October IV: 543.

33. Some of this is briefly discussed in Paul Lüth, *Geschichte der Geriatrie* (Stuttgart, 1965), 101-124.

34. Aristotle, *On the Soul. Parva naturalia. On Breath*, ed. and trans. W.S. Hett (Cambridge, Mass., 1935). 387-426.

35. For Averroes' commentary see Harry Blumberg, ed., *Averroes' Epitome of the Parva Naturalia* (Cambridge, Mass. 1961); and Aemilia Ledyard Shields, ed., *Corpus commentariorum Averrois in Aristotelem*, VII. 1 (Cambridge, Mass., 1949).

36. Johannes de Magistris, *Questiones perutiles supra tota philosphia naturali* (Venice, 1490), *De longitudine et brevitate vite.*

37. Pedro Hispano, *Obras filosoficos. III.*, ed. Manuel Alonso (Madrid, 1952), 404-490. Peter is also the author of a *Regimen sanitatis* addressed to Frederick II. See Maria Helena da Rocha Pereira, "Um manuscrito inedito do 'Liber de conservanda sanitate' de Pedro Hispano," *Studium generale*, 9 (1962), 99-105. The commentary by Adam of Buckfield, *Oxford, Corpus Christi*, 114, ff. 235r-237r terms warmth the "nobilissimum elementum" because of its life-giving properties; cf. Giles of Rome, *Commentationes physicae et metaphysicae* (Rome, 1582), 861-4; John of Jandun, *Quaestiones in libros Aristotelis* (Venice, 1562), 86-7.

38. Albertus Magnus, *De aetate, sive de juventute et senectute liber*, in *Opera omnia*, 38 vols., ed. August Borgnet (Paris, 1890), IX, 305-319; on childhood, see *De caelo et mundo*, 82, in *Opera*, V, 45 ff; *De animalibus*, ed. Hermann Stadler, 2 vols. (Münster, 1916), I, 823-7 on

the ages of man; this is based on Avicenna's *De animalibus*, a commentary on Aristotle, and Thomas of Cantimpré's *De natura rerum*; see Pauline Aiken, "The Animal History of Albertus Magnus and Thomas of Cantimpré," *Speculum*, 22 (1947), 205-225.

39. Sarton, III.1, 954.

40. Roger Bacon, *De retardatione accidentium senectute* ..., ed. A.G. Little and E. Withington, *Opera hactenus inedita Rogeri Baconi*, fasc. 9 (Oxford, 1928), 1-89. See also his treatises on old age, *De universali regimine regum et seniorum* (*ibid.*, 90-95), and *De balneis senum et seniorum* (*ibid*, 96-97); on Roger, see Stewart Easton, *Roger Bacon and his Search for a Universal Science* (Westport, Ct., 1952), 24, 193; A.C. Crombie and J.D. North, "Bacon, Roger," *DSB*, I, 377-385.

41. Roger Bacon, *Liber (Sermo) de conservatione iuventutis*, in *Opera*, fasc. 9, 120-143.

42. Roger Bacon, *Opus maius*, VI. xii.2, 3 vols., ed. J.H. Bridges (London, 1897-1900), II, 204 ff. : "Et ideo patres corrumpuntur, et generant filios corruptos et habentes dispositionem ad mortis festinationem."; see also extract from *Liber sex scientiarum*, in *Opera*, fasc., 9, 181-186.

43. Roger Bacon, *Epistola, de secretis operibus artis et naturae et de nullitate magiae*, ed. J.S. Brewer, in *Rerum Britannicarum Scriptores*, 15 (London, 1859), 538-542.

44. Roger Bacon, *Secretum secretorum* ..., ed. Steele, *op. cit.*, 105.

45. *De retardatione*, 15-56. Reporting on recent studies of the biology of aging, Erik Eckholm says that "scientists ... regard reports from Asia, the Soviet Union and Ecuador of this or that Shangri-la as discredited, and describe various potions for life extension as snake oil" in "Aging Studies Point towards Ways to Slow It," *New York Times, Science Times Supplement*, June 10, 1986, pp. 15, 17.

46. *Sex scientiarum*..., 182; *De secretis* ..., 538 ff.; *Opus maius*, 290.

47. Engelbert of Admont, *Liber de causis longaevitatis hominum ante diluvium*, in Bernard Pez, ed., *Thesaurus anecdotorum novissimus*, 8 vols. (Augsburg, 1721), I. 1, 437-502.

VIII. Conclusion

The late thirteenth and early fourteenth centuries were an optimistic time, when the potential for human development and rehabilitation through the application of reason, philosophical knowledge and medical therapy were recognized. The translation, publication, commentary and assimilation of a wide range of materials drawn largely from patristic, Arabic and classical sources, such as the *Regimen sanitatis*, the *Secretum secretorum*, the treatise by "Bryson" and the Aristotelian *Parva naturalia*, brought a host of recipes for self-improvement before a wider audience. Through such reference tools, as concordances, indices, encyclopedias, collections of *exempla* and saints' lives, the speculations of the learned were transmitted to a more popular audience.

A concern for personal development coincided with the appearance of autobiographical confessions, which assumed the feasibility of correcting sin through the cure of the soul, just as the medical tradition assumed the correction of physical ills through the application of medical therapy. The emphasis on sacramental confession afforded an opportunity for the simple believer to undertake a retrospective examination of his past, to put it into some schematic perspective. This same meliorism was found in the mirrors for princes, which counselled the rectification of the sovereign's moral faults and suggested schemes to insure the public good through proper governance of the state. The education of the young, both male and female, and a proper understanding of the virtues and vices of each stage of life were regarded as necessary concomitants to good government.

The scholastic synthesis of the thirteenth century schools was based on the kind of cross-fertilization of disciplines which allowed both the theologian and the philosopher to deal with the ages of man in his own peculiar way, while drawing on ancillary sciences. Thus, such diverse figures as Thomas of Cantimpré, Vincent of Beauvais, Conrad of Megenberg, John of San Gemignano, and Raymund Lull, many of whom were associated with the friars, reflected on the ramifications of each stage of life within different literary and intellectual frameworks. On the other hand, the two traditions of hagiography and natural philosophy maintained an independent character. On the one hand, Thomas of Cantimpré in his *Vita* of Lutgard of Aywières divided the saint's life into three periods, in accordance with the three phases of spiritual development: the *vita inchoantium*, the *vita proficientium* and the *vita perfectorum*.[1] The first stage dealt with her life as a Benedictine, the second as a Cistercian, and the third as a time of spiritual perfection. In his *De natura rerum*, on the other hand, Thomas presented a scheme of seven ages based on Isidore of Seville and Avicenna, each with its own characteristics; and in his exemplaristic *Bonum universale de apibus*, in accordance with the tradition of natural philosophy, he attempted to derive moral principles of human behavior from the life of the bees.

Nevertheless, one occasionally finds the appropriation of images drawn from natural history by hagiographers as a means of placing their subjects in a wider cosmic context. Caesarius of Heisterbach in his *Sermo de translatione Beati Elyzabethe* (1238) likened Elizabeth of Thuringia's moral virtues to the properties of the date-palm, the cedar and cypress trees.[2] A hint of John of San Gemignano's biological knowledge is found in his comparison of Seraphina of San Gemignano and Jesus to the showers which bless the world with fertility.[3] Conrad of Megenberg likewise described Erhard of Bamberg as a blooming rose among youths.[4]

In the face of the efflorescence of interest in the healthful enjoyment of life and its prolongation, the apologetic argument, grounded in Scripture, that the extension of life is undesireable, contrary to human nature, a violation of the natural order, and a contradiction of the doctrine of original sin, found fewer adherents.[5] Such an optimistic faith in man's possibilities, already voiced by the natural philosophers of the twelfth century, was paralleled by a belief in the reparative value of progressive revelation. It was given material confirmation by great material and demographic advancement, which only began to slow down around 1300. The sharp population rise had two direct consequences which encouraged interest in the human life cycle: 1) an increasing number of youngsters required child-care and education outside the monastic framework; and, 2) a larger number of persons survived into middle and old age, demanding greater attention to the problems of senescence and the maintenance of good health in mid-life.

A summary portrait of the human life cycle achieved universal currency by the late thirteenth century. By combining the moral, biological and spiritual ramifications of each age found in such sources, the public acquired a multilevel understanding of the organic growth of the individual from birth to death, a reflection of the dynamic tale of genesis, development and dessication found in nature and history.

Prenatal life was perhaps the best example of the dynamic organic character of human life, in which the biological, spiritual and moral work in tandem. Just as the four humors should be kept in equilibrium in order to insure physical health, so vice should be balanced in order to insure spiritual well-being. Just as the seeds of future greatness are revealed before birth through prenatal omens and portents; so the menstrual blood which nourishes the foetus is a harbinger of evil and suffering. After birth, original sin may be washed away with baptism; in the same way, proper attention to the needs of the neonate will guarantee his physical survival. Indeed, a new concern for the dangers of childbirth and infancy achieved wide currency. In childhood, the tradition of Spartan monastic education was now tempered by the secular emphasis on parental love. Parents and teachers were urged to rear each child in accordance with his own individual potential and character; and to guide the malleable, undisciplined child in a more fruitful direction.

Adolescence was characterized as a time of stress and danger, when the young stood at a critical crossroads, when professional, familial and religious decisions must be made. While the choice had once been between celibacy and marriage, the sacramentalization of marriage had introduced the path of marital chastity as a viable Christian option. If the encyclopedia and the moral treatise railed against the sexual turbulence and excess of youth, saints' lives now provided living examples of those who overcame temptation; attention was now devoted not simply to the problems of male adolescence, but also to the rearing of women.

In the Jewish tradition and among those like Bernard Gordon who were strongly influenced by Aristoteliansm, adulthood was a time when one undertakes the responsibilities of family and community. The greatest stress was laid on the maintenance of good health, evidenced by the large number of *regimina* for health which appeared. As a consequence of the interest in Aristotle and the new Arabic medical sources, old age ceased to be characterized exclusively as a time of physical decay in anticipation of death, but was tempered by the hope that human life span could be extended.

VIII. Notes

1. Thomas of Cantimpré, *Vita Lutgardis*, in *ASS*, 16 June IV: 189.

2. Caesarius of Heisterbach, *Sermo de translatione beate Elyzabeth*, in A. Huyskens, ed., *Die Schriften des Cäsarius von Heisterbach über die heilige Elisabeth von Thüringen*, in *Publikationen der Gesellschaft für rheinische Geschichtskunde*, 43, pt. 3, (1937), 281-90.

3. John of San Gemignano, *Vita S. Finae*, in *ASS*, 12 June II: 233.

4. Conrad of Megenberg, *Vita S. Erardi*, in *ASS*, 8 January I: 941.

5. Gerald Gruman, *A History of Ideas About the Prolongation of Life*, in *Transactions of the American Philosophical Society*, New Series, 56, pt. 9 (Philadelphia, 1966), 19 ff.; for a list of some treatises on aging, see Joseph Freeman, *Aging, Its History and Literature* (New York, 1979).

Bibliography

Manuscripts

Adam of Buckfield, *Commentaria super De longitudine et brevitate vite*, in *Oxford, Corpus Christi*, 114, ff. 235r-237r.

Distinctiones, in *B.M. Royal*, 7. C. V.

Domenico di Bandino, *Fons memorabilium universi*, in *Oxford, Baillol*, 238 E.

Giles of Rome, *Exameron*, in *B.N. Lat.*, 3160, 1r-65r.

Guy of Vigevano, *Texaurus regis Francie acquisicionis terre sancte de ultra mare...*, in *B.N. Lat.*, 11015, 32r-54r.

"Jacobus", *Omnebonum*, in *B.M. Royal*, 6. E. VI, 6. E. VII.

Radulphus Ardens, *Compendium philosophiae*, in *B.N. Lat.*, 3329.

Thomas of Cantimpré, *Liber de natura rerum*, in *B.M. Royal*, 12. F. VI.

Thomas of Cantimpré, *Liber de natura rerum*, in *B.M. Royal*, 12. E. XVII.

Thomas of Ireland, *Manipulus florum*, in *B.M. Royal*, 7. C. III.

William of Conches, *Dragmaticon, Stanford University Ms.*, M 412.

Primary Sources

Abraham ha-Kohen, *Orhot haim*, ed. E. Schlesinger (Berlin, 1902).

Abrahams, I., ed., *Hebrew Ethical Wills*, 2 vols. (Philadelphia, 1926).

Absalom of Springiersbach, *Sermones de tempore*, in *MPL*, 211: 13-294.

Adam of Perseigne, *Epistolae*, in *MPL*, 211: 579-694.

Adam of Perseigne, *Lettres*, ed. J. Bouvet (Paris, 1960).

Adelard of Bath, *Questiones naturales*, ed. M. Müller, *Beiträge*, 31.2. (Munich, 1934).

Aharon Halevi of Barcelona, *Sefer ha-Hinukh* (Jerusalem, 1966).

Alan of Lille, *Liber parabolarum*, in *MPL*, 210: 579-594.

Alberigo, J., et al., eds., *Conciliorum oecumenicorum decreta*, 3rd ed. (Bologna, 1973).

Albertus Magnus, *De animalibus*, ed. H. Stadler, 2 vols. (Münster, 1916).

Albertus Magnus, *Opera omnia*, 38 vols., ed. A. Borgnet (Paris, 1890-1898).

Albertus Magnus, *Sermones de tempore*, ed. P. Jammy, new ed. (Toulouse, 1883).

Aldobrandinus of Siena, *Le régime du corps*, ed. L. Landouzy and R. Pepin (Paris, 1911).

Ambrose, *De Josepho*, in *CSEL*, 32. 2 (Leipzig, 1897).

Ambrose, *Hexaemeron*, in *Opera omnia de Sant' Ambrogio. I sei giorni della creazione*, ed. G. Banterle (Milan, 1979).

Ambrose, *Hexaemeron*, trans. J.F. Savage (New York, 1961).

Ambrose, *In Psalmum CXVIII Expositio*, in *MPL*, 15: 1197-1526.

Ambrose, *Opera*, ed. C. Schenkl, *CSEL*, 32.1. (Leipzig, 1897).

Ambrose, *Sermones in Psalmum cxviii*, in *MPL*, 15: 1257-1603.

Andrew of Strumi, *Vita S. Joannis Gualberti*, in *MPL*, 146: 765-960.

Angelo of Clareno, "Apologia pro sua vita," ed. V. Doucet, *Archivum franciscarum historicum*, 39 (1948), 63-100.

Angelo of Clareno, *Historia septem tribulationum fratrum minorum*, in I. von Döllinger, ed., *Beiträge zur Sektengeschichte des Mittelalters*, 2 vols. (Munich, 1890), II, 417-528.

Annaeus Seneca, *Tragoediae*, ed. R. Peiper and G. Richter (Leipzig, 1902).

Anonymous of Molesmes, *Vita S. Roberti*, in *MPL*, 157: 1269-1288.

Anonymous of Oliva, *Vita Gullelmi de Oliva*, in *ASS*, 11 February I: 495-500.

Anonymous disciple of Stephan of Obazine, *Vita S. Stephani*, in *ASS*, 8 March I: 799-808.

Anselm, *De similitudinibus*, in *MPL*, 159: 605-708.

Aristotle, *Ars rhetorica*, ed. L. Spengel, 2 vols. (Leipzig, 1867).

Aristotle, *De generatione animalium*, ed. A.L. Peck (London, 1963).

Aristotle, *De generatione animalium*, trans. William of Moerbeke, ed. H.J.D. Lulofs, *Aristoteles latinus*, 17.2. v. (Leiden, 1966).

Aristotle, *Ethica Nicomichea*, trans. Robert Grosseteste, ed. R.A. Gautier, 3 vols., in *Aristotles latinus*, 26. 1-3, (Leiden, 1972-1973).

Aristotle, *Historia animalium*, ed. A.L. Peck, 2 vols. (Paris, 1965-1970).

Aristotle, *Parva naturalia*, in A.L. Shields, in *Corpus commentariorum Averroes in Aristotelem*, VII. 1. (Cambridge, Mass., 1949).

Aristotle, *On the Soul. Parva naturalia. On Breath*, ed. and trans. W.S. Hett (Cambridge, Mass., 1935).

Aristotle, *Opera*, ed. Academia regia Borussica, 5 vols. (Berlin, 1831)

Aristotle, *Opera cum Averroes commentariis*, 10 vols. + 3 Suppl. (Venice, 1562-1574).

Aristotle, *Politica*, trans. William of Moerbeke, ed. P. Michaud-Quantin, in *Aristotles latinus*, 19.1. (Bruges, 1961).

pseudo-Aristotle, *Oecumenica*, ed. B.A. van Groningen and A. Wartelle (Paris, 1968).

pseudo-Aristotle, *Oecumenica*, ed. F. Süsemihl (Leipzig, 1887).

Arnold of Foligno, *Vita Angelae de Fulgineo*, in *ASS*, 4 January I: 186-234.

Arnold of Villanova, *Opera omnia* (Lyons, 1511).

Athanasius, *Vita S. Antonii*, in *MPG*, 25: 835-976.

Atto of Pistoia, *Vita S. Joannis Gualberti*, in *MPL*, 146: 667-703.

Augustine, *Confessiones*, ed. C. Watts (Cambridge, 1950).

Augustine, *De civitate Dei*, in *Corpus christianorum. Series latina*, 48 (Turnhout, 1955).

Augustine, *De diversis questionibus*, in *MPL*, 40: 11-100.

Augustine, *De diversis questionibus*, ed. A Mutzenbecher, in *CCL*, 44A (Turnhout, 1975), 3-249.

Augustine, *De genesi contra Manichaeos libri duo*, in *MPL*, 34: 173-246.

Augustine, *De trinitate*, ed. W.J. Mountain, *CCL*, 50, 50A (Turnhout, 1968).

Augustine, *De trinitate*, in *MPL*, 42: 819-1098.

Augustine, *De vera religione*, ed. K.D. Daur, *CCL*, 32 (Turnhout, 1962), 187-260.

Augustine, *De vera religione*, in *MPL*, 34: 121-172.

Augustine, *Ennarationes in Psalmos*, ed. E. Dekkers and J. Fraipont, *CCL*, vols. 38-40 (Turnhout, 1956).

Augustine, *Ennarationes in Psalmos*, in *MPL*, vols. 36-39.

Augustine, *The Good of Marriage (De bono conjugali)*, trans. C. Wilcox, in *Treatises on Marriage and Other Subjects* (New York, 1955), 3-51.

Augustine, *Homiliae super Joannen*, in *MPL*, 35: 1376-1977.

Avicebron [Ibn Gebirol], *Fons vitae*, trans. John of Spain and Dominicus Gundissalinus, ed. C. Baeumker, in *Beträge*, 1 (1895).

Avicenna, *De animalibus super de animalibus Aristotelis*, trans. Michael Scot (Venice, 1508).

Avicenna, *Liber canonis*, trans. Gerard of Cremona (Venice, 1506).

Bahya ben-Asher, *Perush Rabbenu Bahya al Masekhet Avoth* (Jerusalem, 1962).

Barach, C.S., ed., *Costa ben-Lucae: De differentia animae et spiritus liber*, in *Bibliotheca philosphorum mediae aetatis*, 3 (Innsbruck, 1878).

Barberino, F., *Reggimento e costumi di donna*, ed. E. Sansone (Turin, 1957).

Bartholomaeus Anglicus, *De rerum proprietatibus*, ed. G. Barthold (Frankfurt, 1601).

Bartholomeo Albizi, "Il trattato dei miracoli del G. Gerardo Cagnoli...," ed. F. Rotolo, *Miscellanea francescana*, 66 (1966), 128-192.

Bartholomei Albizi, "La Leggenda del B. Gerardo...", ed. F. Rotolo, *Miscellanea francescana*, 57 (1955), 367-446.

Basil of Caesarea, *Homélies sur l'Hexaeméron*, ed. S. Gret (Paris, 1949).

Basil of Caesarea, *Sur l'origine de l'homme (Hom. X et XI de l'Hexaeméron)*, ed. A. Smets and M. van Esbroeck (Paris, 1970).

Bede, *De temporibus liber*, ed. C.W. Jones (Cambridge, 1943).

Bede, *Expositio in S. Joannis Evangelium*, in *MPL*, 92: 633-938.

Bede, *Hexameron*, in *MPL*, 91: 9-190.

pseudo-Bede, *Commentaria in Pentateuchem*, in *MPL*, 91: 189-394.

pseudo-Bede, *De mundi coelestis terrestrisque consuetudine liber*, in *MPL*, 90: 881-910.

pseudo-Bede, *De sex dierum creatione*, in *MPL*, 93: 207-304.

Berengar of Landorre, *Lumen animae*, ed. M. Farinato (Augsburg, 1477).

Bernard Gordon, *De conservatione vitae* (Leipzig, 1570).

Bernard of Clairvaux, *De consideratione libri quinque*, in *MPL*, 182: 727-809.

Bernard of Clairvaux, *Life of Malachy of Armagh*, trans. H.J. Lawlor (London, 1920).

Bertagna, M., ed., "Note e documenti intorno a S. Lucchese," *Archivum franciscanum historicum*, 62 (1969), 3-114, 449-502.

Bianchi, L., ed., *Le prediche di San Bernardino da Siena*, 3 vols. (Siena, 1880).

Biblia sacra cum glossis interlineari et ordinaria, 7 vols. (Venice, 1588).

Bieler, L., ed., "Libri Epistolarum sancti Patricii episcopi. I. Introduction, Text and Commentary", *Classica et mediaevalia*, 11 (1951). 1-150.

de la Bigne, M., ed., *Bibliotheca maxima patrum*, 28 vols. (Lyons, 1677).

pseudo-Boethius, *Disciplina scolarium*, in *MPL*, 64: 1223-1239.

Bowden, W.B., ed. and trans., *The Book of Margery Kempe* (New York, 1944).

Blumberg, H., ed., *Averroes' Epitome of the Parva naturalia* (Cambridge, Mass., 1961).

Boffito, P., ed., "Il 'De principiis astrologiae di Cecco d'Ascoli," *Giornale storico della letteratura italiana Supplemento*, 6 (Turin, 1903), 1-73.

Bonaventure, *The Mind's Road to God*, trans. G. Boas (New York, 1953).

Bonaventure, *Opera omnia*, 10 vols., ed. PP. Collegii S. Bonaventurae (Quaracchi, 1968).

de la Borderie, A., et al., eds., *Monument originaux de l'histoire de S. Yves* (Saint-Brieuc, 1887).

Bouquet, M., et al., eds., *Recueils des historiens des Gaules et de la France*, 24 vols. (Paris, 1869-1904).

Brown, C., ed., *English Lyrics of the XIIIth Century* (Oxford, 1932).

Brown, C., ed., *Religious Lyrics of the XIVth Century*, 2nd rev. ed. (Oxford, 1957).

Brown, C., ed., *Religious Lyrics of the XVth Century* (Oxford, 1959).

Brunetto Latini, *Li livre dou trésor*, ed. F.J. Carmody (Berkeley, 1948).

Brunholzl, F., "Florilegium Treverense," *Mittellateinische Jahrbuch*, 1 (1964), 65-77; 3 (1966), 129-217.

Bruno of Carthusian, *Expositio in Psalmos*, in *MPL*, 152: 637-1420.

Bruno of Segni, *Commentaria in Matthaeum*, in *MPL*, 165: 63-314.

Bruno of Segni, *Expositio in Genesim*, in *MPL*, 164: 147-233.

Bruno of Segni, *Homiliae XXII*, in *MPL*, 165: 747-864.

Buber, M., ed., *Ecstatic Confessions*, ed. P. Mendes-Flohr (New York, 1985).

Bullarium romanum..., ed. A. Thomasetti, 24 vols. (Turin, 1857-1872).

Caesarius of Heisterbach, *Sermo de translatione beate Elyzabeth*, in A. Huyskens, ed., *Die Schriften des Cäsarius von Heisterbach über heilige Elisabeth von Thüringen*, in *Publikationen des Gesellschaft für Geschichtskunde*, 43. 3 (1937), 281-290.

Caesarius of Heisterbach, *Vita, Passio et Miracula S. Engelberti*, in *ASS*, 7 November III: 623-684.

Cambell, J., ed., *Enquête pour le procès de canonisation de Dauphine de Puimichel Comtesse d'Ariano (+ 26. XI. 1360)* (Turin, 1978).

Casagrande, C., ed., *Prediche alle donne del secolo XIII* (Milan, 1978).

Cecco d'Ascoli, *Acerba*, ed. P. Rosario (Lanciano, 1913).

Celestine V (?), *Opuscula*, in M. de la Bigne, ed., *Bibliotheca maxima patrum*, 28 vols. (Lyons, 1677), 25: 769-867.

Chauvin, Y., ed., *Livre des miracles de Sainte-Catherine-de-Fierbois (1375-1470)* (Poitiers, 1976).

Christopher of Parma, "Legenda beati Francisci de Senis," *AB*, 14 (1895), 166-197.

Chronica XXIV generalium ordinis minorum, in *Analecta franciscana*, 3 (Quaracchi, 1897).

Cicero, *Cato maior*, new ed., 2 vols. (Oxford, 1957).

Cicero, *De senectute*, ed. E. Behrens (Leipzig, 1883).

Collin-Rosset, S., ed., "Le *Liber Thesauri occulti* de Pascalis Romanus (Un traité d'interprétation des songes du XIIe siècle)," *AHDLMA*, 30 (1963), 111-198.

Conrad of Castellario, *Vita Benvenutae de Foro-Julii*, in *ASS*, 29 October XIII: 152-185.

Conrad of Megenberg, *Ökonomik*, ed. S. Krüger, 2 vols., in *MGH. Staatsschriften des späten Mittelalters*, 3 (Stuttgart, 1973).

Conrad of Megensberg, *Vita S. Erardi*, in *ASS*, 8 January I: 541-544.

Constantine the African, *Opera*, 2 vols. (Basel, 1536-1539).

Constitutiones Hirsaugensis, in *MPL*, 150: 923-1146.

Coquelines, C., ed., *Bullarium romanum*, 14 vols. (Rome, 1739-1744).

Corbett, J.A., ed., *The De instructione puerorum of William of Tournai O.P.* (Notre Dame, Ind., 1955).

Cyprian (?), *De duodecim abusionibus saeculi tractatus*, in *MPL*, 4: 869-882.

Dante Alighieri, *Il Convivio*, ed. G. Busnelli and G. Vandelli, 2nd ed. (Florence, 1964).

Deschamps, E. *Oeuvres complètes*, 11 vols., ed. M. de Queux de Saint-Hilaire (Paris, 1878-1903).

Dinur, B.-Z., ed., *Masehket Avoth* (Jerusalem, 1974).

Doncoeur, P., ed., *Le livre de la bienheureuse Angèle de Foligno* (Toulouse, 1925).

Douie, D.L., and Farmer, H., eds., *Magna vita sancti Hugonis*, 2 vols. (London, 1961).

Eadmer, *Vita sancti Anselmi*, ed. R.W. Southern (London, 1962).

Eberhard of Bethune, *Graecismus*, ed. J. Wröbel (Bratislava, 1887).

Edmund of Abingdon, *Speculum ecclesie*, ed. Helen P. Forshaw (London, 1973).

Ellinson, E., ed., *Ish ve-Ishto, Mekorot halachtiim mevooarim* (Jerusalem, 1979).

Engelbert of Admont, *Liber de causis longaevitatis hominum ante diluvium*, in B. Pez, ed., *Thesaurus anectoroum novissimus*, 8 vols. (Augsburg, 1721), I, 437-502.

Eustace of Faversham, *Vita sancti Edmundi*, in Lawrence, C.H., ed., *St. Edmund of Canterbury* (Oxford, 1960), 203-221.

Eva of St. Martin, *Vita Beatae Iulianae Corneliensis*, in *ASS*, 5 April I: 441-475.

Faloci-Pulignani, M., ed., *L'Autobiografia e gli scritti della B. Angela da Foligno* (Città di Castello, 1932).

Fazio degli Uberti, *Dittamondo*, ed. Silvestri (Milan, 1926).

Field, C., ed. and trans., *The Confessions of Al-Ghazzali* (Lahore, n.d.).

Firmicius Lactantius, *Divinae institutiones*, ed. S. Brandt, *Opera omnia*, in *CSEL*, 19 (Leipzig, 1890).

Fluck, R., "Guillaume de Tournai et son traité 'De modo docendi pueri'," *Revue des questions religieuses*, 27 (1953), 333-356.

Franceschini, E., ed., "Il 'Liber philosophorum moralium antiquorum'," *Atti del Reale Istituto veneto di scienze, lettere ed arti*, 91.2 (1931), 393-597.

Franknoì, G., ed., *Inquisitio super vita, conversatione et miraculis beatae Margarethae virginis*, in *Monumenta romana episcopatus Vesprimiensis*, 6 vols. (Budapest, 1896), I, 160-384.

Friedberg, E. and Richter, E., eds., *Corpus iuris canonici*, 2 vols. (Leipzig, 1879-1881).

Frugoni, A., ed., *Celestinana* (Rome, 1954).

Fulgentius, *Opera*, ed. J. Fraipont, *Corpus christianorum. Series latina*, 91 (Turnhout, 1968).

Fulgentius, *Opera*, ed. R. Helm (Leipzig, 1898).

de Gaiffier, B., ed., "Vita beati Raimundi Lulli," *AB*, 48 (1930), 13-178.

Galen, *Opera omnia*, ed. C.C. Kühn, 20 vols. (Leipzig, 1821-1833).

Gautier of Metz, *Mirror of the World*, ed. O.H. Prior, *EETS*, 110 (1913).

Geoffrey de la Tour Landry, *The Book of the Knight and of the Tower*, ed. T. Wright, *EETS*, 33 (1906).

Germann, P., ed., *Die sogenannten Sententiae Varronis* (Paderborn, 1967).

Gervase of Tillbury, *Otia imperialia*, ed. F. Lieberman and R. Pauli, *MGH. Scriptores*, 27 (Hannover, 1885), 359-394.

Giarrantano, C., ed., *Calpurnii et Nemesiani*, 3rd ed. (Turin, 1951).

Gilbert of Limerick, *Liber de statu eccelsiae*, in *MPL*, 159: 997-1004.

Giles of Rome, *Commentationes physicae et metaphysicae* (Rome, 1582).

Giles of Rome, *De regimine principum* (Rome, 1607).

Giles of Rome, *Hexameron, sive de mundo sex diebus condito*, in *Opera*, I (Rome, 1555).

Girvan, R., ed., *Ratis Raving and Other Early Scots Poems on Morals*, in *Scottish Texts Society*, 3rd series, 11 (Edinburgh, 1937).

Gisbertus, et al., *Vita et miracula Ambrosii Sansedonii*, in *ASS*, 20 March IV: 181-201.

Godefred of Admont, *Homiliae dominicales*, in *MPL*, 174: 131-144.

Godefrey of St. Victor, *Microcosmus*, ed. P. Delhaye (Lille, 1951).

Gohlman, W., ed. and trans., *The Life of Ibn Sina* (Albany, 1974).

Golb, N., ed., "Megillat Ovadia ha-Ger," in *Mehkarei Adoth ve-Genizah*, ed. S. Morag (Jerusalem, 1981), 78-107.

Gori, P., ed., *Dodici avvertimento...* (Florence, 1885).

Gregory the Great, *Dialogi*, 2 vols., ed. A. de Vögué and P. Antin (Paris, 1978-1980).

Gregory the Great, *XL Homilarum in Evangelia*, in *MPL*, 76: 1075-1312.

Gregory the Great, *Moralium libri*, in *MPL*, 75: 499-1162.

Gregory of Nyssa, *De opificio hominis*, in *MPG*, 44: 125-256.

Guilelmus Alvernus, *Opera omnia*, 2 vols. (Paris, 1674).

Gummere, R.M., ed., *Senecae Epistulae*, 3 vols. (Cambridge, 1953).

Haly Abbas, ['Ali ibn al-Abbas], *Liber regalis*, trans. Stephen of Antioch, in *Liber totius medicine...* (Lyons, 1523).

Harrington, J., trans., *The School of Salernum. Regimen Sanitatis Salerni* (Salerno, 1859).

Haymo of Halberstadt, *Homiliae de tempore*, in *MPL*, 118: 11-747.

Hermann of Carinthia, *De essentiis*, ed. C. Burnet (Leiden, 1982).

Hermannus Judaeus, *De conversione sua*, ed. Neimeyer, *MGH. Quellen zur Geistesgeschichte des Mittelalters*, 2 (Weimar, 1963).

Herrad of Landsberg, *Hortus deliciarum*, ed., A. Straub and G. Keller (Strassbourg, 1879-1899).

Heysse, A., ed., "Documenta de vita S. Ludovici episcopi Tolosani," *Archivum franciscanum historicum*, 40 (1947), 118-142.

Hildebert of Lavardin, *Sermones*, in *MPL*, 171: 339-964.

Hilka, A., ed., *Das Leben und Sentenzen des Philosophen Secundus* (Breslau, 1910).

Hilka, A., ed., *Liber de monstruosis hominibus orientis* (Berlin, 1933).

Hippeau, C., ed., *Chevalier du cynge et Godefroid de Bouillon*, 2 vols. (Geneva, 1969).

Hippocrates, *Oeuvres complètes*, ed. E. Littré, 10 vols. (Paris, 1834-1861).

Honorius of Autun, *De imagine mundi*, in *MPL*, 176: 115-188.

Honorius of Autun, *De vita claustrali*, in *MPL*, 172: 1247-8.

Honorius of Autun, *Gemma animae*, in *MPL*, 172: 543-738.

Honorius of Autun, "Imago mundi," ed. V.I.J. Flint, *AHDLMA*, 49 (1982), 48-151.

Horace, *Carmina*, ed. F. Vollmer (Leipzig, 1912).

Horace, *Epistulae*, ed. H.R. Fairclough (Cambridge, 1955).

Hugh of Floreffe, *Vita Idae*, in *ASS*, 29 October XIII: 100-135.

Hugh of Foliot(?), *De medicina animae*, in *MPL*, 176: 1183-1202.

Hugh of St. Victor, *De institutione novitiorum*, in *MPL*, 176: 925-952.

Hugh of St. Victor, *Didascalicon*, ed. and trans. J. Taylor and H. Buttimer (New York, 1961).

Iacopo di Dante Alighieri, *Il Dottrinale*, ed. G. Crocioni (Città di Castello, 1895).

Isidore of Seville, *Differentiarum sive de proprietate sermonum libri duo*, in *MPL*, 83: 1-98.

Isidore of Seville, *Etymologiarum sive originum libri II*, ed. W.H. Lindsay, 2 vols. (Oxford 1911).

Isidore of Seville, *Quaestiones in vetus Testamentum in Genesim*, in *MPL*, 83: 207-287.

Jacobs, L., ed., *Jewish Mystical Testimonies* (New York, 1977).

Jaime I, King of Aragon, *Chronicle*, 2 vols., trans. John Forster (London, 1983).

James of Vitry, *Vita Mariae Oigniacensis*, in *ASS*, 23 June V: 630-684.

James of Voragine, *Legenda aurea*, ed. Th. Graesse, 3rd ed. (Leipzig, 1890).

Jehan Maillart, *Le Roman du Comte d'Anjou*, ed. M. Rogues (Paris, 1931).

Jerome, *Contra Iovinianum*, in *MPL*, 23: 221-352.

Jerome, *Liber interpretationis hebraicorum*, ed. P. de Lagarde, in *Corpus christianorum. Series latina*, 72 (Turnhout, 1959), 57-161.

Jerome, *Vita Pauli Thebaei*, in *MPL*, 20: 159-176.

pseudo-Jerome, *Expositio quattuor Evangelii*, in *MPL*, 30:: 549-608.

Joachin of Flora, *Tractatus super quattuor Evangelia*, ed. E. Buonaiuti (Rome, 1930).

Johannes Balbi, *Catholicon* (Strasbourg, 1483).

Johannes Gallensis, *Communiloquium sive Summa Collationum* (Strassbourg, 1489).

Johannes Gobi, *Scala coeli* (Lübeck, 1476).

Johannes de Magistris, *Questiones perutiles supra tota philosophia naturali* (Venice, 1490).

Johannes of Marienwerder, *Vita prima B. Dorotheae*, in *ASS*, 30 October XIII: 493-499.

John of Cluny, *Vita Odonis*, in *MPL*, 133: 43-86.

John of Fruttuaria, *Tractatus de origine vitae et morum instructione*, in *MPL*, 184: 559-584.

John of Jandun, *Questiones in libros Aristotelis* (Venice, 1562).

John of Lodi, *Vita Petri Damiani*, in *ASS*, 23 February III: 412-433.

John of San Gemignano, *Opusculum de operibus sex dierum* (Paris, 1512).

John of San Gemignano, *Summa de exemplis et rerum similitudinibus* (Venice, 1584).

John of San Gemignano, *Vita S. Finae,* in *ASS,* 12 March II: 435-442.

Juncta of Bevagna, *Vita Margaritae,* in *ASS,* 22 February III: 302-363.

Keever, E., *Imago Mundi by Petrus Alliacus* (Wilmington, N.C., 1948).

Kiessling, A., ed., *Annaei Senecae Oratorum et Rhetorium Sententiae, Divisiones, Colores* (Leipzig, 1872).

Licitra, V., ed., "Il Liber legum moralium e il De regimine vite et sanitatis di Bellino Bissolo," *Studi medievali,* ser. 3, 6 (1965), 405-454.

Mahzor Vitry, ed. S. Hurwitz (Nuremberg, 1923).

Malter, H., ed., "Shem tov ben Joseph Palquera II. His 'Treatise of the Dream'," *Jewish Quarterly Review,* N.S. 1 (1910/11), 451-501.

Manzalaoui, M.A., ed., *Secretum secretorum, nine English versions,* in *EETS,* 276 (Oxford, 1977).

Marbod of Rennes, *Liber Marbodi episcopi decem capitulum,* in *MPL,* 171: 1693-1716.

Martène, E., *De antiquis monachorum ritibus* (Bassano, 1758).

Martin de Bosco Gualteri, *Vita Mariae de Mailliaco,* in *ASS,* 28 March III: 737-747.

Matthew Paris, *Vita sancti Edmundi,* in *St. Edmund of Abingdon,* ed. C.H. Lawrence (Oxford, 1960), 222-289.

May, H.M., "The Confession of Prous Boneta Heretic and Heresiarch", in *Essays in Medieval Life and Thought Presented in Honor of Austin Patterson Evans,* ed. J.H. Mundy, et al. (New York, 1955), 3-30.

Menachem ben Shlomo ha Meiri, *Beit ha-Bechira al-Masekhet Avoth,* 2nd ed. (Jerusalem, 1965).

Michael Scot, *Physiognomia* (Paris, 1505).

Migne, J.P., ed., *Patrologiae cursus completus. Series graeca,* 161 vols. (Paris, 1857-1905).

Migne, J.P., ed., *Patrologiae cursus completus. Series latina,* 221 vols + 4 Suppl. (Paris, 1844-1905).

Monumenta poloniae historica, 6 vols. (Cracow, 1864-1894).

Meech, S., and Allen, E.H., eds., *The Book of Margery Kemp*, in *EETS, O.S.*, 212 (1940).

Millers, E., ed., "Un 'Speculum novitii' inédit d'Etienne de Salley," *Collectanea ordinis Cisterciensrim reformatorum*, 8(1946), 17-68.

Miracula ex processu canonizationis Thomae episcopi Herefordensis, in *ASS*, 2 October I: 585-696.

Molenaer, S.P., ed., *Li Livres de Gouvernement des Rois* (Paris, 1899).

Möller, R., ed., *Mitteldeutsche Prosaübersetzung des Secretum secretorum* (Berlin, 1963).

Moshe ben Maimon, *Hanhagat ha-Briut be Tirgumo shel Moshe ibn-Tibbon*, ed. S. Muntner (Jerusalem, 1957).

Muntner, S., "Al-ha-Melancholia, le Regel Yovel ha-Elef le-Moto shel Yizhak ben-Shlomo Yisrael," *Ha-Rofeh ha-Ivri*, 25 (1952), 85-94.

Nemesius of Emesa, *De natura hominis*, ed. G. Verbeke and J.R. Moncho (Leiden, 1975).

Nicholas of Lyra, *Glossa seu postilla perpetua in Veterum et Novum Testamentum*, 3 vols. (Nuremberg, 1471-1472).

Odo II of Cluny, *Vita Geraldi Aurilacensis*, in *MPL*, 133: 639-710.

Offard, M.Y., ed., *The Parlement of the Thre Ages*, in *EETS*, 246 (London, 1959).

Osburn of Gloucester, *Panorma*, ed. A. Mai, *Thesaurus novus latinitatis. Classicorum auctorum e vaticanis codicibus editorum*, 8 (Rome, 1836).

Ovid, *Ars amatoria*, ed. J.H. Mozley (Cambridge, Mass., 1962).

Ovid, *Epistulae*, ed. R. Ehwald (Leipzig, 1897).

Ovid, *Fasti*, ed. J.G. Frazer (Cambridge, 1931).

Ovid, *Heroides and Amoris*, ed. G. Showerman (Cambridge, 1971).

Ovid, *Tristia*, ed. A. Wheeler (Cambridge, 1953).

Pack, R.A., ed., "De prognosticatione sompniorum libellus Guillelmus de Aragonia adscriptus," *AHDLMA*, 33 (1968), 237-293.

Pack, R.A., "Pseudo-Aristotelis Epistola ad Alexandrum de regimine sanitatis a quodam Nicolao versificata," *AHDLMA*, 45 (1979), 307-325.

Paetow, L.L., ed., *Morale scolarium of John of Garland (Johannes de Garlandia)* (Berkeley, 1927).

Palmieri, M., *Vita civile*, ed. G. Belloni (Florence, 1982).

Papias, *Elementarium doctrinae rudimentum* (Venice, 1496).

Peter Abelard, *Expositio in Hexaemeron*, in *MPL*, 178: 720-784.

Peter Comestor, *Historia ecclesiastica*, in *MPL*, 198: 1053-1722.

Peter Damian, *De bono religiosi status*, in *MPL*, 145: 763-792.

Peter Damian, *De laude flagellum*, in *MPL*, 145: 679-685.

Peter Damian, *Vita Sancti Romualdi*, in *MPL*, 144: 953-1008.

Peter of Florence, *Vita Margaritae de Faventia*, in *ASS*, 10 June II: 847-851.

Peter of Monte Rubiano, *Vita et miracula Nicolai de Tolentino*, in *ASS*, 10 September II: 644-664.

Peter of Porto (?), *Regula clericorum*, in *MPL*, 163: 703-748.

Peter of Spain, *Obras filosoficos III*, ed. M. Alonso (Madrid, 1952).

Peter the Venerable, *De miraculis*, in *MPL*, 189: 851-954.

Petronius, *Satyricon*, ed. M. Heseltine (London, 1919).

Petrus Alfonsi, *Dialogi*, in *MPL*, 157: 535-671.

Pez, B., *Thesaurus anecdotorum novissimus*, 8 vols. (Augsburg, 1721).

Philip of Harvengt, *Vita S. Amandi*, in *MPL*, 203: 1237-1276.

Philippe de Navarre, *Les quatres âges de l'homme*, ed. M. de Fréville (Paris, 1887).

Pierre Bersuire, *Opera omnia*, 6 vols. (Cologne, 1731).

Pierre d'Ailly, *Imago mundi*, ed. E. Buron, 2 vols. (Paris, 1930).

Plato, *Timaeus*, ed. R. Klibansky, in *Corpus platonicum medii aevi*, 4 (London, 1962).

Plessner, M., ed., "Der OIKONOMIKOC des Neupythagorers 'Bryson' und sein Einfluss auf die islamische Wissenshaft," *Orient und Antike*, 5 (Heidelberg, 1928).

Pliny, *Naturalis historia*, ed. L. Ian and C. Mayhoff, 6 vols (Stuttgart, 1967).

Ponce de Leon, C., ed., *Physiologus* (Rome, 1587).

Poncelet, A., ed., "Vita Beatae Margaretae virginis de Civitate Castelli," *AB*, 14 (1900), 21-36.

Processus canonizationis de vita et miracula Ivonis Trecorensis, in *ASS*, 19 May IV: 541-577.

Prümmer, D., ed., *Fontes Vitae S. Thomae Aquinatis* (Toulouse, 1911).

Publilius Syrus, *Sententiae*, ed. E. Woefflin (Leipzig, 1869).

Quintillian, *Institutio oratoria*, ed. H.E. Butler, 2 vols. (Cambridge, 1921-1922).

Rabanus Maurus, *Commentariorum in Mathaeum*, in *MPL*, 197: 727-1156.

Rabanus Maurus, *De universo libri XXII*, in *MPL*, 111: 179-185.

Ralph Bocking, *Vita Ricardi episcopi Cicestrensis*, in *ASS*, 3 April I: 282-318.

Rappaport, S., trans., *A Treasury of the Midrash* (New York, 1968).

Rather of Verona, *Confessio eiusdem*, in *MPL*, 136: 393-444.

Raymund of Capua, *Legenda Agnetis de Montepolitano*, in *ASS*, 20 April II: 792-812.

Raymond Lull, *Doctrina pueril*, ed. G. Schib (Barcelona, 1972).

Raymond Lull, *Doctrine de l'enfant, version médiévale*, ed. A. Llinares (Paris, 1969).

al-Razi [Muhammed ibn Zakariya Abu Bakr], *Liber Rasis ad Almansorem* (Venice, 1497).

Remi of Auxerre, *Commentarius in Genesim*, in *MPL*, 133: 51-131.

Reypens, L., ed., *Vita Beatricis. De Autobiografie van de Z. Beatrijs van Tienen O. Cist. 1200-1268* (Antwerp, 1964).

Richard of Mediavilla, *Super quattuor libros Sententiarum*, 4 vols. (Brescia, 1591).

di Rienzi, S., ed., *Flos medicinae scholae Salerni*, 2nd ed. (Naples, 1856).

Rius-Serra, J., ed., *Sancti Raymundi di Penyaforte Opera omnia* (Barcelona, 1949-1954).

Robert of Blois, *Robert von Blois sämtliche Werke*, ed. J. Ulrich, 3 vols. (Berlin, 1885-1895).

Robert Grosseteste, *Hexaemeron*, ed. R.C. Dales and S. Gieben (London, 1982).

Richard of St. Victor, *Liber exceptionum*, ed. J. Châtillon (Paris, 1958).

Roger Bacon, *Compendium studii philosophiae*, ed. J.S. Brewer (London, 1959).

Roger Bacon, *Moralis philosophiae*, ed. J.E. Massa (Turici, n.d.).

Roger Bacon, *Opera*, ed. J.S. Brewer, in *Rerum Britannicarum Scriptores*, 15 (London, 1859).

Roger Bacon, *Opera hactenus inedita Rogeri Baconi*, ed. R. Steele, fasc. 5 (Oxford, 1920).

Roger Bacon, *Opus maius*, ed. J.H. Bridges, 3 vols. (London, 1897-1900).

Saadia Gaon, *The Book of Beliefs and Opinions*, ed. S. Rosenblatt (New Haven, 1967).

Sallust, *Catalina*, ed. A. Ahlberg (Leipzig, 1919).

Samau'al al-Maghribi Ifham al-Yahud, *Silencing the Jews*, ed. and trans. M. Perlman (New York, 1964).

Sbath, P., ed., "Le livre des caractères de Qosta ibn Louqa," *Bulletin de l'Institut d'Egypte*, 23 (1940/1), 140-163.

Sefer ha-Hasid, ed. R. Margalith (Jerusalem, 1957).

Seneca, *Declamationes*, ed. W. Winterbottom, 2 vols. (Cambridge, 1974).

Seppelt, F.X. ed., *Momumenta Coelestiniana. Quellen zur Geschichte des Papstes Coelestin V* (Paderborn, 1921).

Shemtov ben Joseph Falaquera, *Iggeret Battei Hanhagat ha-Guf ve-he-Nefesh, oh Battei Hanhagat ha-Guf ha-Bari*, ed. S. Muntner (Jerusalem, 1950).

Sicard of Cremona, *Mitrale, sive summa de officiis ecclesiasticis*, in *MPL*, 213: 9-436.

Sicco Polentino, "Vita beati Antonii Peregrini," *AB*, 13 (1894), 417-425.

Sigismondi, G., ed., "La Legenda Beati Raynaldi. Le sue fonti e il suo valore storico," *Bolletino della societa umbra di storia patria*, 59 (1959), 5-111.

Simon of Trebnitz, *Legenda maior S. Hedwigis*, in *ASS*, 17 October VIII: 224-264.

Singleton, C., ed., *Canti carnascialeschi del Rinascimento* (Bari, 1936).

Société des bibliophiles français, eds., *Le ménagier de Paris*, 2 vols. (Paris, 1847).

Socii Bollandiani, eds., *Acta sanctorum quotquot tote orbe colluntur*, 66 vols. to date, new ed. (Paris, 1863-1940).

Solinus, *Collectanea rerum memorabiluim*, ed. Th. Mommsen (Berlin, 1895).

Stachnik, R., ed., *Die Akten des Kanonisationsprozess Dorotheas von Montau von 1394 bis 1521*, in *Forschungen and Quellen zur Kirchen und Kulturgeschichte Ostdeutschlands*, 15 (Cologne, 1878).

Statius, *Thebais*, ed. A. Klotz (Leipzig, 1973).

Stephan de Bourbon, *Anecdotes historiques, légendes et apologues*, ed. A. Lecoy de la Marche (Paris, 1877).

Sulpicius Severus, *Vita S. Martini*, ed. J. Fontaine, 3 vols. (Paris, 1967-1969).

Süsemihl, F., ed., *Aristolelis Politicorum libri octo cum translatione Guillelmi de Moerbeke* (Leipzig, 1872).

Thomas Aquinas, *Expositio super librum Boethii de trinitate*, ed. B. Decker (Leiden, 1959).

Thomas Aquinas, *Opera omnia*, 26 vols. (Parma, 1852-1873).

Thomas Aquinas, *Opera omnia*, ed. S.E. Fretté, 28 vols. (Paris, 1875).

Thomas Aquinas, *Super Epistolam S. Pauli Apostoli ad Hebraeos Commentaria*, 2 vols. (Turin, 1929).

Thomas of Argentina, *Compendium theologiae veritatis* (Strassbourg, 1489).

Thomas of Cantimpré, *Bonum universale de apibus* (Douai, 1627).

Thomas of Cantimpré, *Liber de natura rerum. Text*, ed. H. Boese (Berlin, 1973).

Thomas of Cantimpré, *Vita Liutgardis*, in *ASS*, 16 June IV: 234-262.

Thomas of Celano, *Vita prima S. Francisci*, in *AF*, 10 (Quaracchi, 1926-1941), fasc. 1.

Ubertino da Casale, *Arbor vitae crucifixae* (Venice, 1485).

Valerius Maximus, *Factorum et dictorum memorabilium libri novem*, ed. C. Kempf (Leipzig, 1888).

Victorinus of Pettau, *Tractatus de fabrica mundi*, in *MPL*, 5: 301-314.

Vincent of Beauvais, *Speculum maius*, 4 vols. (Douai, 1624).

Virgil, *Opera*, ed. O.E. Ribbeck (Leipzig, 1894).

Vita beati Alpaidis, in *ASS*, 3 November II, 1: 174-209.

Vita beati Angeli de Furcio, in *ASS*, 6 February I: 936-939.

"Vita beati Antonii peregrini," *AB*, 13 (1894), 417-425.

Vita beati Geraldi de Salis, in *ASS*, 23 October X: 254-259.

Vita et miracula B. Ioanne de Signa, in *ASS*, 9 November IV: 283-288.

Vita et miracula Sanctae Cunegundae ducissae Cracoviensis, ed. W. Ketrzynski, in *MPH*, IV: 690-694.

"Vita S. Albertis confessoris ordinis Carmelitarum," *AB*, 17 (1899), 317-336.

Vogel, C., ed., *Le pêcheur et la pénitence au moyen âge* (Paris, 1969).

Vollner, F., ed., *Q. Horatii Flacii Carmina* (Leipzig, 1912).

Walter Daniel, *Vita Ailredi Abbatis Rievall*, ed. F.M. Powicke (London, 1963).

Way, A., ed., *Promptuarium parvulorum sive clericorum*, in *EETS*, *O.S.*, 89 (London, 1865).

Welter, J., ed., *Tabula exemplorum de habundancia...secundum alphabeti ordinata* (Paris, 1926).

Westpfal, H., ed., *Vita Dorotheae Montoviensis magistri Johannis Marienwerder* (Cologne, 1964).

Wiebert, *Vita Sancti Leonis*, in *MPL*, 142: 465-504.

William Brito, *Summa, sive Expositio vocabulum Biblii*, ed. L.B. Daly, 2 vols. (Padua, 1975).

William of Conches, *Das Moralium dogma philosophorum*, ed., J. Holmberg (Uppsala, 1929).

William of Conches, *De philosophia mundi*, in *MPL*, 172: 39-102.

William of Conches, *Elementorum philosophiae libri quattor*, in *MPL*, 90: 1127-1178.

William of Conches, *Sacramentarium*, in *MPL*, 172: 738-806.

William Peraldus, *De eruditione principum*, in Thomas Aquinas, *Opera omnia*, ed. S.E. Fretté, 28 vols. (Paris, 1875), XVII, 551-673.

William Peraldus, *Sermones*, in Guilelmus Alvernus, *Opera*, 2 vols. (Paris, 1674), II, 1-476.

William of St. Thierry, *De natura corporis et animae libri duo*, in *MPL*, 180: 695-726.

William of Tocco, *Vita S. Thomae Aquinatis*, in *ASS*, 7 March I: 657-686.

Wilmart, A., ed., "Exorde et conclusion du traité de Jean l'Homme de Dieu," *Revue bénédictine*, 38 (1926), 310-320.

Yitzhak Ben Shlomo me-Toledo, *Perushim el-Masekhet Avoth* (Jerusalem, 1965).

Yuhanna ibn Masawaih [John Mesue], *De consolatione medicinarum antidotorum*, ed. D. Jacquart and G. Troppeau (Paris, 1980).

Secondary Sources

"Aging Studies Point towards Ways to Slow It," *New York Times, Science Times Supplement*, June 10, 1986, pp. 15, 17.

Aiken, P., "The Animal History of Albertus Magnus and Thomas of Cantimpré," *Speculum*, 22 (1947), 205-225.

d'Alatri, M., ed., *I frati penitenti di San Francesco nella società del due e trecento* (Rome, 1977).

d'Alatri, M., *Il movimento francescano della penitenza nella società medievale* (Rome, 1980).

Allen, J.B., *The Ethical Poetic of the Later Middle Ages. A decorum of convenient distinction* (Toronto, 1982).

d'Alverny, M.T., "Translation and Translators," in R.L. Benson and G. Constable, eds., *Renaissance and Renewal in the Twelfth Century* (Cambridge, Mass., 1982), 421-462.

Anagnine, E., *Dolcino e il movimento ereticale del trecento* (Florence, 1964).

Ancelet-Hustache, J., *Master Eckhart and the Rhineland Mystics*, trans. H. Graf (New York, 1957).

Anderson, M., *Approaches to the History of Western Family, 1500-1914* (London, 1980).

Allers, R., "Microcosmus: From Anaximarder to Paracelsus," *Traditio*, 2 (1944), 319-407.

Ariès, P., *Centuries of Childhood*, trans. R. Baldick (New York, 1965).

Ariès, P., *Images et l'homme devant la mort* (Paris, 1983).

Arnold, K., *Kind und Gesellschaft im Mittelalter und Renaissance* (Paderborn, 1980).

Aron, M., *Un animateur de la jeunesse au XIIIe siècle. Vie, voyages du Bx. Jourdain de Saxe* (Paris, 1930).

Atkinson, C., *Mystic and Pilgrims, the Book and World of Margery Kemp* (Ithaca, 1983).

Auty, R., et al., *Lexikon des Mittelalters*, 3 vols + 3 fasc. to date (Munich, 1977-1988).

d'Auvray, D., and Tausche, M., "Marriage Sermons in *Ad Status* Collections of the Central Middle Ages," *AHDLMA* 47 (1981), 71-119.

von Auw, L., *Angelo Clareno et les spirituels italiens* (Rome, 1979).

Baer, T., "Ha-megama ha-datit chevratit shel 'Sefer ha-Hassidim'," *Zion*, 3 (1937/8), 1-48.

Baker, D., ed. *Medieval Women* (Oxford, 1978).

Banani, A. and Vyronis, S., Jr., eds., *Individualism and Conformity in Classical Islam* (Wiesbaden, 1977).

Baratier, E., "Démographie médiévale dans le midi méditerranéen. Sources et méthodes," in Perroy, E., ed., *La démographie médiévale. Sources et méthodes* (Nice, 1970), 9-16.

Batany, J., "Regards sur l'enfance dans le littérature moralisante," *ADH*, 8 (1973), 123-132.

Battlori, M., "Sur l'édition de l'Autobiographie de Raymonde Lulle par le père de Gaiffier," *AB*, 10 (1982), 683-689.

Baudrillart, A., et al., eds., *Dictionnaire d'histoire et de géographie ecclésiastiques*, 21 vols. + 3 fasc. to date (Paris, 1912-1988).

Bauer, U., *Der Liber Introductorius des Michael Scotus in der Abschrift Clm. 10268 der bürgerlichen Staatsbibliothek München* (Munich, 1983).

Bautier, R.H., *The Economic Development of Medieval Europe*, trans. H. Karolyi (London, 1971).

Begnami-Odier, J., *Études sur Jean de Roquetaillade (Johannes de Rupescissa* (Paris, 1952).

Bell, R., *Holy Anorexia* (Chicago, 1985).

Bennett, M.K., *The World's Fool* (New York, 1954).

Benson, R., and Constable, G., eds., *Renaissance and Renewal in the Twelfth Century* (Cambridge, Mass., 1982).

Benton, J.F., "Individualism and Conformity in Medieval Western Europe," in Banani, A., and Vyronis, S., Jr., eds. *Individualism and Conformity in Classical Islam* (Wiesbaden, 1977), 145-158.

Berger, A., "The Messianic Self-Consciousness of Abraham Abulafia," in Blau, J., et al., eds., *Essays in Jewish Life and Thought presented to Salo W. Baron* (New York, 1959), 55-62.

Berges, W., *Die Fürstenspiegel des hohen und späten Mittelalters* (Stuttgart, 1938).

Beriou, N., "Autour de Latran IV (1215): la naissance de la confession moderne et sa diffusion," in Groupe de la Bussière, eds., *Pratiques de la confession* (Paris, 1983), 73-93.

Bertrand, G., et al., eds., *Histoire de la France rurale. La formation de campagnes françaises des origines au XIVe siècle* (Paris, 1975).

vander Bijl, M., "Petrus Berchorius - les Sermons de Bersuire," *Vivarium*, 22.2 (1984), 113-120.

Biraben, J.N., "La medicine et l'enfant au moyen âge," *ADH*, 8 (1973), 73-75.

Blau, J., et al., eds., *Essays in Jewish Life and Thought presented to Salo W. Baron* (New York, 1959).

Blintz, J., *Die Leibesübugen des Mittelalters* (Gutersloh, 1880).

Blumenkranz, B., "Jüdische und christliche Konvertiten," in *Miscellanea mediaevalia Jüdentum im Mittelalter*, ed. P. Wilpert (Berlin, 1966), 264-280.

Blumenthal, D.R., ed., *Approaches to Judaism in Medieval Times*, 2 vols. (Chico, Ca., 1985).

Boese, H., "Zur Textüberliefung von Thomas Cantimpratensis' *Liber de naturis rerum*," *Archivum fratrum praedicatorum*, 39 (1969), 53-68.

Böll, F., "Die Lebensalter, Ein Beitrag zur Ethologie und zur Geschichte de Zahlen," *Neue Altertumsgeschichte und deutsche Literatur*, 16 (1913), 89-145.

Bolton, B., "Mulieres sanctae," *Studies in Church History*, 10 (1973), 77-95.

Bolton, B., "*Vitae Matrum.* A Further Aspect of the Frauenfrage," in Baker, D., ed., *Medieval Women* (Oxford, 1978), 253-224.

Bernstein, D., *The Lady in the Tower. Medieval Courtesy Literature for Women* (Hamden, Ct., 1983).

Boutruche, R., *Seigneurie et feodalité*, 2 vols. (Paris, 1970).

de Boüard, M., "Encyclopédies médiévales. Sur la connaissance de la nature et du monde au moyen âge," *Revue des questions historiques*, 112 (1930), 258-304.

de Boüard, M., *Une encyclopédie médiévale: le Compendium philosophiae* (Paris, 1936).

Bowen, J., *A History of Western Education*, 3 vols. (London, 1975).

Boyer, G.E., "Bartholomaeus Anglicus and his Encyclopedia," *Journal of English and Germanic Philology*, 14 (1920), 168-189.

Brackmann, A., ed., *Papsttum und Kaisertum...* (Munich, 1926).

Breitscher, J.K., "'As a twig is bent': Children and their Parents in an Aristocratic Society," *Journal of Medieval History*, 2 (1976), 181-191.

Brewer, E.C., *A Dictionary of Miracles* (London, 1966).

Brown, P., "The Saint as Exemplar in Late Antiquity," *Representations*, 1.2 (1983), 1-25.

Brundage, J., *Law, Sex and Christian Society in Medieval Europe* (Chicago, 1987).

Burrow, J.A., *The Ages of Man: A Study in Medieval Writing and Thought* (Oxford, 1986).

Burton, R., *Classical Poets in the "Florilegium Gallicum"* (Frankfurt, 1983).

Bynum, C.W., *Docere Verbo et Exempla. An Aspect of Twelfth Century Spirituality* (Cambridge, Mass., 1979).

Bynum, C.W., *Holy Feast and Holy Fast. The Religious Significance of Food to Medieval Women* (Berkeley, 1987).

Bynum, C.W., *Jesus as Mother. Studies in the Spirituality of the Middle Ages* (Berkeley, 1982).

Cabanis, P.J.G., *Oeuvres complètes*, 5 vols. (Paris, 1845).

Caraffa, F., et al., *Bibliotheca sanctorum*, 12 vols. (Rome, 1962-1970).

Carmody, F.J., *Arabic Astronomical and Astrological Sciences in Translation* (Berkeley, 1956).

Chambers, J.C., *Population, Economy and Society in Pre-Industrial England*, ed. W.A. Armstrong (Oxford, 1972).

Charlond, Th., *Artes praedicandi contribution à l'histoire de la rhétorique au moyen âge*, in *Publications d'Institut d'Etudes médiévales d'Ottawa*, 7 (Ottawa, 1936).

Chew, S., *The Pilgrimage of Life* (Port Washington, N.Y. 1973).

Chiffoleau, J., *La comptabilité de l'au dela les hommes, la mort et la religion dans la region d'Avignon à la fin du moyen âge (vers 1320 - vers 1489)* (Paris, 1980).

Classen, P., *Gerhoch von Reichersberg* (Wiesbaden, 1960).

Collison, R., *Encyclopedias, their History throughout the Ages* (New York, 1966).

Colomer, E., "Die Beziehung des Ramon Llull zum Jüdentum and Rahmen des spanischen Mittelalter," in P. Wilpert, eds., *Miscellanea Mediaevalia. Jüdentum im Mittelalter* (Berlin, 1966), 183-227.

Constable, G., "Renewal and Reform in Religious Life, Concepts and Realities," in *Renaissance and Renewal in the Twelfth Century*, ed. R. Benson and G. Constable (Cambridge, Mass., 1982), 37-67.

Cumont, F., *Lux perpetua* (Paris, 1949).

Curtius, E.R., *European Literature and the Latin Middle Ages*, trans. R.E. Trask (New York, 1968).

Dales, R.C., "The Medieval View of Human Dignity," *Journal of the History of Ideas*, 38 (1977), 557-572.

Davidsohn, R., *Geschichte von Florenz*, 8 vols. (Berlin, 1908).

Delahaye, H., *Études sur le légendier romain des saints de novembre et décembre* (Paris, 1936).

Delany, S., "Undoing Substantial Connection: the Late Medieval Attack on Analogical Thought," *Mosaic*, 5.4 (1972), 31-52.

Delany, S.P., *Married Saints* (New York, 1935).

Delaruelle, E., *La pieté populaire au moyen âge* (Turin, 1975).

Delhaye, P., "Le dossier anti-matrimonial de l'*Adversus Jovinianum* et son influence sur quelque écrits latins de XIIe siècle," *Mediaeval Studies*, 13 (1951), 65-86.

Delumeau, J., *La peur en Occident (xive-xviiie siècles). Une cité assiegée* (Paris, 1978).

Demaitre, L., "Child Care in the Middle Ages," *Journal of Psychohistory* (1976/7), 461-490.

Demaitre, L.E., *Doctor Bernard de Gordon. Professor and Practitioner* (Toronto, 1980).

Dempf, A., *Sacrum imperium* (Darmstadt, 1954).

Dilthey, W., *Selected Writings*, ed. and trans. H.P. Rickman (Cambridge, 1976).

Dinzelbacher, P., ed., *Frauenmystik im Mittelalter* (Ostfielden, 1985).

Donaldson, C., *Martin of Tours, Parish Priest, Mystic and Exorcist* (London, 1980).

Dondaine, A., "Guillaume Péyraut, vie et oeuvres," *Archivum fratrum praedicatorum*, 18 (1948), 162-236.

Dondaine, A., "La vie et les oeuvres de Jean le San Gemignano," *Archivum fratrum praedicatorum*, 9 (1939), 128-183.

Douie, D.L., *The Nature and Effect of the History of the Fraticelli* (Manchester, 1932).

Ducange, C. de Fresne, *Glossarium mediae et infimae latinitatis*, 10 vols. (Paris, 1883-1887).

Duby, G., "Au XIIème siècle: les 'jeunes' dans la société aristocratique," *Annales (Économies, Sociétés, Civilisations)*, 19 (1964), 835-846.

Duby, G., *The Early Growth of the European Economy*, trans. H.G. Clark (London, 1973).

Duby, G., "In Northwestern France: the Youth in Twelfth Century Aristocratic Society," in *Lordship and Community in Medieval Europe*, ed. F. Cheyette (New York, 1968), 198-209.

Duby, G., *Rural Economy and Country Life in the Medieval West*, trans. C. Postan (London, 1968).

Duby, G., "Structure de parenté et noblesse dans la France du Nord aux XIe et XIIe siècles," in *Hommes et structures du moyen âge* (Paris, 1973), 267-285.

Duby, G., and Le Goff, J., eds., *Famille et parenté dans l'Occident médiévale* (Rome, 1972).

Dupaquier, J., and Le Roy Ladurie, E., "Quatre-Vingts villages (XIIIe-XX siécles)," *Annales (Économies, Sociétés, Civilisations)*, 24 (1969), 423-434.

Eisenstadt, S.N., "African Age Groups: A Comparative Study," *Africa*, 24 (1954), 100-113.

Eskoli, A.Z., *Ha-Tnuot ha-Meschichiot be-Yisrael* (Jerusalem, 1956).

Ettinger, E., et al., eds., *Yitshak Baer Jubilee Volume* (Jerusalem, 1960).

Falk, Z., *Jewish Matrimonial Law in the Middle Ages* (Oxford, 1966).

Festugière, A.J., *La Sainteté* (Paris, 1949).

Fliche, A., *La Réforme grégorienne*, 3 vols. (Louvain, 1924-1937).

Forest, A., et al., *Le mouvement doctrinal du XIe au XVe siècle* (Paris, 1956).

Fosbrooke, H., "Die Altersgliederung als gesellschaftliches Grundprinzip. Ein Untersuchung am Beispiel des Hirtenvolkes der Maasai in Ostafrika," in Rosenmäyr, L., *Die menschlichen Lebensalter: Kontinuität und Krisen* (Munich, 1978), 80-104.

Fossier, "La Démographie médiévale. Problèmes de méthode (Xe - XIIIe siècles)," *ADH*, 10 (1975), 143-165.

Fowler, G.B., "Manuscript Admont 608 and Engelbert of Admont (c. 1250-1331). Part II. Appendices 6-13," *AHDLMA*, 45 (1978), 250-306.

Freeman, J., *Aging: Its History and Literature* (New York, 1979).

Frugoni, C., "La giovinezza di Francesco nelle fonte (testi e immagini)," *Studi medievali*, Ser. 3, 25.1 (1984), 115-144.

Gabriel, A.L., *The Educational Ideas of Vincent of Beauvais* (Notre Dame, Ind., 1962).

Gabriel, A.L., and Rytko, E., *L'educazione nel medio evo e l'educazione d'oggi* (Rome, 1962).

de Gaiffier, B., *Études critiques d'hagiographie et d'iconologie* (Brussels, 1967).

de Gaiffier, B., "Intactum sponsam reliquens. À propos de la vie de S. Alexis," *AB*, 65 (1947), 157-195.

de Gandillac, M., et al., *La pensée encyclopédique au moyen âge* (Neûchatel, 1966).

Garfagnini, G.C., *Cosmologie medievali* (Turin, 1978).

Garin, E., "La dignitas hominis e la letteratura patristica," *La Rinascità*, 1.4 (1938), 102-146.

Gauthier, R.A., "Deux témoignages sur la date de la première traduction latine des Économiques," *Revue philosophiqe de Louvain*, 50 (1952), 273-283.

Génicot, L., "La population en Occident du XIème au XIIème siècle," *Cahiers d'histoire mondiale*, (1953), 446-462.

Génicot, L., *Le XIIIe siècle européen* (Paris, 1968).

Génicot, L., "On the Evidence of Growth of Population in the West," in Thrupp, S., ed., *Change in Medieval Society* (New York, 1964), 14-29.

Gersh, S., *From Iamblichus to Eriugena: An Investigation of the Prehistory and Evolution of the Pseudo-Dionysian Tradition* (Leiden, 1978).

de Ghellinck, J., "Inventus, gravitas, senectus," in *Studia mediaevalia in honorem admodum reverendi patris Raymundi Josephi Martin* (Bruges, 1948), 39-59.

Gil'adi, A., *Makhschevet ha-Hinukh shel al-Ghazzali* (Hebrew University of Jerusalem, unpublished doctoral dissertation, 1983).

Gillespie, C.C., ed., *Dictionary of Scientific Biography*, 16 vols. (New York, 1970-1980).

Glasser, M., "Marriage in Medieval Hagiography," *Studies in Medieval and Renaissance History*, Ser. 2, 4 (1981), 3-34.

Glorieux, R., *La faculté des arts et ses maîtres du XIIIe siècle* (Paris, 1971).

Goodich, M., "Bartholomeux Anglicus on Child-Rearing," *Journal of Psychohistory*, 3 (1975), 75-84.

Goodich, M., "Childhood and Adolescence among the Thirteenth Century Saints," *History of Childhood Quarterly*, 1 (1973), 283-309.

Goodich, M., "Un dialogue entre occident et orient: Anselme de Havelberg et l'idée de progrès," *Actes du premier colloque franco-polonais d'histoire* (Nice, 1983), 173-81.

Goodich, M., *Vita perfecta: the Ideal of Sainthood in the Thirteenth Century*, in *Monographien zur Geschichte des Mittelalters*, 15 (Stuttgart, 1982).

Grabmann, M., *Guglielmo di Moerbeke O.P. il traduttore delle opere di Aristotele* (Rome, 1946).

Gransden, A., *Historical Writing in England*, 2 vols. (London and Ithaca, 1974-1982).

Gregory, T., "La nouvelle idée de nature et de savoir scientifique au XIIe siècle," in Murdoch, J.E. and Sylla, E.D., eds., *The Cultural Context of Medieval Learning*, in *Boston Studies in the Philosophy of Science*, 26 (Boston, 1972), 193-218.

Grignaschi, "La diffusion du *Secretum secretorum* (Sirr al-'asrar) dans l'Europe occidentale," *AHDLMA*, 47 (1980), 7-69.

Grignaschi, M., "L'origine et les metamorphoses du <<Sirr-al asrar>>," *AHDLMA*, 43 (1976), 7-112.

Groupe de la Bussière, eds., *Pratiques de la confession* (Paris, 1983).

Gruman, G., *A History of Ideas About the Prolongation of Life,*, in *Transactions of the American Philosophical Society*, New Series, 56, pt. 9 (Philadelphia, 1966).

Grundmann, H., *Religiöse Bewegungen im Mittelalter* (Hildesheim, 1961).

Guglielmiti, M., "L'Autobiographie en Italie, XVe-XVIIe siècles", in Olney, J., ed., *Autobiography: Essays Theoretical and Critical* (Princeton, 1980), 101-114.

Guillaume, P., and Pousson, J.P., *Démographie historique* (Paris, 1970).

Guiraud, J., *Histoire de l'Inquisition au moyen âge* (Paris, 1935-1938).

Gulliver, P.H., *Social Control in an African Society: A Study of the Arusha: Agricultural Masai of Northern Tanganyika* (London, 1963).

Hallack, G., and Anson, P., *These Made Peace* (Peterson, N.J., 1957).

Hanning, R., *The Individual in Twelfth-Century Romance* (New Haven, 1977).

Hanson, R.P.C., *Saint Patrick, His Origins and Career* (Oxford, 1968).

Harvey, B., "The Population Trend in England between 1300 and 1348," *Transactions of the Royal Historical Society*, 16 (1965), 23-42.

Harvey, E.R., *The Inward Wits- Psychological Theory in the Middle Ages and Renaissance* (London, 1975).

Hatcher, John, *Plague, Population and the Economy 1348-1530* (London, 1977).

Hentsch, A.A., *De la littérature didactique du moyen âge s'adressant specialement aux dames* (Halle, 1903).

Herlihy, D., *Medieval Households* (Cambridge, Mass., 1985).

Herlihy, D., "Viellir à Florence au Quattrocento," *Annales (Économies, Sociétes, Civilisations)*, 24 (1969), 1338-1352.

Herlihy, D., and Klapisch-Zuber, C., *Les toscanes et leurs familles* (Paris, 1978).

Hewson, M.A., *Giles of Rome and the Medieval Theory of Conception* (London, 1975).

Higounet-Nadal, A., "Les facteurs de croissance de la ville Périgeux," *ADH*, 17 (1982), 11-20.

Hillgarth, J.N., "The Position of Isidorean Studies: A Critical Review of the Literature 1936-1975," *Studi medievali*, Ser. 3, 24.1 (1983), 816-905.

Hillgarth, J.N., *Ramon Lull and Lullism in Fourteenth Century France* (Oxford, 1971).

Hilton, R.H., eds., *Peasants, Knights and Heretics* (Cambridge, 1976).

Hinderer, D., "On Rehabilitating Margery Kempe," *Studia mystica*, 5, no. 3 (1982), 27-43.

Hodgett, G.A.J., *A Social and Economic History of Medieval Europe* (London, 1972).

Hofmeister, G., "Rasis' Traumlehre. Traümbucher des Spätmittelalters," *Archiv für Kulturgeschichte*, 51 (1969), 137-159.

Hofmeister, A., "Puer, Iuvenis, Senex. Zum Verständnis der mittelalterlichen Altersbezeichnungen," in *Papsttum und Kaisertum. Forschungen zur politischen Geschichte und Geisteskultur des Mittelalters. Paul Kehr zum 65. Geburtstag dargestellt*, ed. A. Brackman (Munich, 1926), 287-316.

Hollingsworth, T.H., *Historical Demography* (London, 1969).

Hostie, R., *Vie et mort de ordres religieux* (Paris, 1972).

"The Human Life Span in History," *Interdisciplinair centrum voor historisch oenderzoek naar de menselijk levensloop Bulletin*, 1, (1984).

Jacquart, D., and Thomasset, C., *Sexualité et savoir medical au moyen âge* (Paris, 1985).

Javelet, R., *Image et ressemblance au douzième siècle: De Saint Anselme à Alain de Lille*, 2 vols. (Strassbourg, 1967).

Jedin, H., ed., *Handbuch der Kirchengeschichte*, III, 2 (Freiburg, 1966-1968).

Jones, R., *Mystical Religion* (London, 1909).

Kamlah, W., *Apokalypse und Geschichtstheologie*, in *Historische Studien*, 285 (Berlin, 1935).

Kanarfogel, E., "Attitudes toward Childhood and Children in Medieval Jewish Society," in D.R. Blumenthal, ed., *Approaches to Judaism in Medieval Times*, 2 vols. (Chico, Ca., 1985), II, 1-34.

Kasher, M.M., and Mandelbaum, J.B., eds., *Sarei ha-Elef*, 2 vols., 2nd ed. (Jerusalem, 1978-1979).

Kasher, M., *Perushei ha-Rishonim le-Masekhet Avoth* (Jerusalem, 1973).

Kemp, E.W., *Canonisation and Authority in the Western Church* (London, 1948).

Kershaw, "The Great Famine and Agrarian Crisis in England 1315-1355," in Hilton, R.H., ed., *Peasants, Knights and Heretics: Studies in Medieval English Social History* (Cambridge, 1976), 85-132.

Kett, J., *Rites of Passage. Adolescence in America, 1790 to the Present* (New York,, 1977).

Kieckhefer, R., *Unquiet Souls, Fourteenth Century Saints and their Religious Milieu* (Chicago, 1984).

Klinck, R., *Die lateinische Etymologie des Mittelalters* (Munich, 1970).

Koch, G., "Die Frau im mittelalterlichen Katholismus und Waldensertum," *Studi medievali*, Ser. 3, 5 (1984), 741-774.

Koch, G., *Frauenfrage und Ketzertum im Mittelalter* (Berlin, 1962).

Krauss, H., ed., *Neues Handbuch der Literaturwissenschaft. Europäisches Hochmittelalter, VII* (Wiesbaden, 1981).

Kroll, J., "The Concept of Childhood in the Middle Ages," *Journal of the History of the Behavioral Sciences*, 13 (1977), 384-393.

Kuttner, S., "La réserve papale du droit de canonisation," *Revue historique de droit français et étranger*, 4th ser. 7 (1938), 172-228.

Lacombe, G., "Medieval Latin Versions of the *Parva naturalia*,", *New Scholasticism*, 5 (1931), 384-411.

Ladner, G.B., *The Idea of Reform*, rev. ed. (New York, 1967).

Lagenkrantz, H., and Slotkin, T.A., "The 'Stress' of Being Born," *Scientific American*, 254, no. 4 (April, 1986), 100-107.

Lagorio, V.M., "Medieval Continental Women Mystics," in Szarmach, P., ed., *An Introduction to the Medieval Mystics of Europe* (Albany, 1984), 161-194.

Lambert, M., *Medieval Heresy, Popular Movements from Bogomil to Hus* (New York, 1976).

Langlois, C.V., *La vie en France au moyen âge*, 4 vols. (Paris, 1926-1928).

Lanzoni, F., "Il sogno presago della madre incinta nella letteratura medievale e antica," *AB*, 45 (1927), 225-261.

Lawrence, C.H., *St. Edmund of Canterbury* (Oxford, 1960).

Lea, H.C., *The History of Sacramental Celibacy in the Christian Church*, 2 vols., 3rd ed. (New York, 1970).

Leach, A.F., *The School of Medieval England* (New York, 1915).

Leclercq, J., "L'Écriture sainte dans l'hagiographie monastique du haut moyen âge," in *La Bibbia nell' Alto Medioevo. Centro italiano di studi sull'Alto Medioevo. Settimane di studio*, 10 (Spoleto, 1963), 103-138.

Leclercq, J., *La spiritualité du Pierre de Celle (1115-1183)* (Paris, 1946).

Lecoy de la Marche, A., *La chaire français au moyen âge* (Paris, 1886).

Leff, G., *Heresy in the Later Middle Ages*, 2 vols. (Manchester, 1967).

Le Goff, J., "Petits enfants dans la littérature des XIIe-XIIIe siècles," *ADH*, 8 (1973), 129-132.

Lehman, P., "Autobiographies of the Middle Ages," *Transactions of the Royal Historical Society*, Ser. 5, 3, (1953), 41-52.

Leitzmann, A., ed., *Winsbekische Gedichte nebst Tirol und Fridebrant*, ed. I. Reifferstein, new ed. (Gottingen, 1962).

Lemoine, M., "L'oeuvre encyclopédique de Vincent de Beauvais," in de Gandilhac, M., ed., *La pensée encyclopédique du moyen âge* (Neûchatel, 1966), 77-85.

Lerner, R. *The Heresy of the Free Spirit in the Later Middle Ages* (Berkeley, 1972).

Le Roy Ladurie, E., *Montaillou, village occitan de 1294 à 1324* (Paris, 1976).

Levinson, D.J., *The Seasons of a Man's Life* (New York, 1978).

Lindberg, D., ed., *Science in the Middle Ages* (Chicago, 1978).

Little, L., *Religious Poverty and the Profit Economy in Medieval Europe* (Ithaca, 1978).

Lloyd-Jones, H., ed., *History and Imagination: Essays in Honor of H.R. Trevor-Roper* (London, 1981).

Lochrie, K., "*The Book* of Margery Kemp: the marginal woman's quest for literary authority," *Journal of Medieval and Renaissance Studies*, 16, 1 (1986), 33-55.

Lohr, C., "Medieval Latin Aristotle Commentaries," *Traditio*, 23 (1967), 313-413; 26 (1970), 135-216; 27 (1971), 251-352; 28 (1972), 281-396; 24 (1973), 93-108; 30 (1974), 119-144.

Lohr, C. "Medieval Latin Aristotle Commentaries. Addenda and Corrigenda," *Bulletin de philosophie médiévale*, 14 (1972), 116-126.

Löw, L., *Die Lebensalter in der jüdische Literatur* (Szegedin, 1875).

de Lubac, H., *La posterité de Joachim de Flore I. De Joachim à Schelling* (Paris, 1978).

Lüth, P., *Geschichte der Geriatrie* (Stuttgart, 1965).

Maffei, R., *Commentariorum urbanorum* (Venice, 1515).

Makdisi, G., et al., eds., *L'Enseignement en Islam et en Occident au moyen âge* (Paris, 1976).

Makowski, E., "The conjugal debt and medieval canon law," *Journal of Medieval History*, 3 (1977), 99-114.

Ma Millas i Vallierosa, J., "The Doctrine of the 'Lullian Dignities' and the Sefiroth," in *Yitshak Baer Jubilee Volume*, ed. Ettinger, E., et al. (Jerusalem, 1960), 186-190.

Martin, H. "Confession et contrôle à le fin du moyen âge," in Groupe de la Bussière, eds. *Pratiques de la confession* (Paris, 1983), 117-134.

de Mause, L., ed. *History of Childhood* (New York, 1974).

McCarthy, J., *Humanistic Emphasis in the Educational Thought of Vincent of Beauvais* (Leiden, 1976).

McLaughlin, M., "Abelard as Autobiographer: the Motives and Meaning of his 'Story of Calamities,'" *Speculum*, 42 (1967), 463-488.

McLaughlin, M., "Survivors and Surrogates: Children and Parents from the Ninth to Thirteenth Centuries," in *History of Childhood*, ed. L. de Mause (New York, 1974), 101-181.

Meersseman, G.G., *Le dossier de l'ordre de la pénitence au XIII siècle* (Fribourg, 1961).

Melamed, A., "Hebrew Italian Renaissance and Early Modern Encyclopedias," *Revista storia della filosofia*, 1 (1985), 93-112.

Metz, R., "L'Enfant dans le droit canonique médiéval. Orientation de recherche," in *L'Enfant. Recueils de la société Jean Bodin et l'histoire comparative des institutions* , 26.2 (Brussels, 1976), 9-96.

Mialart, G. and Vial, J., eds., *Histoire mondiale de l'éducation*, 4 vols. (Paris, 1981).

Michaud-Quantin, P., "Les petites encyclopédies du XIIIe siècle," *Cahiers d'histoire mondiale*, 9 (1965/6), 580-595.

Michaud-Quantin, P., "À propos des premiers 'Summae confessorum'," *Recherches de théologie ancienne et médiévale*, 26 (1959), 264-309.

Michaud-Quantin, P., *Sommes de casuistique et manuels de confession au moyen âge (XII-XVI siècles)* (Louvan, 1962).

Miles, M.R., "Infancy, Parenting and Nourishment in Augustine's Confessions," *Journal of the American Academy of Religion*, 10 (1982), 349-364.

Milis, L., "Het kind in de Middelleeuven Beschouwingen over methode en ondersock," *Tijdschrift voor geschiednis*, 94 (1981), 377-390.

Miller, E., "The English Economy in the XIIIth Century," *Past and Present*, 28 (1964), 21-40.

Minio-Palluelo, L., "Iacobus Veneticus Grecus: Canonist and Translator of Aristotle," *Traditio*, 8 (1952), 265-304.

Minois, G., *Histoire de viellesse* (Paris, 1987).

Misch, G., *Geschichte der Autobiographie*, 4 vols. (Bern, 1949/1969).

Mols, R., *Introduction à la démographie historique des villes d'Europe du XIVe au XVIIIe siècle*, 3 vols. (Louvain, 1954-1956).

Momigliano, A., "A Medieval Jewish Autobiography," in *History and Imagination. Essays in Honour of H.R. Trevor-Roper*, ed. H. Lloyd-Jones, et al. (London, 1981), 30-36.

Montague, A., *Growing Young* (New York, 1981).

Moore, R.I., *The Birth of Popular Heresy* (London, 1975).

Morag, S., ed., *Mehkarei Adoth ve-Genizah* (Jerusalem, 1981).

Morris, C., "Individuality in Twelfth Century Religion," *Journal of Ecclesiastical History*, 31 (1980), 195-206.

Müchow, H., "Über der Quellenwert der Autobiographie für die Zeitgeistforschung," *Zeitschrift für Religions - and Geistesgeschichte*, 17 (1966), 297-310.

Mueller, J.M., "Autobiography of a New 'Creatur'. Female Spirituality, Selfhood and Authorship in *The Book of Margery Kemp*", in M.B. Rose, et al., *Women in the Middle Ages and the Renaissance* (Syracuse, N.Y., 1986), 155-172.

Mundy, J.H., et al., eds., *Essays in Medieval Life and Thought Presented in Honor of Austin Patterson Evans* (New York, 1955).

Mundy, J.H., *Europe in the High Middle Ages, 1150-1309* (London, 1973).

Murdoch, J.E., and Sylla, E.D., eds., *The Cultural Context of Medieval Learning*, in *Boston Studies in the Philosophy of Science*, 26 (Boston, 1975).

Murphy, J., "Aristotle's *Rhetoric* in the Middle Ages," *The Quarterly Journal of Speech*, 52 (1966), 109-115.

Naz, R., et al., *Dictionnaire de droit canonique*, 7 vols. (Paris, 1924-1965).

Nock, A.D., *Conversion* (Oxford, 1933).

Noonan, J.T., "Intellectual and Demographic History," in Glass, V., and Revelle, R., eds., *Population and Social Change* (London, 1972), 115-135.

Novati, F., "Nuovi studi su Albertino Mussato. II," *Giornale storico della letteratura italiana*, 7 (1886), 31-47.

Ohlin, G., "No Safety in Numbers: Some Pitfalls in Historical Statistics," in Rosovsky, H., ed., *Industrialization in Two Systems: Essays in Honor of Alexander Gerschenkorn* (New York, 1966), 68-90.

Oliger, L., "De pueris oblatis in ordine minorum," *Archivum franciscanum historicum*, 8 (1915), 389-447; 10 (1917), 271-288.

Olney, T., ed., *Autobiography: Essays Theoretical and Critical* (Princeton, 1980).

Orme, N., *English Schools in the Middle Ages* (London, 1973).

Pascal, R., *Design and Truth in Autobiography* (London, 1960).

von Pauly, A.F., and Wissowa, G., eds., *Realencyclopädie...*, 48 vols. (Stuttgart, 1958-1974).

Payen, J.C., "La crise de mariage à la fin du XIIe siècle d'après la littérature française de temps," in Duby, G., and Le Goff, J., eds., *Famille et parenté dans l'Occident médiévale* (Rome, 1972), 413-430.

Peck, R.A., "Number as Cosmic Language," in D.A. Jeffrey, ed., *By Things Seen. Reference and Recognition in Medieval Thought* (Ottawa, 1979), 47-80.

Peiper, A., *Chronik der Kinderheilkunde* (Leipzig, 1955).

Pelliccia, G., et al., eds., *Dizionario degli istituti di perfezione*, 7 vols. to date (Rome, 1974-1983).

Pelzer, A., "Un traducteur inconnu, Pierre Gallego," *Miscellanea Francesco Ehrle*, 2 vols. (Rome, 1924), I, 407-456.

Pelzer, C., and Kaeppel, T., "Conrad de Mégenberg," *Revue d'histoire ecclésiastique*, 45 (1950), 554-616.

Perroy, E., *La démographic médiévale. Sources et méthodes* (Nice, 1970).

Philibert, M., *L'échelle des âges* (Paris, 1968).

Pirenne, J., "L'Instruction des marchands au moyen âge," *Annales d'histoire économique et sociale*, 1 (1924), 20-28.

Plassman, T.B., "Bartholomaeus Anglicus," *Archivum franciscanum historicum*, 12 (1919), 68-109.

Platzeck, E.W., *Raymond Lull*, 2 vols. (Düsseldorf, 1962).

Postan, M., et al., *Cambridge Economic History of Europe*, 7 vols. to date (Cambridge, 1941-1978).

Power, E., *Medieval Women*, ed., M.M. Postan (Cambridge, 1975).

Prawer, J., "The Autobiography of Obadiyah the Norman, a Convert to Judaism at the Time of the First Crusade," in *Studies in Medieval Jewish History and Literature*, ed. I. Twersky, 1 (Cambridge, 1979). 110-134.

Prins, A.H.J., *East African Class Systems: An Inquiry into the Social Order of Galla, Kipsigis and Kikuyu* (Groningen, 1953).

Reames, S.L., *The legenda aurea. A Reexamination of its Paradoxical History* (Madison, Wisconsin, 1985).

Reeves, M.E., *The Influence of Prophecy in the Middle Ages* (Oxford, 1969).

Reeves, M.E., *Joachim of Fiore and the Prophetic Future* (London, 1976).

Rein, A., "Über die Entwicklung der Selbstbiographie im ausgehenden deutschen Mittelalter," *Archiv für Kulturgeschichte*, 14 (1919), 193-213.

Reynolds, L.D., and Wilson, N.G., *Scribes and Scholars. A Guide to the Transmission of Greek and Latin Literature*, 3rd rev. ed. (Oxford, 1974).

Riché, P., "L'Enfant dans la société monastique au XIIe siècle," in *Pierre Abélard. Pierre la Vénérable* (Paris, 1975), 692-700.

da Rocha Pereira, H., "Um manuscrito inedito do 'Liber de Conservanda sanitate' de Pedro Hispano," *Studium generale*, 9 (1962), 99-105.

Roggen, H., "Die Lebensform der hl. Franziskus von Assisi in ihrem Verhältnis zur feudalen und bürgerlichen Gesellschaft Italiens," *Franziskanische Studien*, 46 (1964), 1-54, 287-321.

Rosenmäyr, L., "Die menschlichen Lebensalter: in Deutungsversuchen der europäischen Kulturgeschichte," in Rosenmäyr, L., ed., *Die menschlichen Lebensalter: Kontinuität und Krisen* (Munich, 1978), 23-79.

Rosenmäyr, L., ed., *Die menschlichen Lebensalter: Kontinuität und Krisen* (Munich, 1978).

Rosenwein, S. and Little, L., "Social Meaning in Monastic and Mendicant Spiritualities," *Past and Present*, 63 (1974), 4-32.897

Ross, J.B., "The Middle Class Child in Urban Italy. Fourteenth to Early Sixteenth Century," in L. de Mause, ed., *History of Childhood* (New York, 1974), 183-228.

Roth, C., et al., eds., *Encyclopedia Judaica*, 16 vols. (Jerusalem, 1972).

Roth, N., "The 'Ages of Man' in Two Medieval Jewish Poems," *Hebrew Studies*, 24 (1983), 41-44.

Rouse, M.A., and Rouse, R.H., "The Texts called 'Lumen animae'," *Archivum fratrum praedicatorum*, 41 (1971), 5-113.

Rouse, R.H., "La diffusion en occident au XIIe siècle des outils de travail facilitant l'accès aux texts autoritatifs," in G. Makdisi, et al., eds., *L'Enseignement en Islam et en Occident au moyen âge* (Paris, 1976), 114-147.

Rouse, R.H., "Florilegia and Latin Classical Authors in Twelfth and Thirteenth Century France," *Viator*, 10 (1979), 131-160.

Rouse, R.H., and Rouse, M.A., *Preachers, Florilegia and Sermons: Studies in The Manipulus florum of Thomas of Ireland* (Toronto, 1979).

Russell, J.C., *Ancient and Medieval Population* (Philadelphia, 1958).

Russell, J.C., *Population in Europe 500-1500* (London, 1969).

Sarton, G., *Introduction to the History of Science*, 3 vols. (Baltimore, 1953).

Saxl, F., "Beiträge zu einer Geschichte Planetendarstellungen in Orient und Okzident," *Der Islam*, 3 (1912), 151-177.

Schipperges, H., *Die Assimilation der arabischen Medizin durch das lateinische Mittelalter* (Weisbaden, 1964).

Schmitt, C.B., "Aristotle among the Physicians," in A. Wear, et al., eds., *The Medical Renaissance of the Sixteenth Century* (Cambridge, 1985), 1-15.

Schmitt, J.C., *Le saint Lévrier, Guinefort guérison d'enfants depuis le XIIIe siècle* (Paris, 1979).

Schmitz, P., *Histoire de l'ordre de Saint Benoît*, 7 vols. (Maredsous, 1948-1956).

Schmücki, O., ed., *L'ordine della penitenza di San Francesco d'Assisi nel secolo XIII* (Rome, 1973).

Schneyer, J.B., *Repertorium der lateinischen Sermones des Mittelalters für die Zeit von 1150-1350*, 9 vols., in *Beiträge*, 43 (Munich, 1969-1980).

Scholem, G., *Ha-kabbalah shel Sefer ha-Tmunah shel Avraham Abulafia*, ed. I. Ben-Shlomo (Jerusalem, 1968).

Scholem, G., *Major Trends in Jewish Mysticism* (New York, 118-155).

Scholem, G., "'Shaarei Tsedek'. Maamar be-Kabbalah me-Ascolat R. Abraham Abulafia meyoohas le-R Shem-Tov", *Kiryat Sefer*, 1 (1924), 127-139.

Sears, E.L., *The Ages of Man. Medieval Interpretations of the Life Cycle* (Princeton, 1986).

Sears, R., and Fellman, S.S., eds., *The Seven Ages of Man* (Los Altos, Ca., 1973).

Shahar, S., "Le catharisme et le début de la cabale,'" *Annales (Économies, Sociétés, Civilisations)*, 29 2 (1974), 1185-1210.

Shahar, S., "Infants, Infant Care and Attitudes towards Infancy in the Medieval Lives of Saints," *Journal of Psychohistory*, 10 (1983), 281-309.

Shore, M.F., "Biography in the 1980s. A psychoanalytic perspective," in T.K. Rabb and Robert I. Rotberg, eds., *The New History. The 1980s and Beyond* (Princeton, 1982), 89-113.

Slicher van Bath, B.H., *The Agrarian History of Western Europe*, trans. O. Ordish (London, 1963).

Smith, M., *Prudentius' Psychomachia. A Reexamination* (Princeton, 1976).

Southern, R., *Medieval Humanism* (New York, 1970).

Spengemann, W.G., *The Forms of Autobiography* (New Haven, 1980).

Staum, M.S., *Cabanis. Enlightenment and Medical Philosophy in the French Revolution* (Princeton, 1980).

von Steenberghen, F., *Aristotle in the West*, trans. L. Johnson (Louvain, 1955).

von Steenberghen, F., *La philosophie au XIIe siècle* (Louvain, 1966).

von Steenberghen, F., "La philosophie de la nature au XIIIe siècle," in *La filosofia della natura nel medioevo. Atti del terzo congresso internazionale di filosofia medioevale* (Milan, 1966), 114-132.

Stow, K.R., "The Jewish Family in the Rhineland in the High Middle Ages. Form and Function," *American Historical Review*, 92 (1987), 1085-1110.

Strayer, J., ed., *Dictionary of the Middle Ages*, 3 vols. to date (New York, 1982-1983).

Sudhoff, K., *Erstlinge der pädiatrische Literatur* (Munich, 1925).

Sudhoff, K., "Zum Regimen sanitatis Salernitanum," *Archiv für Geschichte der Medizin*, 7 (1914), 360-362; 8 (1915), 29, 352-373; 9 (1916), 221-245; 10 (1917), 91-101; 12 (1919), 149-180.

Szarmach, P., ed., *An Introduction to the Medieval Mystics of Europe* (Albany, 1984).

Tentler, T., *Sin and Confession on the Eve of the Reformation* (Princeton, 1977).

Tentler, T., "The Summa for Confessions as an Instrument of Social Control," in Trinkaus, C., amd Oberman, H., eds., *The Pursuit of Holiness in Late Medieval and Renaissance Religion* (Leiden, 1974), 102-126.

Thesaurus linguae latinae, 10 vols. to date (Leipzig, 1900-1984).

Thomasset, C., "La representation de le génération dans la pensée scientifique médiévale," in *Love and Marriage in the Twelfth Century*, ed. W. van Haecke and A. Welkenhuysen (Louvain, 1981), 1-17.

Thorndike, L., *A History of Magic and Experimental Science*, 8 vols. (New York, 1954-1964).

Thorndike, L., *Michael Scot* (London, 1965).

Thorndike, L., "More Manuscripts of Thomas of Cantimpré's *De natura rerum*," *Isis*, 54 (1963), 269-277.

Thouzellier, C., *Catharisme et Valdéisme en Languedoc* (Paris, 1969).

Titow, J.Z., "Some Evidence of the Thirteenth Century Population Increase," *Economic History Review*, 14 (1961/2), 217-223.

Toynbee, P., *Dante Studies and Researches* (London, 1902).

Trinkaus, C., *In Our Image and Likeness. Humanity and Dignity in Italian Humanist Thought*, 2 vols. (Chicago, 1970).

Trinkaus, C., amd Oberman, H., eds., *The Pursuit of Holiness in Late Medieval and Renaissance Religion* (Leiden, 1974).

Tuaf, A., "Remazim le-Tnuah Meschichit be-Roma be-Shnat 1260," *Bar Ilan Sefer ha-Shana shel Universitat Bar-Ilan*, 14/15 (1976), 114-121.

Turnbull, C., *The Human Cycle* (New York, 1983).

Ullman, B.L., "Classical Authors in Medieval *Florilegia*," *Classical Philology*, 27 (1932), 1-42.

Vacant, A., et al., *Dictionnaire de théologie catholique*, 15 vols. (Paris, 1908-1950).

Vauchez, A., *La sainteté en occident aux derniers siècles du moyen âge d'après les procès de canonisation et des documents hagiographiques* (Rome, 1981).

Viller, M., et al., *Dictionnaire de spiritualité*, 13 vols. to date (Paris, 1937-1987).

Violante, C., "Quelque characteristiques des structures familles en Lombardie, Émilie et Toscane aux XIe et XIIe siècles," in Duby, G., amd Le Goff, J., eds., *Famille et parenté dans l'Occident médiéval* (Rome, 1972), 87-112.

Wackernagel, W., *Die Lebensalter, Ein Beitrag zur vergleichenden Sitten-und Rechtsgeschichte* (Basel, 1862).

Wakefield, W., *Heresy, Crusade and Inquisition in Southern France, 1100-1250* (Berkeley, 1974).

Walstra, G.J.J., "Thomas de Cantimpré. De naturis rerum. État de la question," *Vivarium*, 5.2 (1967), 146/171; 6.2 (1968), 46-71.

Warner, G., and Gilson, J., *British Museum Catalogue of Western Manuscripts in the Old Royal and King's Collections* (London, 1921).

Wear, A., et al., eds., *The Medical Renaissance of the Sixteenth Century* (Cambridge, 1985).

Weinstein, D., and Bell, R., *Saints and Society* (Chicago, 1982).

Weintraub, K.J., "Autobiography and Historical Consciousness," *Critical Inquiry*, 1 (1975), 821-848.

Weintraub, K.J., *The Value of the Individual, Self and Circumstance in Autobiography* (Chicago, 1978).

Weisheipl, J.A., "Curriculum of the Faculty of Arts at Oxford in the Early Fourteenth Century," *Mediaeval Studies*, 26 (1964).

Welter, J., *L'exemplum dans la littérature religieuse et didactique du moyen âge* (Paris, 1927).

Wendt, B., *Idee und Ertwicklungsgeschichte der enzyklopedischen Literatur* (Wurzburg, 1941).

West, D.C., and Swartz, S.Z., *Joachim of Fiore, A Study in Spiritual Perceptions and History* (Bloomington, Ind., 1983).

Wilpert, P., ed., *Miscellanea mediaevalia. Jüdentum im Mittelalter* (Berlin, 1966).

Wilson, A., "The Infancy of the History of Childhood: An Appraisal of Philippe Ariès," *History and Theory*, 19 (1980), 132-153.

Wilson, S., ed., *Saints and Their Cults: Studies in Religious Sociology, Folklore and History* (Cambridge, 1983).

Zimmerman, T.C.P., "Confession and Autobiography in the Early Renaissance," *Renaissance Studies in Honor of Hans Baron*, ed. A. Molho and J.A. Tedeschi (Florence, 1971), 119-140.

Index

Abel, 110
Abelard, 32, 71
Absalom of St. Victor, 71
Abulafia, Abraham, 10-11, 32, 34, 149
Acestes, 144
Achas, 101 n. 39
Adam and Eve, 85-6, 122-3, 143
Adam de la Halle, 28
Adam of Perseigne, 88, 93
Adelard of Bath, 10-11
adolescence, 2-4, 30-1, 35, 59, 70-1, 105-114, 121-34, 160-1
Adrastus (King), 106
adulthood, 143-146
Aeacus, 148
Aeneas, 106, 144
age, terminology of, 59-63
Agillolfus, 110
Agnes of Montepulciano, 83-4
Ailred of Rievaulx, 94
Alan of Lille, 60-1
Albertus Magnus, 38, 67, 69, 72
Alcabitius, 116 n. 15, 75 n. 17
alchemy, 153
Aldobrandino of Siena, 37-8
Alemanni, Antonio, 43
Alexander of Roes, 7, 9
Alexis, 131
Alfano of Montecassino, 11
Alfonse of Poitiers, 153
Alfonso VII (King), 28
Alfonso the Wise (King), 56 n. 84
Allen, Judson Boyce, 68-9
Alphanta, Garsenda, 131
Ambrose, 41, 62, 69, 209, 147
Ambrose of Siena, 92
analogy, 68-73
Anchises, 144
Angela of Foligno, 12, 29, 33
Angelo of Clareno, 10, 33, 34
Angelo of Furci, 84
Anselm of Canterbury, 93-4, 111
Anselm of Havelberg, 8
Anthony, 125
Anthony of Padua, 34, 117 n. 23
apocalypticism, 10-12

Apostolic Brethren, 9
Arabic sources, 90, 95
Ardent, Raoul, 68
Ariès, Philippe, 2, 96
Aristotle, 11, 35-9, 43-4, 59-62, 65-6, 83-7, 90-1, 109, 114, 122-3, 140, 144-5, 150-4, 159
Armengaud Blasius, 38, 145
Arnold of Villanova, 10, 38, 40
Artephius, 153
Ascanius, 144
assimilation, 108
astrology, 4, 11, 53, 61
Athanasius, 29, 125
Augustine, 8, 10-11, 15, 30, 32, 39, 69-71, 84-90, 121, 130, 132
Augustinian order, 111-2
autobiography, 10-12, 15, 27, 31-35, 112-2, 128, 150-1, 159
Avenzoar, 21 n. 29, 38
Averroes, 11, 37
Avicenna, 11-12, 42, 59-61, 75 n. 18, 87-91, 146-7, 153

Bacon, Roger, 7-10, 36-7, 151, 152-3
Bahya ben Asher ben Hlava of Saragossa, 62
Balbi, Joannes, 60
Bandino, Domenico di, 39, 54 n. 67, 76 n. 25
Barberino, Francesco, 122
Bartholomaeus Anglicus, 39-43, 64, 74 n. 1, 143
Basil, 41, 63, 69-70
Basilian order, 92
Beatrice of Planisolles, 32
Beatrice of Provence (Countess), 38
Bede, 71
Ben Bag Bag, 62-3
Benedict of Nursia, 29-30, 125
Benedictine order, 92-3
Berengar of Landorre, 40, 43, 64, 106-9
Berges, Wilhelm, 35

Bernard of Clairvaux, 85-6, 128
Bersuire, Pierre, 40-1, 62, 68, 84-7, 91, 105-8, 121, 143-4
bestiary, 63-4, 86
Bible, see Scripture
biography, 28, 34, 59; see autobiography
birth, 85-7, 91
Bissolo, Bellino, 38, 87, 107, 122, 146
Bocking, Ralph, 83
Bojano, Benvenuta, 50 n. 44, 92, 129
Bocados de Oro, 56 n. 84
Boleslas of Cracow, 132
Bonafos ibn Kaspi, Joseph, 113
Büll, Franz, 3
Bonaventure, 27, 60, 71, 77 n. 29, 93
Boniface VIII (Pope), 7, 40
Boutaric, Edgar, 43
Boutruche, Robert, 2
Brethren of the Sack, 12
Bridget of Sweden, 129
Brito, William, 61
Bruno of Segni, 72
Bryson, 38, 112, 114, 121, 144, 159
Burgundio of Pisa, 56 n. 85
Burley, Walter, 28
Burrow, J.A., 3-4
Bynum, Caroline, 30

Cabanis, Pierre-Jean George, 1
Caecilia, 131
Caesarius of Heisterbach, 83, 110, 124-5, 159-60
Cagnoli, Gerard, 96
Camaldulensians, 127-9
canonization, 31
Cantilupo, Thomas, 18 n. 10, 96
Capella, Martianus, 4, 77 n. 29
Carmelites, 149
Cathars, 124
Catherine of Alexandria, 124
Catherine of Siena, 110
Cato, 148
Celestine V (Pope), 10, 5 n. 65, 32, 34, 84, 128, 145, 149

Censorinus, 4
Charles II (King), 131
Charles of Blois (Duke), 129
Charroi de Nîmes, 43
chastity, female, 129-32
Chew, S., 3
Chiffoleau, J., 148
childhood, 1-4, 30, 35, 89-96, 146, 160
Cicero, 4, 61
Cistercians, 128
classical tradition, 3-4, 29, 60-70
Clement of Alexandria, 129
Climacus, Johannes, 10
Cluniacs, 93, 126
Colonna, James, 34
confession, 13-15, 85, 148-50; see autobiography; penance
Conrad of Castellario, 50 n. 44
Conrad of Halberstadt, 41
Conrad of Megenberg, 94-6, 122-3, 160
Constantine, 42
Constantinus Africanus, 38-9, 66, 84-8, 145; 151
conversi, 87-8
conversion, 126
Cunegunda (Queen), 132
Cyprian, 88, 147-8
Cyrus (King), 91

Damian, Peter, 63, 126-7
Daniel, Walter, 94
Daniel of Morley, 11
Dante Alighieri, 7, 9-10, 67-8, 105, 107, 144, 148, 151
Dauphine of Languedoc, 31, 131
decrepita, 72, 146-50
Demetrius, 124
demography, 4, 5-7, 13, 95, 105
dentition, 82
Deschamps, Eustace, 43
Dicta, 33
dictionaries, 59-61
Dido, 144
dignity of man, 65-8
Dilthey, Wilhelm, 31-2
Distinctiones, 75 n. 11
Dodici..., 122

Dominicans, 112, 129
Dorothy of Montau, 31, 132
dreams, 133
Dubois, Pierre, 7, 10
Duby, Georges, 2, 13
Ducange, C. du Fresne, 59

Eberhard of Bethune, 10
Ecclesiastes Rabbah, 62
Edmund of Canterbury, 24 n. 64, 45, 61, 92, 117
education, 20 n. 28, 89-96, 109-114, 122, 160
Edward II (King), 28
Elizabeth of Thuringia, 29, 83, 89, 124, 132, 159-60
Elzéar, 131-2
encyclopedias, 27, 39-42, 63-4
Engelberg of Admont, 4, 7, 27, 30, 36, 51 n. 47, 83, 110, 153-4
Erhard of Bamberg, 160
etymology, 68, 83-5, 95; *see* dictionaries; Isidore of Seville
Eugenius III (Pope), 85
Eustace of Faversham, 45 n. 6
Eva of St. Martin, 110; *see* Juliana of Cornillon
Evergislus, 110
Everyman, 68
exegesis, 69-73, 84-5, 147
exempla, 2, 64, 110, 159
expectancy, life, 7
extension of life, 68, 150-154

Facio of Cremona, 128
ibn Falaquera, Shemtov, 10, 62, 146
al-Farabi, 10
Fazio degli Uberti, 43
Flagellants, 15
Flamenca, 122
Floci, Evenus, 149
florilegia, 4
Francis of Assisi, 13-14, 33, 83-4, 92, 128
Franciscans, 34, 93
Fulgentius, 143

Galen, 11, 85
games, 5, 87-9
Gellius, 61
Gematria, 11-12, 62-3; *see* numerology
Génicot, Leopold, 5
Geoffrey Plantagenet, 66
Gerald of Aurillic, 30, 126
Gerald of Salles, 30
Gerard of Cremona, 11, 61
Gerhoh of Reichersberg, 8-9
Gervase of Tillbury, 18 n. 9, 41
al-Ghazzali, 11-12
de Ghellinck, Joseph, 3
Gilbert of Limerick, 123
Giles of Rome, 35-9, 44, 84, 87, 95, 105, 107, 111-3, 121-3, 144, 151
Giovanna da Signa, 149-50
Glorieux, R., 43
Gobi, Johannes, 2
Godfrey of St. Victor, 71
Gordon, Bernard, 10-11, 27, 38, 69, 113, 123, 146, 148, 161
Goswin of Metz, 43
Gratian, 60, 130
Gregory of Nyssa, 86
Gregory the Great, 28-30, 129
Grosseteste, Robert, 63, 72-3
Gualberti, John, 127
Guibert of Nogent, 32
Guibert of Tournai, 123, 191 n. 48
Guido of Montefeltro, 148
Guillaume of St. Martial, 131
Guinefort, 96
Guy de Vigevano, 37
Guy Vere of Valence, 36

hagiography, 2, 15, 27-31, 83-92, 96, 107, 110, 124-6, 131, 159; *see* James of Voragine
Halevi, Aharon of Barcelona, 141 n. 68
Halevy, Judah, 62
Haly Abbas, 11, 42, 88, 90, 147
Hanning, Robert, 33

health, manuals for, 7
Hedwig of Silesia, 29, 132
Henri de Gauchy, 51 n. 48
Henry III (Emperor), 91
Henry IV (Emperor), 91
heresy, 32, 34, 88, 124
Herlihy, David, 28
Hermann of Carinthia, 11
Hermann of Scheda, 32, 133
Herrad of Landsberg, 63
hexameron, commentaries on, 61-9 *passim*, 147
Higounet-Nadal, A., 6
Hildebert of Lavardin, 111
Hildegard of Bingen, 63
Hippocrates, 11, 61, 85
Hirschau, 93
history, philosophy of, 3, 8-10, 70-3
Hofmeister, Adolph, 3
Hollingsworth, T.H., 6
Honorius III (Pope), 15, 63
Honorius Inclusus, 40
Honorius of Autun, 8, 63, 71, 92
Horace, 147
hortatory treatises, 19, 35-39
Hostiensis, 59
Hugh of Lincoln, 92, 94
Hugh of St. Victor, 8-9, 41, 86, 93-4, 110
Huguccio of Pisa, 60
Humbert of Romans, 14-15, 123
humors, four, 1, 66-90, 106, 126, 145, 148, 150-5

Images of youth, 107-9
individualism, 4, 13-16
infancy, 1-2, 6, 30, 59ff, 83-9, 94; *see* neonate
Innocent III (Pope), 80, 147
Innocent V (Pope), 60
Isabella of Navarre, 122
Isidore of Seville, 8, 11, 39, 41-2, 59-61, 68, 83, 87-9, 95, 121, 143
iunior, 59
iuventus, 60, 70-3

"Jacobus", *see Omnebonum*

James of Aragon (King), 33, 38
James II (King), 145
James of Venice, 38
James of Vitry, 15
James of Voragine, 29, 69, 83-4, 72, 128
Jane Mary of Maillé, 140 n. 61
Jean of Chatillon, 152
Jerome, 8, 29, 71, 83, 125, 129
Jewish sources, 3, 11-13, 34-5, 62, 132-4, 161
Joachim of Flora, 9, 10, 12
John II of France (King), 41
John XXII (Pope), 40
John of Capua, 145
John of Fruttuaria, 109-10
John of Marienwerder, 31
John of Rupescissa, 33
John of San Gemignano, 40, 64, 68-9, 87-8, 147-8, 160
John of Spain, 36
John of Wales, 61
Jones, Rufus, 128
Judah ben Asher ben Yehiel, 84, 113
Judah the Maccabee, 110
Juliana of Cornillon, 89, 94
Juncta of Bevagna, 34

Kabbalah, 11, 62
Kempe, Margery, 33, 140 n. 61
Kett, Joseph, 59

Lactantius, 4
Lancelot, 148
Latini, Brunetto, 43
Lehmann, Paul, 32
Liber Hermetis..., 4, 11
Liber philosophorum..., 41
Livy, 41, 91
Louis IX of France (King), 40, 122
Louis of Bavaria, 94-5
Louis of Toulouse, 30, 92
Low, Leopold, 3
Lucchesio of Poggibonsi, 128
Lull, Raymund, 7, 10-13, 27, 32-4, 40, 112, 128, 149, 159

Lutgard of Aywières, 29, 159

Maffei, Raffaelo, 39
al-Maghribi, Samau'al, 32, 133
Magistri, Johannes, 151
Mahzor Vitry, 62
Maimonides, 10, 12, 42, 113, 145
Manipulus florum, 19, n. 18
Marbod of Rennes, 42
Margaret of Cortona, 34
Margaret of Hungary, 31, 129
marriage, 122-5, 129-32, 143, 160
Martin of Tours, 28-9, 125
Mary of Oigniès, 29, 140, n. 61
McLaughlin, Mary, 126-7
medievalists, life cycle and, 2-5
melancholia, 1, 145, 149
Menachem ben Hameiri, 62
mendicant orders, 13-15, 27, 64-5, 93-4, 111-2; see Augustinians, Carmelites Dominicans, Franciscans, Servites
Merlin, 10
menstruation, 86
Metz, René, 59-60
microcosm, 63-6, 145
middle age, 1, 143-6
Midrash, 62
miracles, 2, 96
mirrors for princes, 21 n. 29, 35-7, 44, 144-5
Misch, Georg, 33
monasticism, 92-5, 109-111, 127

ibn-Naghrillah, Samuel, 62
Nahmanides, 113
nature, 8, 37, 63-5, 95, 107-8
Neckham, Alexander, 63
Nemesius of Emesa, 11, 42
Nemus, 153
neonate, 85-9, 160, *see* infant
New Society, 2
Nicholas III (Pope), 11
Nicholas IV (Pope), 40
Nicholas of Lisieux, 93
Nicholas of Lyra, 55 n. 79, 72
Nicholas of Myra, 124
Nicholas of Tolentino, 84

Ninus of Bactria, 86
Noonan, John, 5
novices, 111
numerology, 62-3, 72-3; *see* Gematria
nurses, 86-7

oblation, 59-60, 92-5
Odil of Cluny, 111
Odo of Cluny, 126
Odo II of Cluny, 30
Oecumenicus Galeni, 38
old age, 35, 108, 146-50
Omnebonum, 40, 121
optimism, philosophical, 7-10, 160
Orsini, Napoleone, 34
Osburn of Gloucester, 60
Osmund of Mortimer, 93
Ovadia the Convert, 32
Ovid, 41, 91, 129

Palmieri, Matteo, 61
Papias, 60
Pascal, Roy, 32
Paschalis Romanus, 11
Pastrengo, 39
Patrick of Ireland, 32
Paul the Hermit, 125
Peck, Russell, 72
penance, 14-15, 129-30; *see* confession
Peraldus, William, 35, 51 n. 47, 72, 113-4, 122-3
Peter Cantor, 34
Peter Comestor, 86
Peter Lombard, 60
Peter of Abano, 40
Peter of Celle, 47, n. 21
Peter of Palude, 93
Peter of Porto, 117, n. 27
Peter of Ravenna, 83
Peter of Spain, 38, 151
Peter of Verona, 15
Peter the Venerable, 29
Peter Waldo, 128
Petrarch, 99 n. 25
Philip de Greve, 152

Philip III of France (King), 35-6
Philip IV of France (King), 37
Philip of Tripoli, 36
Philippe de Navarre, 51 n. 49, 112
Philo, 4, 85
philosophy, 63-4, 130
Pierre Gallego (Bishop), 38
Pierre des Près (Cardinal), 41
Pirqe Avoth, 62
Plato, 66-7
Pliny, 85, 109, 153
Polentino, Sicco, 124-5
Polo, Marco, 33
popularization, 3-4, 42-4
pre-natal life, 83-5, 160
primogeniture, 13
progress, idea of, 4, 8-10, 14-15
Promptuarium..., 61
Prudentius, 68
Ptolemy, 151
pueritia, 59-60, 70-5, 84-96, 105; see *iuventus*
Pythagoreanism, 38

Quintillian, 61
Qosta ibn Luqa, 66-7

Rabanus Maurus, 40, 60
Rashi, 76 n. 23
Rather of Verona, 14
Raymund of Capua, 83, 110
Raymund of Penyaforte, 96
Raymund of Toulouse, 124
al-Razi, 11, 42, 68, 87-8, 99, 105
Regimen Sanitatis, 37-8, 144, 159
Remi of Auxerre, 80 n. 51
Remus, 91
Richard I (King), 28
Richard of Chichester, 30, 83
Richard of St. Victor, 41, 72
Ricordi, 3
rites of passage, 1-2
Robert of Sicily (King), 28
Robert of Uzès, 33
Romuald of Salerno, 127
Russell, J.C., 5-7

Saadia Gaon, 145-6
Sainte-Catherine of Fierbois, 74
Saints, *see* hagiography
Salimbene de Adam, 24 n. 60, 32
Samuel Hakatan, 62
Samuel Hanagid, 113
Sarton, George, 151-2
Scot, Michael, 3, 38-9, 86
Scripture:
  Acts 15.37:110
  Acts 16.3: 110
  Acts 40:110
  I *Corinthians* 7.3-6: 130
  Daniel 10.5-7: 143
  Deuteronomy 18.18: 133
  Ecclesiasticus 6.18: 108
  Ecclesiasticus 25.3: 108
  Ecclesiasticus 30.11-12: 108
  Ecclesiasticus 40.1: 85
  Galatians 2.1: 110
  Genesis 34: 65, 69-71
  Genesis 2: 70
  Genesis 24.1: 147
  Genesis 34: 62
  Hebrews 9
  Isaiah 9.6: 89
  Isaiah 11.2: 46 n. 11
  Job 38.8-9: 85
  Job 39.9-12: 108
  Jeremiah 1.7: 89
  John 2.20: 85
  John 2.1-2: 70, 72
  John 14.1-2: 4, 71
  Luke 1.24: 70
  Luke 12.35-8: 70
  Luke 14.26: 47 n. 15
  Luke 23.44: 67
  Mark 6.46: 1
  Matthew 2.2: 70
  Matthew 4.22: 47 n. 15
  Matthew 5.8: 94
  Matthew 10.35-7: 47 n. 15
  Matthew, 20.1-16: 3 70-2
  Matthew 23.9: 47 n. 15
  Numbers 8.25: 62
  Proverbs: 113
  Proverbs 22.3-6: 92, 108
  Proverbs 24.13: 108
  Psalms 103.5: 105
  Revelations 21.13: 70

Wisdom 4.9: 147
Wisdom 7.2: 85
Sears, Elizabeth, 3
Sefer Yetsirah, 12
Seneca, 48, 121
senectus, 64-6, 146-50
senior, 59
senium, 66
Seraphina of San Gemignano, 160
sermons, 69
Servites, 15
sexuality, 30, 141-5; adolescent, 106, 110-1, 121-34; childhood, 89-93; male, 125-9; *see* chastity
Sicard of Cremona, 71-2
Siger of Brabant, 38
Silvestris, Bernard, 77, n. 29
Simhah b. Samuel of Vitry, 62
Socrates, 67
Solinus, 41, 85
Solomon (King), 110
Sophocles, 147
Stephen of Antioch, 11
Stephen of Obazine, 93
Stephen of Salley, 111
Stephen Tempier (Bishop), 11
Sufism, 133
Sulpicius Severus, 28-29, *see* Martin of Tours
Sybil, 10
syncretism, 4, 10-12

Tabula exemplorum, 64
Talmud, 62-3
teachers, 66, 87-90, 113-4
tertiary orders, 14-15
Tertullian, 129
Thabit b. Abi Thabit, 62
Thomas Aquinas, 8-9, 24 n. 60, 35, 84, 93
Thomas Becket, 110
Thomas of Argentina, 63-4
Thomas of Cantimpré, 36, 39-43, 63, 89, 121, 146, 159

Thomas of Celano, 92
Thomas of Ireland, 56 n. 83
ibn-Tibbon, 113, 145
topoi, 4, 29-30, 36, 83-5, 89
toys, *see* games

Ubertino da Casale, 9

Valerianus, 131
Vallumbrosians, 127-8
Varro, 4
vernacular sources, 42-3
Victorinus of Pettun, 69
Vincent of Beauvais, 40-1, 61-2, 66, 85-91, 105-6, 121
Virgil, 4
virtues, 61-2, 83, 91, 105-9, 122-3, 144
visions, 29-33
Vitae patrum, 110

Wackernagel, W., 3
Wicbod, 80 n. 51
William of Conchos, 41, 63-66, 85, 86
William of Oliva, 128
William of St. Thierry, 63, 89
William of Sicily (King), 153
William of St. Amour, 93
William of Volpiano, 93
William the Marshal, 28
wills, 148-9; ethical, 36

Yehudah ha-Hasid, 141 n. 70
Youth, *see iuventus*
Yves of Trécors, 74 n. 2, 96

Zoroaster, 85-6
Zamora, Gil, 28

About the Author

Michael Goodich is a graduate of the City College of New York, the University of Pennsylvania and Columbia University, where he specialized in medieval social history. At the present time he is a professor of medieval history at the University of Haifa in Israel, and dean of the faculty of humanities. His research has concentrated on the social and ideological foundations of medieval Christianity, having published monographs dealing with such subjects as the psychological and social ramifications of Catholic sainthood, and the treatment of sexual nonconformity in canon and secular law. The present study of the human life cycle in late medieval thought is the byproduct of an attempt to reconstruct the foundations of developmental psychology found in contemporary hagiographical, medical and didactic sources.